THE ILLIAC IV

The First Supercomputer

THE ILLIAC IV

The First Supercomputer

R. Michael Hord

Computer Science Press

Computer Science Press
11 Taft Court
Rockville, MD 20850 U.S.A.

1 2 3 4 5 6   87 86 85 84 83 82

12-8-87   1146002

Library of Congress Cataloging in Publication Data

Hord, R. Michael, 1940-
    The Illiac IV, the first supercomputer.

    Includes bibliographical references.
    1. Illiac computer. I. Title.
QA76.8.I5H67 1982   001.64   81-19437
ISBN 0-914894-71-4   AACR2

Table of Contents

List of Figures

x List of Figures

List of Tables

Acknowledgements

CHRIS JESSHOPE
MEL PIRTLE
AL BIRHOLTZ
RICHARD HALE
ANDERS FIELD
FANIS ECONOMIDIS
S. KOVACS
K.G. STEVENS
ED STERNBERG
C.T. MARKEE
HOWARD FALK
DANIEL SLOTNICK
R. GEMOETS
M. OZGA
F.T. LUK
D.H. LEHMER
A.S. HOPKINS
J. LEVESQUE
WIN BERNHARD
PAT HISS
R.A. GUSTAFSON
L. BRIGHT
M. SMITH
C. ROMNEY
D.H. LAWRIE
F. REINHARDT
L.L. REED
D.R. HENDERSON
R.S. ROGALLO
J.L. STEGER
H.E. BAILEY
R.H. MILLER
S. TULLOH
D.K. STEVENSON
G. FEIERBACH
A. KERR

I.   Introduction

The Illiac IV was the first large scale array computer. As the fore-
runner of today's advanced computers, it brought whole classes of
scientific computations into the realm of practicality. Conceived
initially as a grand experiment in computer science, the revolutionary
architecture incorporated both a high level of parallelism and pipelining.

After a difficult gestation, the Illiac IV became operational in
November 1975. It has for a decade been a substantial driving force
behind the development of computer technology. Today the Illiac IV
continues to service large-scale scientific application areas including computational fluid dynamics, seismic stress wave propagation modeling, climate simulation, digital image processing, astrophysics,
numerical analysis, spectroscopy and other diverse areas.

This volume brings together previously published material, adapted
in an effort to provide the reader with a perspective on the strengths
and weaknesses of the Illiac IV and the impact this unique computational resource has had on the development of technology. The history
and current status of the Illiac system, the design and architecture
of the hardware, the programming languages, and a considerable sampling
of applications are all covered at some length. A final section is
devoted to commentary.

The story of the Illiac IV is also in part the story of the
Institute for Advanced Computation. This is the government organization
formed in 1971 by the Defense Advanced Research Projects Agency and the
National Aeronautics and Space Administration Ames Research Center to
develop and operate this computer. The Institute provides access to
the Illiac through a connection to the ARPANET, a national communication
network. The Institute also performs software development, maintenance,
and research in various advanced computation topics.

Considerable effort has been invested by the Institute in documen-
ting the evolution of the Illiac system and providing those publica-
tions to the user community. Frankly, this material has experienced
quite limited circulation and to most of the computer world the Illiac
remains mysterious. This attitude is fostered by the lack of a thorough-
going summary of the Illiac's environment, design and capabilities.
It is in response to that information gap that this book is addressed.

The Illiac IV consists of a single control unit that broadcasts
instructions to sixty-four processing elements operating in lock step.

Each of these processing elements has a working memory of 2K sixty-four bit words. The main memory of the Illiac is implemented in disk with a capacity of eight million words and with a transfer rate of five hundred megabaud. Arithmetic can be performed in 64, 32 or 8 bit mode. In 32 bit mode, on algorithms well suited to the parallel architecture, the Illiac performs at a rate of 300 million instructions per second. Although it uses electronics from the late 1960's, for certain classes of important problems, the Illiac remains the fastest computer to date.

This book is written primarily for computer professionals. Certainly a much wider audience of engineers, scientists, students, program managers and laymen interested in this dynamic technology will find much to engage them. Some sections, however, include considerable detail and assume a fairly sophisticated background in computer science.

II. Background

A. History

The Illiac IV story begins in the mid-1960's. Then, as now, the computational community had requirements for machines much faster and
with more capacity than were available. Large classes of important
calculational problems were outside the realm of practicality because
the most powerful machines of the day were too slow by orders of magnitude to execute the programs in plausible time. These applications
included ballistic missile defense analyses, reactor design calculations, climate modelling, large linear programming, hydrodynamic simulations, seismic data processing, and a host of others.
     This demand for higher speed computation began in this time frame
to encounter the ultimate limitation on the computing speed theoreti-
cally achievable with sequential machines. This limitation is the
speed at which a signal can be propagated through an electrical conductor. This upper limit is somewhat less than the speed of light,
186,000 miles per second. At this speed the signal travels less than
a foot in a nanosecond. Through miniaturization the length of the interconnecting conductors had already been reduced substantially. Integrated circuits containing transistors packed to a density of several
thousand per square inch helped greatly. But the law of diminishing
returns had set in.
     Designers realized that new kinds of logical organization were
needed to break through the speed of light barrier to sequential computers. The response to this need was the parallel architecture. It
was not the only response. Another architectural approach that met
with some success is overlapping or pipelining wherein an assembly
line process is set up for performing sequential operations at different stations within the computer in much the way an automobile is fab-
ricated. The Illiac IV incorporates both of these architectural
features.
     The first section of this chapter introduces the design concept
in somewhat more detail. This detail will be elaborated in the course
of the book. The design concepts were enormously innovative when the
Illiac project was undertaken. It was the first of what today have
come to be called supercomputers.
     The second section of this chapter is based on an article by
Howard Falk that appeared in the IEEE Spectrum,* October, 1976. It
provides chapter and verse in describing the horrendous problems that
were overcome in making the Illiac IV a reality.
[*© 1976 IEEE. Reprinted with permission from IEEE Spectrum.]

3

1. The Design Concept

The Illiac IV computer is the fourth of a series of advanced computers designed and developed at the University of Illinois, and this accounts for the origin of its name. Its predecessors include a vacuum tube machine completed in 1952 (11,000 operations per second), a transistor machine completed in 1963 (500,000 operations per second) and a 1966 machine designed for automatic scanning of large quantities of visual data. The Illiac IV is a parallel processor in which 64 separate computers work in tandem on the same problem. This parallel approach to computation allows the Illiac IV to achieve up to 300 million operations per second.

Conventional computers solve problems by a series of sequential steps in much the way an individual mathematician would solve the same problem. In a parallel processor, however, many computations can be performed simultaneously; on the Illiac IV for example, 64 calculations are done at once.

If the problem at hand is to calculate the price earnings ratio for the stock of a corporation, parallelism is of no advantage since the problem cannot be broken into pieces that the separate processors can address independently. Hence 64 mathematicians can solve the problem no faster than one mathematician. If, on the other hand, the problem is to calculate the average price earnings ratio for all of the stocks listed on the New York Stock Exchange, then by assigning the calculation of the different ratios to different mathematicians, a productive division of labor is achieved and the result is obtained more quickly than one mathematician could obtain it sequentially.

Fortunately, a very large fraction of the world's scientific computational problems satisfy this parallelism requirement. For these problems that are suitable for implementation on the Illiac, very handsome run-time reduction factors have been achieved.

The father of the Illiac IV was Professor Daniel Slotnick who conceived the machine in the mid-1960's. The development was sponsored by the Defense Advanced Research Projects Agency. Subsystems for the Illiac were manufactured in a number of facilities throughout the U.S. These subsystems were then shipped to the Burroughs Corporation in Paoli, Pennsylvania for final assembly. The Illiac was delivered to the NASA Ames Research Center south of San Francisco in 1971.

The logical design of the Illiac IV is patterned after the Solomon computers. Prototypes of these were built in the early 1960's by the Westinghouse Electric Company. This type of computer architecture is

4

referred to as SIMD, Single Instruction Multiple Datastream. In this design there is a single control processor which sends instructions broadcast style to a multitude of replicated processing units termed elements. Each of these processing elements has an individual memory unit; the control unit transmits addresses to these processing element memories. The processing elements execute the same instruction simultaneously on data that differs in each processing element memory.

For comparison, the logical structure of a conventional sequential computer is illustrated in Figure 2.1, while Figure 2.2 shows the architecture of the SIMD machine.

In the particular case of the Illiac IV, each of the processing element memories has a capacity of 2,048 words of 64-bit length. In aggregate, the processing element memories provide a megabyte of storage. The time required to fetch a number from this memory is 188 nanoseconds, but because additional logical circuitry is needed to resolve contention when two sections of the Illiac IV access memory simultaneously, the minimum time between successive operations is somewhat longer.

In the execution of a program it is often necessary to move data or intermediate results from one processor to another. Routing paths for this purpose are provided as shown in Figure 2.3. One way of regarding this interconnection pattern is to consider the processing elements as a linear string numbered from 0 to 63. Each processor is provided a direct data path to four other processors, its immediate right and left neighbors and the neighbors spaced eight elements away. So, for example, processor 10 is directly connected to processors 9, 11, 2, and 18. This interconnection structure is wrapped around, so processor 63 is directly connected to processor 0. To transfer values among processors not directly connected, multiple routing steps are required. For example, to move a number from processor 9 to processor 18 it must first be moved to processor 17 and then to processor 18.

The other major control feature that characterizes the Illiac IV is the enable/disable function. While it's true that the 64 processing elements are under centralized control, each of the processing elements has some degree of individual control. This individual control is provided by a mode value. This mode value for a given processor is either 1 or 0, corresponding to the processor being enabled ("on"), or disabled ("off"). The 64 mode values can be set independently under program control, depending on the different data values unique to each processing element. Enabled processors respond to commands from the control unit; disabled elements respond only to a command to change mode. Mode values can be set on specific conditions encountered during program execution. For example, the contents of two registers can be compared and the mode value can be set on the outcome of the comparison. Hence iterative calculations can be terminated in some processors while the iteration continues in others when, say, a quantity exceeded a specified numerical limit.

In addition to the megabyte of processor element memory, the Illiac IV has a main memory with a sixteen million word capacity. This main memory is implemented in magnetic rotating disks. Thirteen fixed head disks in synchronized rotation are organized into 52 bands of 300 pages each (an Illiac page is 1024 words). This billion-bit storage subsystem is termed the Illiac IV Disk Memory or I4DM. The access time is determined by the rotation rate of the disks. Each disk rotates once in 40

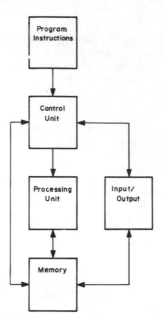

Figure 2.1 Conventional computer architecture

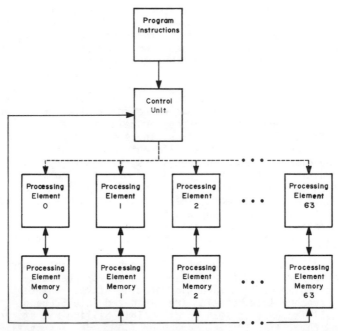

Figure 2.2 Parallel organization of Illiac IV

milliseconds so the average access time is 20 milliseconds. This
latency makes the access time about 100,000 times longer than the access
time for processor element memory. The transfer rate, however, is 500
million bits per second.

   This memory subsystem, the input/output peripherals and the management of the other parts of the system are under the direction of a
Digital Equipment Corporation PDP-10 conventional computer. A Burroughs B-6700 computer compiles the programs submitted to the Illiac
into machine language.

   This design concept came to fruition in November 1975 when the
Illiac IV was pronounced operational.

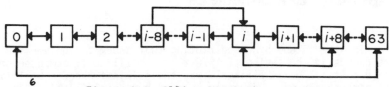

Figure 2.3   Illiac IV routing paths

2. Implementation Difficulties

It was during the firebombing and rioting that shook the University of
Illinois campus in the spring of 1970 that the Illiac IV computer project reached its climax. Illiac IV was the culmination of a brilliant
parallel computation idea, doggedly pursued by Daniel Slotnick for
nearly two decades, from its conception when he was a graduate student
to its realization in the form of a massive supercomputer. Conceived
as a machine to perform a billion operations per second, a speed it was
never to achieve, Illiac IV ultimately included more than a million
logic gates--by far the largest assemblage of hardware ever in a single
machine.
    Until 1970, Illiac IV had been a research and development project,
whose controversy was limited to the precise debates of computer scientists, the agonizing of system and hardware designers, and the question-
ing of budget managers. Afterward, the giant machine was to become a
more or less practical computational tool, whose disposition would be a
matter of achieving the best return on a government investment of more
than $31 million.
    This article will discuss the successes and failures that have made
Illiac IV significant in the development of computer technology, but
first let us return to the campus in Urbana-Champaign, Ill., in 1970,
when Illiac IV was at the center of boiling passions over the relationships between the university, government, and private industry.
    Illiac was funded by the U.S. Department of Defense's Advanced Re-
search Projects Agency (ARPA) through the U.S. Air Force Rome Air Defense Center. However, the entire project was not only conceived, but
to a large extent managed, by academicians at the University of Illinois.
Finally, the system hardware was actually designed and built by manufacturing firms--Burroughs acted as the overall system contractor; key
subcontractors included Texas Instruments and Fairchild Semiconductor.
    When headlines in The Daily Illini, January 6, 1970, proclaimed,
"Department of Defense to employ UI computer for nuclear weaponry,"
tensions rapidly escalated--not only between University of Illinois students and the faculty and school administration, but also between the
parties directly involved in the Illiac IV project itself. Out of the
campus cauldron bubbled heated phrases; some directed at Government's
"dangerous fools," others at industry's "questionable business prac-
tices," and still others at the university's "volatile visionaries."

8

As a university-based project supported by military funds, Illiac IV was large, but by no means unique. Such funds had long been flowing into graduate schools and laboratories, and had always been accompanied by strain and contradiction. On the one hand, there was the university's need to train students and advance basic knowledge; on the other, there was the Department of Defense (DOD) need for new military technology. With the prodding of the Military Procurement Act of 1970, signed into law by President Richard Nixon on November 19, 1969, DOD funding agencies were under increased pressure to demonstrate the military value of all the research and development projects they supported. David Packard, then Deputy Secretary of Defense, was publicly reiterating DOD determination to support only work that had a "direct, apparent, and clearly documented relationship" to military functions and operations. Meanwhile, on the campus, there were antiwar sit-ins, demonstrations, and rising feelings--extending beyond the students to the faculty--that military projects did not belong at the University of Illinois. Confrontation over the military R&D issue was imminent in 1970; and the news of military uses for Illiac IV was explosive.

When the dust settled, what remained for those in industry who had been observing the Illiac IV project was an impression that universities might be bold initiators of new ideas but were not equipped to manage large engineering projects. For those in government, there was a hardening determination to keep Illiac in a protected, secure environment away from any campus. For university administrators and faculty, there was a growing conviction that military R&D support was a very mixed blessing, and one that in many cases might not be worth pursuing.

Despite misgivings, the university prepared itself to receive the giant computer--in a new building specially designed for the machine-- but the move from the Burroughs plant in Paoli, Pa. to Illinois was never to occur. Instead, Illiac IV would find its permanent home at a NASA facility in California.

Lawrence Roberts, then director of ARPA Information Processing Techniques, recalls the decision not to place Illiac IV at Illinois as mainly a question of finding the best possible operational managers for the machine: "University people who might run it . . . are unwilling to look at some kinds of problems; maybe the classified ones, maybe just sensitive ones . . . Was the university the right organization to manage a large operational undertaking? . . . The answer was generally no."

Just as the story of Illiac IV can be divided into the periods before and after the campus turmoil of 1970, so the successes and failures of the project can be measured in two quite separate senses. For the Illiac IV balance sheet, there are the achievements and shortcomings of an R&D project, deliberately designed to press computer architecture and design forward as far and fast as possible. There are also the more practical considerations surrounding a multimillion-dollar conglomeration of hardware that is expected to prove its worth by performing day-to-day computational tasks.

This research-operational ambivalence in the Illiac IV project is reflected in the divided feelings expressed by those involved. For example, Daniel Slotnick says: "I'm bitterly disappointed, and very pleased . . . delighted and dismayed. Delighted that the overall objectives came out well in the end. Dismayed that it cost too much, took too long, doens't do enough, and not enough people are using it."

Perhaps the greatest strength of Illiac IV, as an R&D project, was in the pressures it mounted to move the computer state of the art forward.   There was a conscious decision on the part of all the technical people involved to press the then-existing limits of technology.   Dr. Slotnick, who was the guiding spirit of the project, made it clear to his co-workers that the glamour and publicity attendant to building the fastest and biggest machine in the world were necessary to successfully complete what they had started.

The end results this pioneering urge had on computer hardware were impressive: Illiac IV was one of the first computers to use all semiconductor main memories; the project also helped to make faster and more highly integrated bipolar logic circuits available (a boon to the semiconductor and computer industries, this development actually proved a disaster for Illiac IV--more on this subject later in this section); in a negative but decisive sense, Illiac IV gave a death blow to thin-film memories; the physical design, using large, 15-layer printed circuit boards, challenged the capabilities of automated design techniques.

As it began to take shape in 1965 and 1966, Illiac IV seemed so exciting that engineers, physicists, and computer scientists pressed to be assigned to the project.   Its overall architecture--using many separate processing units all operating simultaneously--was an undeniable demonstration of the possibility of highly parallel computation.   With Illiac IV, exploration of the benefits of parallel computation was underway.

On the software side, the Illiac IV programming work at the University of Illinois spawned a whole new generation of experts in parallel and high-speed computation.   David Kuck and his students at the university stopped full-time work on Illiac IV in 1968, but the impact on software and applications thinking was a lasting one.   Students who wrote their master's theses at Illinois on Illiac IV have gone on to promising careers in the field.   For example, Muraoka is now manager of computer architecture at NTT Laboratories in Japan.   According to Dr. Kuck, work on extracting the ultimate computation speed from programs, in organizing algorithms for ultimate speed, has been greatly stimulated by experience with the Illiac IV project.   He points out that people at other schools, such as Stanford, the Massachusetts Institute of Technology, and Carnegie-Mellon, are now doing theses and research that have been influenced, however indirectly, by Illiac IV.

In terms of hardware, deficiencies in Illiac IV's bipolar logic circuits set off a series of design changes that ultimately delayed by years the completion of the machine, while they also ushered in dramatic changes in memory technology.

Initial plans for Illiac IV circuitry envisioned bipolar emitter-coupled logic (ECL) gates capable of speeds of the order of 2-3 ns.   The ECL circuits were to be packaged with 20 gates per chip--a level of complexity that later would be called medium-scale integration.   Chosen as the subcontractor for these circuits, Texas Instruments seemed eager to do the job and sincere in the belief that it could produce the expected circuits.

As the development process moved ahead, it became evident that the 20-gate chips were not functioning properly.   Noise margins for these circuits were inadequate.   The power distribution design inside the circuit packages was such that crosstalk was excessive.   At the root of such problems was an inability to produce multilevel circuit substrates that could meet the necessary precision requirements for lead definition, resistivity, and level-to-level registration. TI asked for an added year of development time to produce the original circuits. Instead, the decision was to go to a simpler integrated circuit--with only seven gates per chip--while maintaining substantially the same circuit speeds.

Although the initial ECL development effort for Illiac was a failure, the millions of dollars of government money that were invested in that effort played a substantial role in advancing the ECL integrated circuit art, so that within about a year TI was able to solve the substrate problems and to offer commercial medium-scale integrated ECL circuits similar to those the Illiac IV project had hoped to use.

But for Illiac IV, problems with ECL circuits were just beginning. The shift to smaller circuit packages was to have a pervasive impact on other portions of the hardware, such as processing element memories, printed circuit boards, and cabling--and overall system design and capabilities would be drastically affected as well. But even the smaller circuit packages themselves proved to be a continuing source of trouble. The plastic encapsulation for these circuits proved to be very sensitive to the operating environment, particularly to the ambient humidity. This required an unusual effort to provide stable humidity in the final Illiac IV installation at the NASA Ames Research Center at Moffet Field, Calif. Internal short circuits between leads to external circuit pins provided a second major problem--and one that was more subtle since it developed only over a period of time. Test procedures were devised to adjust power-supply voltages to maximum and minimum marginal values in an attempt to show up potential short circuits. Dynamic impedance between leads was also checked, using a variable-current supply source while monitoring voltage output. For the design and production schedule of the overall Illiac IV system, the shift from medium-scale to small-scale ECL chips was a disaster that led to delays probably totaling about two years.

Illiac IV initial specifications called for a 2048-word, 64-bits-per-word, 240-ns cycle-time memory for each of its processing elements. In 1966, when the initial design study for the system was underway, the only technology that seemed to be available to meet these requirements was the thin-film memory. At that time, a few developmental semiconductor memory chips were being studied, but no computer manufacturer would yet consider them seriously for main memory use.

Fortunately, Burroughs, the Illiac IV system contractor, had already developed thin-film memories for its B8501 computer. Two years and about a million dollars later, the memory design had been modified to meet initial Illiac IV requirements and prototype memories were in operation.

The change to smaller ECL circuit chips proved to be a death blow to the thin-film memory. When the smaller chips' requirements for added space on circuit boards and interconnections were taken into account, it turned out that there was not enough room for the smallest feasible thin-film memory configuration. Attempts to increase the overall size of the processing elements were frustrated by limitations on propagation time through system interconnections and cables. Even when use of the small-scale ECL circuits forced the designers to drop the system clock rate from 25 MHz down to its present value of 16 MHz, the thin-film memory still could not be made to fit. Not only was the thin-film

development money wasted, but thin-film memory technology received what
has since proved to be a fatal blow--at least as far as its use in computer main memories is concerned.

Strangely, the failures and disappointments of the ECL circuits and
thin-film memories also set the stage for a brilliant hardware success:
Illiac IV was to be one of the first computers to use all-semiconductor
main memories. While interviewing EE students at the University of
Illinois for jobs at Fairchild's Semiconductor Division, Rex Rice also
happened to meet an old friend and former co-worker, Daniel Slotnick.
When the conversation turned to the computer memory art, Rice, who was
managing advanced development projects at Fairchild, described, in con-
fident and optimistic terms, the work then underway on bipolar semiconductor memories. The conversation may have been just interesting
shoptalk at the time, but the idea that high-speed semiconductor memories
had become a feasible alternative was to play a key role in Illiac IV
developments.

When it became clear that thin-film memories could not be used
without drastically slowing down the entire system, the stage was set
for semiconductor memories. Proposals were taken from Texas Instruments,
Motorola, and Fairchild for the development and production of memories
that would meet Illiac IV specifications. Over the contrary advice of
some of the engineers working on the project, Slotnick chose Fairchild
as the semiconductor memory subcontractor.

Called for were 2048 words (64 bits/word) of memory for each of the
64 Illiac processing elements, a total of 131,072 bits per processing
element. And the memory was to operate with a cycle time of 240 ns and
an access time of 120 ns. A complication, in the packaging of the memories, was the need to provide access to each memory not only from its
own processing element but from the overall system control unit and the
system input-output connections as well. Meeting these requirements
meant some extension of the semiconductor art, as well as overcoming a
host of design and production problems.

When Fairchild was awarded the contract, its facilities for the
project consisted of an empty room, a naked facility that was to be converted for development and production of new devices.' Within a few
months, with an all-out effort, the company would churn out some 33,000
memory chips (256 bits per chip).

Slotnick recalls that development proudly: "I was the first user
of semiconductor memories, and I took a lot of criticism for thinking
that we'd have them on time and within specifications. Illiac IV was
the first machine to have all-semiconductor memories. Fairchild did a
magnificent job of pulling our chestnuts out of the fire. The Fairchild
memories were superb and their reliability to this day is just incredi-
bly good." For the semiconductor industry, this dramatic demonstration
of memory capabilities had a decisive effect. It put Fairchild firmly
into the memory business and, together with IBM's announcement of 64-bit
bipolar memory chips for its 360-85 system, the effect was to speed up
the pace toward the widespread acceptance that semiconductor memories
now enjoy in computers and related systems.

One of the most formidable problems faced by the Illiac IV designers was that of packaging and interconnecting the control unit and the
64 processing elements. Speed was a prime objective of the design, and
in the early stages there was no indication that the project would be

moving into massive cost overruns, so guaranteeing 25-MHz operation appeared to be an unconditional design criterion. Optimization was to be strictly on performance, not cost.

Configuration studies revealed that the principal packaging problems were to minimize the volume of the equipment and the length of the interconnections so as to reduce propagation delays. Because of the tight system control requirements and the limited space available for interconnections, the designers felt forced into the use of multiple-layer printed circuit boards. For the control unit, four signal layers were needed to make connections between the 165 circuit package positions accommodated by each board (the final control unit boards averaged about 140-150 circuits each).

Because of impedance problems, ground layers had to be spaced between the signal layers and the board designs grew until they included 15 different layers. They were expensive and extremely difficult to produce. Furthermore, the designs turned out to be so complex that board layout by human beings was virtually impossible. Initially, a number of wiring patterns were attempted by designers and draftsmen, but these proved to contain so many errors that they were unusable. In addition to the 15-layer complexity, wiring rules were complicated by the use of 50-ohm transmission lines loaded with 100-ohm stubs throughout the design. There were limitations on how close, and how far, loads could be placed from sources--because of the problem of transmission reflections. The human designers simply could not cope with all the rules and requirements.

Fortunately, computer-based design automation techniques were available at the time the Illiac control unit boards were being designed. At first, a printed-wiring routing program supplied by a subcontractor proved inadequate, but with the help of the University of Illinois faculty and students, as well as the Burroughs design team, a satisfactory routing program was finally developed. The boards were designed and produced--a minor triumph for the design automation art.

That was not the end of the printed circuit board story, however. In its final incarnation at NASA Ames, Illiac IV continued to be plagued by board problems, and faults, such as small cracks in the printed circuit connections, were uncovered in the process of bringing the computer into regular daily operation.

In looking back at the history of the Illiac IV project, Lawrence Roberts, former director of ARPA Information Processing Techniques, feels that Illiac's strongest virtue--its pioneering role in pressing forward the computer state of the art--became in the end its greatest weakness. Dr. Roberts now feels that the best course would have been to build the machine using transistor-transistor logic (TTL) rather than ECL circuits. TTL logic was, in the late 1960s, a straightforward, widely employed technology, and its use could have considerably reduced the cost and duration of the project. Says Roberts: "I feel it is absolutely clear that it should have been done with older technology. I've used that lesson many times since then. People complain bitterly but it has always worked out better."

When Illiac IV was delivered to its final home at the NASA Ames Research Center in California in the spring of 1972, the question in the mind of Dr. Pirtle, former Director of NASA's Institute for Advanced Computation, was whether or not the machine could actually be made to perform useful work. By the following summer, the educated outlook was positive. Illiac was then operating at reduced speed, but it would almost always execute its control sequences correctly, and--occasionally-- it would actually deliver correct results. At that time, the machine was made available to a few users, just to demonstrate that useful programming codes could be made to run--but knowing full well that most of the computed results would be erroneous or inaccurate.

Then, in June 1975, a concerted effort began to check out Illiac fully and make it operational. Over the next four months, thousands of manufacturing faults were uncovered in printed circuit boards and connectors; 110,000 low-reliability terminator resistors, wire-wrapped to backplanes, were replaced by circuit-board-mounted resistors; and logic design faults--principally involving signal-propagation times--were corrected, as were improper line terminations and inadequate power-supply filtering in the disk controllers.

The system now operates from Monday morning to Friday afternoon, including 60 to 80 hours of good, verified up-time for the users, along with 44 hours of maintenance and downtime.

Above all, speed was to be the most crucial characteristic of Illiac IV. A billion instructions per second was Slotnick's initial goal. As the system design took shape, that target was expressed more specifically as 256 parallel processing elements that would each perform a 64-bit floating point addition in 240 ns.

Then, when the size of the machine had to be dropped from 256 to 64 processing elements, this goal faded from sight, retreating even further as the clock speed was dropped from 25 to 16, and finally to 13, MHz. Still, even in 1970--after major hardware disappointments with the available circuitry had been absorbed into the systems design--the system was still believed by its creator to be capable of performing 200 million instructions per second. Today this has been achieved. Performance is discussed in detail in Section III.

When the University of Illinois trustees signed the initial Illiac IV contract with the U.S. Air Force in February 1966, the cost of the project was estimated at just over $8 million, a number that was remarkably close to the gate of the Clay--Liston world championship heavyweight title bout held just months earlier. By January 1970, funding for the project had grown far beyond the dimensions of a prizefight, to over $24 million, and by April 1972, when the huge computer had been delivered to its permanent site in California, its estimated cost had reached $31 million.

Clearly, inflation played a role in these escalating costs, as did the millions that were spent for development of key components such as the ECL circuits, and for components that were discarded, such as the thin-film memories.

At the same time, Illiac was originally planned to include 256 processing elements. As it became evident that costs were rapidly rising, the number of processing elements was cut back to 64--so the machine ended up at one-fourth its original size, although costing about four times as much as initially estimated.

University-based project managers apparently had no clear idea of the costs of developing and manufacturing in an industry environment. Slotnick felt that the primary source of the cost overruns was at Burroughs where the cost-plus-fixed-fee environment in the company's defense-space operations set it up to jump on the Illiac IV contract "with both feet." From the Burroughs viewpoint, it was a "hairy" project; their aim was to avoid losing money. Actually, Burroughs management consistently underestimated the man-hour costs of the project.

It wasn't until 1971 that those costs came under more accurate control. At that time, a group was set up at DOD's Advanced Research Projects Agency to review the Illiac IV situation every few months and make estimates of costs to completion. Their figures proved to be accurate, probably because they were from a relatively uninvolved source.

From the system software standpoint, Illiac IV is quite rudimentary. There is almost no operating system. A user takes hold of the machine, runs his problem, and then lets it go; the next user does the same. No shared use of Illiac's 64 processing elements is provided. In smaller computers that surround Illiac's control unit and processing elements, there is more complex software that forms a queue of users waiting to get at the big machine and allows them to perform nonarithmetic "companion" processes. But the actual Illiac operating software itself is very simple, capable of such basic operations as monitoring input/output and loading data into the processing element memories. An operating system, along with two Illiac IV languages called TRANQUIL and GLYPNIR, was written at the University of Illinois beginning in 1966. This effort amounted to perhaps a dozen man-years of programming. Later, when the system was moved to California and connected to the ARPA network, it was decided that entirely new system software was needed, since PDP-10 and -11 computers were used--in place of the original B6500 machine--to connect Illiac IV to the outside world.

There, the NASA Ames users decided to write a new Illiac IV language, which would be called CFD, to efficiently communicate problems involving the solution of partial differential equations to the big machine. This was accomplished with approximately two man-years of programming effort.

These equations were important to the NASA Ames users, who now take up about 20 percent of Illiac IV operating time solving aerodynamic flow equations.

The remaining 80 percent of Illiac IV time is taken up by a diverse, and often anonymous, group of users, many of whom still use the GLYPNIR language.

A giant computer should be useful for tackling giant computing problems, and that is pretty much the story of Illiac IV applications programs. Beyond the NASA Ames aerodynamic flow problems, users of the big computer have been running several small weather-prediction and climate models with improved and larger models still under development.

Several types of signal processing computations, including fast Fourier transforms, are now a regular part of Illiac IV's diet, and a large-scale experiment with real-time data is now underway. Other applications problems that have actually found their way to Illiac IV include beam forming and convolution, seismic research, radiation transport for fission reactors, and linear programming software capable of handling 50,000 or more constraints is under development.

As Slotnick sees it, applications have gone just about as he thought they would--"No huge new computational areas have succumbed to Illiac, but nothing we thought would work has not worked."

B. Current Status

The Illiac IV became operational in November, 1975. This was defined to mean that a minimum of sixty hours per week would be made available to users; today the average is about eighty hours per week of verified user time.

The first major application effort culminated in September, 1976 in the successful use of the Illiac in support of a real-time, interactive experiment for the Department of Defense. Thereafter the Institute for Advanced Computation made the Illiac available to government agencies for large-scale computation efforts. Many agencies use it today for diverse application projects (see Section V).

The Institute for Advanced Computation is charged with the responsibility for developing, operating and enhancing the Illiac. This government body was formed in 1971 on the basis of an interagency agreement between the Defense Advanced Research Projects Agency and the NASA Ames Research Center. The Illiac and the Institute are located at NASA Ames, about forty miles south of San Francisco. The interagency agreement expired in 1979, and today NASA is solely responsible for the Illiac's continued development and operation.

The Institute's staff numbers about eighty-five under the guidance of a contractor general manager and a civil servant director. The Institute for Advanced Computation (IAC) is an element of the NASA/Ames Research Support Directorate.

The IAC staff provides analysis and programming support in addition to operations, development and research activities. These activities include new language development, application project management and maintenance of a full computational environment with ARPANET communications and digital graphics capabilities.

The preeminent application of the Illiac IV is wind tunnel simulation in support of the Computational Fluid Dynamics Branch of NASA/Ames. This activity has given rise to substantial advances in the state of the art of aerodynamic design.

Today the Institute continues to improve the capabilities of the Illiac and is participating in the development of successor machines and in the progress of advanced computation technology in general.

Figures 2.4-2.7 show various views of the Illiac IV facility.

Figure 2.4   Rear view of Illiac IV   Figure 2.5   Long view of Illiac IV

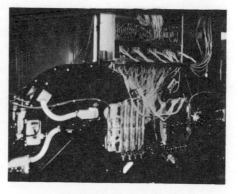

Figure 2.6   IAC computer room   Figure 2.7   Internal view of
Illiac IV

III.　The Computer

This chapter describes the hardware aspects of the Illiac IV and its environment. As the reader can well imagine, a complex of system elements having the first supercomputer as a component is highly complex and in many ways quite sophisticated. This treatment will necessarily leave much unsaid.

Each of the 64 processing elements of the Illiac itself contains more than 100,000 discrete electronic parts assembled into approximately 12,000 switching circuits. This complexity implies serious concern about reliability. Any system containing more than six million parts that must all work for the whole to work is expected to fail every few hours. Consequently a great deal of attention has been directed to testing and diagnostic procedures. A Test and Maintenance Unit is incorporated into the design of the Control Unit. Each of the 64 Processing Elements is subjected every two hours to an elaborate battery of automatic tests. If any malfunction is indicated by any of these tests, the Processing Element is unplugged and replaced by a hot spare; once repaired the unplugged unit becomes a spare.

One measure of the Illiac's reliability is the week-in week-out performance compared with its operational goal. Illiac status is color-coded by the operations staff. Green hours are actual hours of verified batch time available to users. Red hours are logged during the repair of an unplanned down period. Blue time is for development and enhancement. Yellow time is counted for maintenance, weekends and holidays, and batch hours preceding a failed verify. The operational goal is a minimum of 60 green hours per week.

In calendar year 1977, data is available for 48 weeks. Missing weeks include a scheduled Christmas shutdown, etc. In this period, which begins more than a year after the announcement of operational status, the Illiac is reported to have delivered 3480 green hours for an average of 72.5 hours per week. The tentative nature of this operational status, however, is indicated by the 14 weeks (30%) in which the Illiac failed to meet its 60 goal. For 23 weeks of 1978 for which data is at hand the Illiac averaged about 66 green hours per week with 26% of the weeks failing to achieve 60 hours.

The Illiac IV could not have been designed were it not for the use of other computers. Artwork for the system's printed circuit boards was designed with computer assistance. Diagnostic programs for the logic and other hardware were developed on other computers. Even application

18

codes were written with the help of SSK, an Illiac simulator running on a conventional computer. Two Burroughs B 5500 computers were devoted virtually full time for two years to development activities.

This chapter is organized into four parts. The first section addresses the IAC Computational System, i.e., the Illiac environment. Section two describes the Illiac per se. The third section describes how the Illiac is a pipelined machine as well as a parallel machine. Finally performance is documented through benchmarks.

A. The System

1. Introduction

This section addresses the overall environment of computational resources
at the Institute for Advanced Computation (IAC) to support the Illiac IV
user community. IAC operates a remotely accessible conventional computer center that affords the users the underlying basic services to permit the effective use of the unconventional Illiac. This section is
based on "The IAC Computer Facility, An Overview" by C. T. Markee, IAC
TM 5194, February, 1977.

2. Overview of the IAC Computational Facility

The IAC system is configured as a memory-centered multiprocessor architecture. The system configuration is illustrated in Figure 3.1. It was primarily designed to provide efficient support for the Illiac IV. This system today routinely provides both interactive conventional processing and large scale parallel processing.

There are two unique large-problem oriented computational resources in the IAC system, the gigabit per second bandwidth Illiac IV array processor and the 500 megabit per second Illiac IV synchronized disk system (I4DM).

This computational facility may be conceptually separated into four functional resources. The first of these, the connection to the 50 kilobit per second packet switched ARPANET communications facility provides remote users with network access to the IAC Central system facilities for code development.

Another functional element, the Central system, provides the researcher with tools for the development of Illiac IV software. Included in the support facilities are interactive job preparation, file management, data movement, job staging, edit and debug utilities, and control of executing Illiac IV programs. The Central system consists of over 20 PDP-11 control and communications processors. Additionally, the Central system supports interactive time shared service on several PDP-10 computers.

A third functional element of the IAC system is the file management system. This is embodied in the multilevel memory hierarchy of the computational facility. This hierarchy is illustrated in Figure 3.2. Five physically distinct memory subsystems comprise the three levels of the hierarchy. The third or primary memory level separates into the PEM (Processor Element Memory), the I4DM and the Central Memory.

The Central Memory is a 512K word multiport, 64-way interleaved, synchronous core memory that has a 10.93 megahertz clock. While the single word access time of the Central Memory is approximately 630 nanoseconds, the normal operating mode is pipelined access which yields a transfer bandwidth of over 1500 megabits per second.

The processor element memories are used to hold both Processor Element instructions and operands. Constructed of 256 bit RAM chips, the PEMs store 128 Illiac IV pages of data, can be accessed in 188 nanoseconds, and have a cycle time of 200 nanoseconds.

21

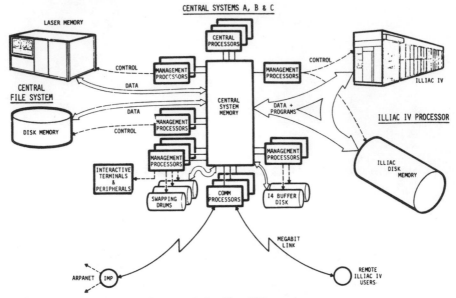

Figure 3.1 The IAC system

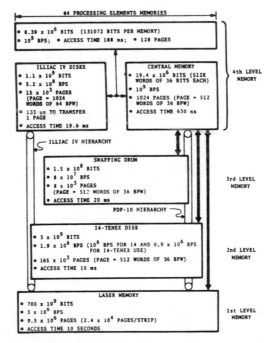

Figure 3.2 Illiac IV system memory hierarchy

The I4DM, the third component of this level in the hierarchy, is used exclusively to support Illiac IV processing. It has a capacity of 16 million 64 bit words. It consists of 13 fixed head disks and has a transfer rate of 500 megabits per second. The swapping drum (4 million 36 bit words capacity, 80 megabit per second transfer rate) and the TENEX disks (165,000 TENEX pages capacity) complete the memory hierarchy.

The final functional element of the IAC system is the Illiac IV parallel computer. A simplified diagram of the Illiac IV is shown in Figure 3.3. The entire Illiac IV computational facility may be viewed as a drum based machine consisting of 64 Processing Elements under the command of a single Control Unit. Each Processing Element has its own 2 K 64-bit word fast semiconductor scratch-pad memory. Transfers between these Processor Element Memories and the I4DM are illustrated in Figure 3.4.

In its capacity as a computational facility, IAC is organized into two divisions: Program Development and Computer Operations. The personnel within these two divisions are directly involved in the operation, maintenance and effective utilization of the computational resource.

The Program Development Division provides the interface between IAC and its computational facility users. Computer Operations has direct responsibility for seven-day-a-week, 24-hour-a-day operation and maintenance of IAC's physical computational facility. Normally, the operations staff has no contact with users.

The conventional user has access to the system via the ARPA network. He LOGS IN, communicates with the IAC System using A Control Language (ACL), and can submit Illiac jobs for deferred processing (BATCH) by simply defining parameters in a Primary Input File (PIF). Corresponding Batch messages and System responses are output into a Primary Output File (POF). The data for processing may be sent via the ARPA network employing a File Transfer Program (CPYNET) or submitted on mag tape.

A special high speed link interface has been developed which provides the facility for a remote computer site to use the Illiac Processor interactively as opposed to normal Batch operation. The Link also enables a user to handle/process classified data on the Illiac.

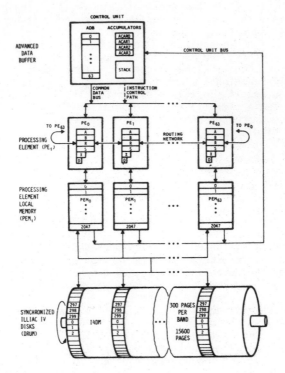

Figure 3.3 Simplified diagram of the Illiac IV

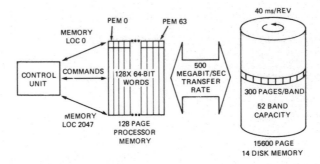

Figure 3.4 PEM to Illiac IV data transfers

3. System Description

The principal computing resource within the IAC computational facility
is the Illiac array processor. The Illiac is integrated into the IAC
computational facility described by this document. This facility includes additional processors, interfacing devices, memory and software
systems, all dedicated to optimizing the support of Illiac's processing
capability.

A. Physical Overview Description

   The physical hardware which comprises the IAC computational facility is located at NASA Ames Research Center, Moffett Field, California. Building N233-A was constructed for this facility.
   The custom-built facility has an 11,700 square foot computer bay.
   The complex requires 1.2 megawatts of power and 281 tons of air
   conditioning.
   An equivalent basement area below the computer bay contains power
   switching gear, air conditioning equipment and 3 motor generator
   sets, which provide approximately 1,000 amps of clean power to the
   machine room.

   1. Environmental Facilities

      Four separate air conditioning systems provide temperature and
      humidity control. Chillers, dryers, moisturizers, fans, etc.
      are distributed in the basement and on the roof. Three of the
      systems provide two acre feet per minute of 60 degree Fahren-
      heit air under the computer room false floor for vented dis-
      tribution through equipment as required. The fourth air con-
      ditioning system moves an acre foot per minute through the
      Illiac with temperature 64 deg F and relative humidity con-
      trolled better than +/-5% to ensure a stable machine environ-
      ment.
      A complex system of sensors, recording devices, and alarms re-
      port status for the entire environmental system on a centrally
      located annunciator panel.

25

2. Personnel Facilities

Most IAC personnel are located in an office facility in Sunnyvale. This separate physical facility provides two benefits.
First, improved system performance is achieved by restricting
machine access only to those directly involved in operation
and maintenance.
And second, the off-site offices afford more convenient liaison with the commercial firms, which provide much of the development support to the Institute.
A communication link provides convenient terminal access to
the computational facility for IAC personnel as well as visit-
ing users.

B. Hardware/Software System

The computational facility has been organized and designed to support high speed computation on the Illiac Processor. The storage,
control and transfer of large data bases (typically, 5-10 million
words) is part of this support. Figure 3.5 is a detailed block
diagram of the current IAC system.

1. Illiac

The Illiac IV parallel computer is described in detail in the
next section. A brief overview is provided here to show the
motivation for various system features.
The Illiac consists of 64 parallel processing units, each a
general purpose, stored program, digital computer devoid of
control, and all under the direction of a single Control Unit,
which is also a stored program digital computer. Local working storage for each processing unit is a semiconductor memory with 2K 64-bit word capacity and 300 nanosecond full cycle.
Local storage typically contains both program and data.
Illiac speed depends upon its basic clock which currently runs
at 12.5 MHz (approximately 80 ns). In addition to the basic
clock rate, Illiac computational speed is achieved in three
ways. First, replication or parallel hardware structure; second, parallel data transfer; and third, overlap operation--
that is, two normally sequential events performed concurrently
in different parts of the machine.
Main memory storage for Illiac processing is currently provided by a 12 disk subsystem (I4DM) with a (maximum) capacity
of 15 million 64-bit words at 500 million bits per second,
synchronized for high bandwidth transfer from multiple disk
drives. This memory with its controls and data paths is
called the I/O subsystem (IOSS).

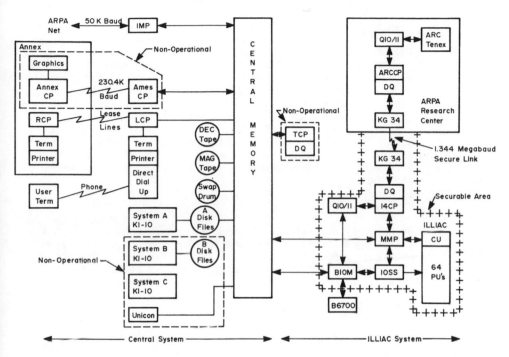

Figure 3.5 Simplified IAC system block diagram

The user and operations deal with each disk or storage unit
(SU) in terms of its bands. Each SU has four bands, each with
a capacity of 300 Illiac pages*, i.e., 1200 Illiac pages per
SU. The user does not see the maximum physical capacity of
32 bands because only a specified quantity of bands are
"released" as operational. The actual bands specified will
vary. Both the bands in use and the spares have been certi-
fied by 8000 passes of random data (10" bits) with no errors.
Remaining bands are undergoing test or maintenance.
The Control Unit directs parallel processing in all or selected Processing Units (PUs). The architecture supports 64, 128
or 512 parallel data systems, respectively 64, 32 or 8 bits
wide. Sixty-four and 32-bit word processing is fully implemented in hardware, while 8-bit capability is limited.
The Illiac Processor is a "raw" computational resource, i.e.,
a computational "job" requires both user data and user program. However, there is a limited operating system which
exists in an external PDP-11 memory management processor (MMP).
It issues high level commands, and processes status, common to
all "jobs".

2. Burroughs 6700

An entirely separate Burroughs 6700 computer complex is maintained operational in the same machine room to provide programming support to users. It supports an Illiac Assembler
(ASK), an Illiac Compiler (GLYPNIR) and an Illiac Simulator
(SSK).

3. Central System

A central system complex provides interactive communications
for users, program and data storage, and high speed data transfer facilities to support the Illiac Processor. Data paths
are established from the ARPA Network and physical mag tapes
via central memory to the Illiac main memory (I4DM) and the
Burroughs 6700 Computer Complex. These paths can be seen in
Figure 3.5.
A concept of "shared memory" is employed within central memory
to accomplish high speed data transfer, concurrent multiprocessing, and communication with central system processes,
which have been "distributed" to PDP-11, peripheral processors.
The central system complex is a memory based system comprised
of a DEC PDP-11 central processing unit with 128K of core memory, a 1 million word swapping drum and 7 each 50 megabyte.

---

*An Illiac page is 1024 64-bit words (or 2048 32-bit words). A TENEX
page is 512 36-bit words. One Illiac page of data can reside within
four pages of TENEX address space.

Century 215 disk drives. This hardware complement supports a
modified BB&N TENEX 1.34, which is a demand page operating
system with fixed page size and a virtual address space implemented by means of page tables.
The central system address space consists of 256 pages of 1
microsecond core memory. Approximately 107 pages are used by
TENEX and other resident functions. Swapping is supported by
a 2048 page drum with an 11 megabit/sec. bandwidth (inst.) and
35 ms worst case rotational latency. Moving head, removable
media disk files provide another 170,520 pages in the virtual
address space.
A special shared memory portion of the central system address
space (BIOM/ME-10) is also accessible by the Burroughs 6700
computer system and the Illiac main memory (I4DM). BIOM ports
provide 40 megabit/sec bandwidth data transfer for Illiac program preparation on the Burroughs 6700 and 640 megabit/second-
bandwidth for on-loading/off-loading either I4DM or PEM.

4. Input/Output Subsystem (IOSS)

Figure 3.6 is a block diagram of the IOSS. It consists of the
following major elements:

a. Storage Units (SU)
b. Disk File Controller (DFC)
c. Electronics Unit (EU)
d. I/O Switch (IOS)
e. Descriptor Controller (DC)
f. Buffer I/O Memory (BIOM)
g. MMP Remote Module
h. Disk Synchronizer

The Illiac IV disk memory (I4DM) is the Illiac processor main
memory. Under direction from the DC, it provides 15 million
64-bit words at 500 megabits per second (inst.) over a 1,024
bit BUS which accesses 16 PEMs simultaneously. Currently, one
DFC with a maximum of 12 SUs is operational.
The BIOM provides data rate buffering over four (4) ports:

a. To I4DM at 640 megabits/second
b. To B6700 at 40 megabits/second
c. To PDP-10 at 32 megabits/second
d. (Not used)

The BIOM is physically constructed of 4 PEMs, i.e., 8K 64-bit
bi-polar memory. Currently TENEX/I4DM transfers via BIOM consist of four Illiac pages (1K x 64 bit each).
I4DM is a fixed head per track disk file system currently consisting of 8 to 12 single disk SUs connected to one DFC.
There are 512 tracks per disk, organized in four bands which
transfer 128 bits parallel. 1200 sectors per revolution x 4
bands = 4800 sectors/disk. Each sector is 128 x 128 bit words.
Total disk capacity is 79,257,600 bits.

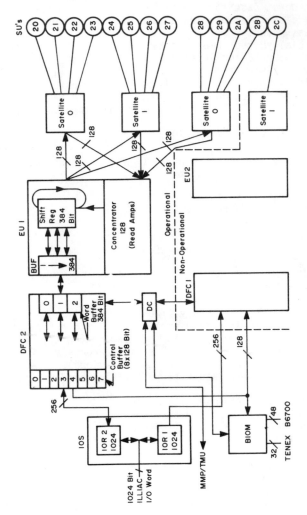

Figure 3.6 Block diagram of Illiac I/O subsystem

An Illiac page, consisting of four contiguous sectors, transfers in approximately 133 milliseconds. Worst case rotational
latency is approximately 40 milliseconds.
A disk synchronizer system synchronizes the SUs for each DFC
within one sector time to avoid full rotational latency during
multi-SU transfer.

5. Illiac Problem Diagnosis Support Software

To understand a "working" machine it is first necessary to
accept the fact that conceptually it is always broken, and
that while broken it is usable depending upon the level of
failure.
The failure of one of the programs listed below can be used to
certify a non-working machine. The successful execution of
one or all of the programs below can be used to certify a level
of failure above which the machine ran during execution of
those programs. Within this context, the following programs
can be used to imply a "working" machine.

Confidence Tests:

   Successful Illiac execution of one or more of the following
   programs is used to establish a level of confidence that
   the machine is "working".

   a. FLIRT - this is a converted segment of user code which will
       halt on one of 64 errors. PE states are compared follow-
       ing each step. Error results are output to a file for use
       by the PESO simulator in isolating stuck-1 stuck-0.
   b. CONBAT - like FLIRT this is a converted segment of user
       code, but it has been optimized for faster execution. The
       diagnostics have been removed and only final results are
       compared. It is a go/no-go test.
   c. I4DMPT - this is an I4DM to PEM array data path transfer
       test. Path testing to the BIOM is currently not opera-
       tional. This test requires TENEX/MMP. It has a user in-
       terface which selects test patterns, number of passes,
       I4DM areas and response to error detection.

Diagnostic Tests:

   Failure during Illiac execution of any of the following programs is used as a diagnostic tool to support efforts to
   isolate and correct problems which occur.

   a. OPAL - this is a basic test of the Control Unit (CU) which
       operates from TENEX via MMP and TMU. All testing uses TMU
       hardware.
       CUTEST is an OPAL subtest.

    b. IOPAL - this is a program of selected tests for Illiac I/O. PEMOZ is an IOPAL job which write 1's or Ø's in the BIOM and loads them into PEM.
PEMVR is an IOPAL job which writes random data in the BIOM.

    c. HACPM - this program tests PEMs, PE mode control and the Control Unit Buffer (CUB) cards. It uses TMU hardware or loads the program directly into IWS. It does not use FINST/PE instructions.

    d. HAPE - this is a PE test which resides in PEM. It employs canned operands and results which test 64- and 32-bit arithmetic Boolean logic functions and transfer paths.
It can be loaded via BIOM (fast) or TMU (slow). Operands and failure results are output to a file for use by the PESO simulator in isolating stuck-1, stuck-Ø.
SINGLE CYCLE MULTIPLY (SCM) is a diagnostic multiply instruction. It executes the first iteration of a floating point multiply.

    e. RUNARA - this program resides in PEM and generates random operands to test PE in 64-bit mode. It uses array routing to check PEs against each other and sends results to a file for use by the PESO simulator in isolating stuck-1, stuck-Ø.

    f. PESO - this is a hardware logic simulation system specifically adapted to simulating the Illiac IV PE but capable of being generalized or converted to simulate other devices. It runs on the working PEs in the Illiac. Its principal application is as a diagnostic aid for locating certain types of hardware failures.
Given a set of known errors in the output of the device being simulated, PESO can be used to simulate all single stuck type faults and report which of these faults produces simulated results consistent with the observed results.

    g. RANDOM INSTRUCTION TEST (RIT) - this is the only CU overlap diagnostic. It has four tables of instructions from which it assembles a random instruction sequence. It compares results in overlap and non-overlap for dissimilarity. It has the ability to reiterate through the sequence looking for the point at which dissimilarity begins.

Special Tests:

    The following diagnostics were written for special purposes:

    a. PROBE - a special diagnostic written to test 64-bit, add-rounding problems.

    b. 7-UP - a special diagnostic to multiply random numbers.

    c. ONEROM - compares the CU ROM output to the known correct output for each instruction decode.

4. Operational System Hardware

A. Burroughs 6700 System

The B6700 is a medium-sized information processing, compiler oriented computer system designed specifically to support problem-
oriented languages, e.g. ALGOL, COBOL and FORTRAN. All programs
are reentrant and support multi-user time sharing. The system
provides dynamic storage allocation, program segmentation and subroutine linkages.
At IAC the Burroughs 6700 supports an Illiac program compiler,
GLYPNIR; an Illiac program assembler, ASK; and an Illiac simulator,
SSK.
Figure 3.7 is a block diagram of the Burroughs 6700 computer system configuration within the IAC computational facility.

1. Processor

The central processor complex consists of a model II processor
(5MHz), a model I multiplexor (10MHz), 4 scratch pad memories,
a peripheral controller (1.67MHz) and a data communications
processor (DCP) with a 9600 baud link to the IAC central system (LCP).

2. Memory Hierarchy

The processing complex is supported by 65.6K x 52-bit core
memory, and 5 each 20-megabyte disk files with 46 millisecond
worst case latency and 408KHz (inst.), transfer rate.

3. Peripherals

In addition to the disk units the peripheral controller has:

a. Three 9-track and one 7-track tape drives selectable for
   556/800 BPI or 75/90/120 IPS
b. 800 line per minute, 132 column line printer
c. 800 card per minute card reader
d. 150 card per minute card punch
e. Console display
f. Hardware diagnostic capability

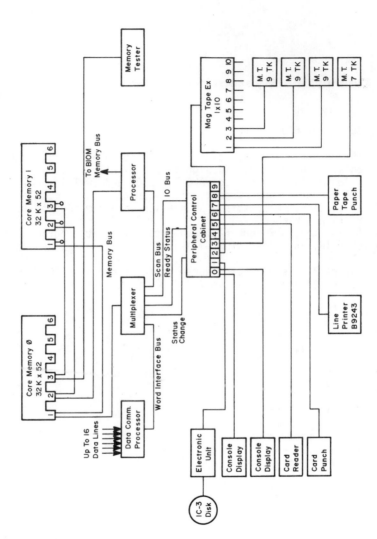

Figure 3.7   B6700 configuration diagram

B. Central System-A

System-A is the primary operational computer system. A BB&N TENEX
operates on DEC-10 hardware to provide a time-sharing system for
both internal and external users to have interactive and batch
access. System-A is the primary host on the ARPANET. It currently provides central file storage and a central communication point
for all of the hardware/software subsystems including the Illiac.

1. Processor

The central processing unit (CPU) is a model KI DEC PDP-10,
general purpose, stored program, binary, digital computer. It
is an asynchronous, 36-bit word processor with an instruction
cycle time of approximately one MHz, 16 general purpose registers (16 accumulators, 15 index registers) and multiplexed
I/O channels featuring programmed priority interrupts with
seven fully nested levels. The system has multi-level in-
direct addressing and features double-precision hardware
floating point arithmetic.
One of its more interesting features is virtual mapping hardware. The most significant 9 bits of the 18-bit memory address points to a user-determined, 13-bit, physical page address, which is concatenated with the original low-order, 9-
bit word address to form a total 22-bit address for physical
memory space.

2. Memory

The System-A operational storage hierarchy consists of 128K of
core memory, a one megaword swapping drum, eight each 50-mega-
byte disk spindles and two IBM compatible Potter mag tape
drives.
MA-10 core memory is 16K per box, 900 ns. full cycle time,
with 4 bits of selection to provide a maximum of 16 MA-10
boxes per system. The MA-10 features a two-way interleave
for overlap memory access and 18 bits of addressability.
The ME-10 is a 16K box with a one microsec full cycle time
and 8 bits of port selection for a total system capacity of
256 16K boxes. The ME-10 features a four-way interleave and
provides 22 bits of addressability.
The Systems Concepts memory is a 64K box with an internal full
cycle time of 700 ns. The swapping drum system consists of an
Applied Logic Corporation controller with a Bryant 1,000,000
word floating head drum interfaced directly to System-A core
memory. The control interface is connected to the standard
KI-10 I/O BUS. The drum is organized in 128 horizontal bands,
each containing eight tracks for parallel simultaneous data
transfer. Five parallel transfers make one 36-bit word; 128
words form a sector; and there are 64 sectors per band, i.e.,
16 TENEX pages per band. Worst case rotational latency is 35
milliseconds, and the instantaneous, bit serial, transfer rate
is 1.4 MHz to provide a bandwidth of 11.2 megabit/second.

A telefile DC-10 disk controller interfaces eight each 215
Century disk drives directly to System-A core memory. The
DC-10 control interface is connected to the standard KI-10
I/O BUS. One 215 disk drive is always off-line as a "hot"
spare.
An IAC modification to the DC-10 controller provides 3 TENEX
pages/track, 60 pages/cylinder, 24,360 pages/spindle. Bandwidth is 2.5 MHz (instantaneous) with 25 ms worst case rotational latency.
An IAC mag tape controller is managed by a PDP-11 processor.
It interfaces two Potter, automatic threading, model 1082,
800 BPI, 150 IPS, vacuum loop tape drives. Current hardware/
software limitations result in a system transfer rate from mag
tape of 28 pages per minute (heavy TENEX loading) or 60 pages
per minute (light TENEX loading).

3. Peripheral Subsystems

The KI-10 processor supports a TD10 DEC tape controller with
eight TU55 DEC tape transports, a 300 character per second,
high-speed, paper tape reader and a DK10 real time clock.
Local and remote communication processes have been implemented
in PDP-11 processors at AMES and the ANNEX facility called the
LCP and RCP respectively. They handle an expanded complement
of devices, which includes terminals, CRTs from 300 to 2400
baud and a system of four line printers implemented on Data
Products 300 line per minute drum printers.
Peripheral communication processes are managed by PDP-11 processors called CPs. These links are discussed separately
below.

4. Special Systems

A separate system called the OPERATOR-11 (OPR-11) monitors
input from major IAC computational facility system elements,
e.g., TENEX-A & B, Illiac (via MMP), the LCP/RCP, the B6700
and the System Status Analyzer (SSA). The OPR-11 logs this
information in real time on a hard-copy terminal, as well as
storing it in a TENEX file for daily status processing. The
SSA is an analog/digital data collection device which multiplexes information from 32 probes/sensors positioned at critical points in the machine room. This system is expandable to
128 probe/sensors.

C. System Communication Links

For overall system operation, effective communication of commands
and data between system nodes is as important as the speed and
capacity of the hardware/software system which comprises that
node.

1. "Shared Memory" Communication

For the most part paths internal to the system are implemented
by means of "shared memory." "Shared memory" is used by the
KI processors, the PDP-11 peripheral processors and the communication processors to transfer commands, data and control
information. Each processor considers the "shared memory" to
be within its address space and access contention is solved
by software "lock" words.
In general each process uses a statically defined area in
one or more of the memory units which it shares with its companion processes. The shared memories are accessed through
TENEX by the use of KLUDGE files. These files have page maps
which point to the associated shared memory unit. Any reference to a page in a KLUDGE file actually references a location
in the shared memory. Using KLUDGE files, the partitioning
and use of shared memories is independent of the actual memory
box used or its physical address.

2. Communication Processors

Communication processors (CPs) have been used to implement
both internal and external system communication paths. A
typical CP consists of a PDP-11 system with the communication
hardware to support the CP operating system software.
The CPs support all the protocol for network type communications which multiplexes and commands both control and data
over a full duplex link. They also offer a uniform hardware/
software interface to support the distribution of processes
previously resident within TENEX.
Two recent important software development projects have made
use of the CP system: first, a high bandwidth, network data
transfer directly with an available port in the TENEX disk
driver (TDD); second, an interactive, real-time, message facility allowing communication between Illiac processing and the
companion process in TENEX.

3. The ARPA Network

Geographically separated computers (hosts) communicate via
the ARPA network. Host computers connect into the network by
means of a small, local computer called an Interface Message
Processor (IMP). Host computers typically differ in type,
speed, word length, etc.

The network is formed by interconnecting IMPs via a 50-kilobit communication link. Each IMP is programmed to store and forward messages to neighboring IMPs in the network, i.e., each message is passed from IMP to IMP through the network until it arrives at its destination IMP.

Host computers communicate via the network by means of regular messages which vary in length from 96 to 8,159 bits. The first 96 bits are control bits called the leader. Leader information is defined by the host and includes destination, handling type and a message ID to identify the message in case of transmission loss.

The IMP converts regular messages to packets which consist of 96 leader bits and 1,008 data bits. The IMP message processing task consists of disassembling outgoing messages into packets, assembling incoming packets into messages, allocating buffer space, detecting lost messages and performing the bookkeeping to support eight messages in transit in either direction. IMPs provide a transmission queue with priorities. They request buffer space for large messages to avoid deadlocks. They provide full network protocol including 30-45 second timeout for no response.

4. The AMES/ANNEX Link

The TENEX low speed I/O capability for line printers and terminals is extended from the IAC computational facility at AMES over a set of telephone lines (type 3002, Schedule 4, voice grade, private line) to the ANNEX facility in Sunnyvale. There are also eight direct dial-up, full duplex, phone lines as well as the 12 AMES/ANNEX phone lines, two of which are full duplex.

The local communication processor (LCP) at AMES multiplexes 300, 1800 and 2400 baud serial transmission paths. Some of these paths communicate with the remote communication processor (RCP) at the ANNEX site, which provides approximately 24 hardwire terminals, eight local exchange dial-ups and a local line printer.

A 230.4 Kbaud wideband link is in the final stages of implementation. The AMES-CP/ANNEX-CP would manage low overhead high bandwidth data transfer with an interactive, real time graphics display system over this link.

5. The AMES/ARC Link

The ARC-CP and the I4CP manage a 1,344 megabaud data link to establish high bandwidth data transfers. This link bypasses the IAC central system facility and provides a remote host TENEX site with direct control of the Illiac system. Control information is passed to the MMP. Data is transferred directly to the ME-10/BIOM.

KG-34 encryption hardware is installed in this link to accommodate the transmission of secure data from a secure remote host for secure Illiac processing.

D. Central System-B

System-B is a secondary computer system. It supports a BB&N TENEX,
operating on DEC-10 hardware. It is a time-sharing system for internal, IAC software development use. It is also used to support
maintenance activity for the Illiac.
Access to this system is limited even within IAC. However, a
TENEX-BATCH facility (T-BATCH) provides deferred processing of
TENEX jobs on System-B.

1. Processor

The Central Processing Unit (CPU) is a model KI DEC PDP-10
identical to the processor described in Section IV-C-1 above.

2. Memory

The System-B operational storage hierarchy consists of 128K of
core memory and 5 each 25-megabyte disk spindles.
The Systems Concepts memory is a 128K of core memory and 5
each 25-megabyte disk spindles.
The Systems Concepts memory is a 128K box with an internal,
full cycle time of 700 ns. Other specifications are unknown.
A Telefile DC-10 disk controller interfaces 5 each 114 Century disk drives directly to System-B core memory. The DC-10
control interface is connected to the standard KI-10 I/O BUS.
One 114 disk drive is kept off-line as a "hot" spare.
An IAC modification to the DC-10 controller provides 3 TENEX
pages per track, 60 pages per cylinder, 12,180 pages per spin-
dle. The bandwidth is 2.5 MHz (inst.) with 25 ms worst case
rotational latency.

3. Peripheral Subsystems

The KI-10 processor supports a 300 character/second, high
speed, paper tape reader and a DK-10 real-time clock.
A local communication process has been implemented in a PDP-11
processor at AMES called LCP-2. It handles an expanded complement of devices including terminals and CRTs from 300 to
2400 baud.

E. Computer Facility Support Systems

The computational facility hardware component systems require support facilities. This includes an environmental control system,
a power distribution system and the necessary alarms to indicate
failures or faults in these systems.

1. Air Conditioning System

A recirculating air flow system removes the machine room heat
load using one of two 281 ton capacity chilling units which
are alternated weekly. The unused unit remains on standby.

The chillers' cool air is driven by the following fan systems:

AC1   22,500 CFM Tech Lab/PEX Lab
AC2   36,000 CFM Machine Room under the west floor
AC3   36,000 CFM Machine Room under the east floor
AC4   7,280 CFM Office area
AC5   7,500 CFM makeup fresh air;

Plus the following special air flow systems:

2 ea.   8,000 CFM Motor Generator Room fans
1 ea.   20,000 CFM Tech Lab/PEX Lab return air;

Plus a special system for the Illiac:

3 ea.   27,500 CFM fans, two of which are operational to provide 55,000 CFM with one fan always on automatic standby.

These systems provide the following environmental control:

AC1   68 +/-5 deg.F with thermostatic control (Tech Lab/
PEX Lab).
AC2, 3   60 +/-5 deg.F and 26 +/-5% relative humidity.
Illiac   64 +/-0 deg.F temperature at 50 +/-5% relative
humidity.

All environmental systems have pneumatic controls.
Temperature alarms are set to go off at 78 deg.F in Illiac and
for a humidity excursion below 20% or above 70% in any area.
Dehumidification is provided by a three stage system on the
roof consisting of bag filters, a charcoal filter and a BRY-
air unit consisting of desiccant and dryer.
A special closed area, in the Tech Lab supplied by ACI, is
equipped with a fume hood for silver solder welding.

2.   Power Distribution

Power is brought to the IAC computational facility wing, Building N233 at AMES, as a 6900-volt feeder input to a four-way
oil switch. The other input is a spare for a future alternate
6900-volt, feeder input.
One output from the oil switch provides 1,600 amps, 480/277
three-phase, four wire service for building power. This service supports fluorescent lighting, air conditioning systems
and utility wall receptacles.
The second output provides 2,500 amp, 120/208 three-phase,
five wire service for three motor generator sets, which provide "clean" computer room power. The motor/generator sets
are equivalent to a load of approximately 1,200-1,300 amps.
Motor generator set #1 provides power for the central system
hardware. Approximately 200 amps of the 521-amp full load
capability is used.

A total of approximately 1,000 amps of "clean" power is delivered by the three motor generator sets to the machine room.
At full load, the motor generator sets will "ride through" a
300 millisecond power discontinuity. The "ride through" is
inversely proportional to the load; therefore, the current
"ride through" would be approximately one-half second.
Approximately 50 utility receptacles distribute "clean" computer power in the PEX Lab and Tech Lab. Each receptacle is
provided with a separate 25 amp, 250 volt, four wire line filter to decouple utility equipment noise from other clean room
power.

3.   Alarm Systems

An alarm system with sensors in all critical areas including
temperature, humidity, unauthorized access, etc., reports to a
centrally located annunciator panel.
A list of annunciator panel alarms follows:

a.   CU OVER TEMPERATURE   (82 Deg.)
b.   CU ALARM TEMPERATURE   (80 Deg.)
c.   CU LOW TEMPERATURE   (65 Deg.)
d.   PUC00-07 OVERTEMPERATURE   (82 Deg.) 8 alarms
e.   PUC00-07 ALARM TEMPERATURE   (80 Deg.) 8 alarms
f.   PUC00-07 LOW TEMPERATURE   (65 Deg.) 8 alarms
g.   FACILITY CONTROL POWER OFF
h.   ILLIAC 3 MINUTE AIR TIMEOUT
i.   ILLIAC SMOKE DETECTION   any PUC
j.   EMERGENCY SHUT DOWN INITIATED
k.   ILLIAC SUPPLY FAN TROUBLE
l.   ILLIAC UNPROTECTED
m.   MG SET ROOM OVERTEMPERATURE
n.   MG SET ALARM TEMPERATURE
o.   ANNUNCIATOR BATTERY CHARGER FAILURE
p.   ANNUNCIATOR POWER ON
q.   SMOKE DAMPERS OPEN

4.   Fire Systems

A halon fire system has been installed to protect the Illiac.
Portable Halon units can be connected to special fixtures installed in the Illiac to flood localized areas with halon for
fire suppression. A manually operated system is also available to flood the entire Illiac from a halon supply in the
basement.

B. The ILLIAC IV

1. Introduction to Parallelism

The Illiac IV belongs to a class of computers termed Single Instruction Multiple Data stream (SIMD) processors. The architecture of the Illiac is shown at a conceptual level in Figure 3.8.

Illiac is a parallel processor. It consists of a control unit (CU), 64 processing elements (PE), 131,072 words of core memory, and 15,974,400 words of disk memory. The control unit has access to all of core memory. Its basic cycle time is 60 nanoseconds. However, greater processing power is achieved through the simultaneous execution of an instruction in each of the 64 processing elements.

The control unit fetches and decodes all instructions. After decoding, some instructions are broadcast for execution in the processing elements while others are executed in the control unit. The arithmetic capability of the control unit is limited to 24 bit two's complement addition and subtraction, masking, and comparison for use in branching. The control unit has no floating point capability. One operand at a time is processed by the control unit. The control unit also initiates data transfers between core and Illiac disk.

The processing power of Illiac resides in 64 identical processing elements. Each PE executes instructions broadcast from the CU. Though each PE has its own index registers and memory to operate upon, all 64 PEs always execute identical instructions in lockstep. Each PE has direct access to 2048 words of core memory.

There are three data paths available for communication among PEs and between the PEs and the control unit (CU). First, the CU can access all of core, so it can load a word from one processing element memory (PEM) and either use it or store it in another PEM. This method of communication is both simple and flexible, allowing for any data movement desired, but, since only one word at a time is transferred, it is relatively slow compared to the two other methods available.

Second, the CU can communicate with all PEs by broadcasting the same word to all PEs simultaneously. This method is faster than the first since sixty-four words are transmitted at once, but provides only a limited form of communication.

Third, the PEs can communicate with each other via the ROUTE instruction which transfers the contents of a register in each PE to the PE determined by the following scheme: If PEN (processing element number) is the number of the source PE and R is the route amount supplied with the instruction, identical in all PEs, the number of the destination PE is MOD_{64} (PEN+R). If the PEs are thought of as arranged in a

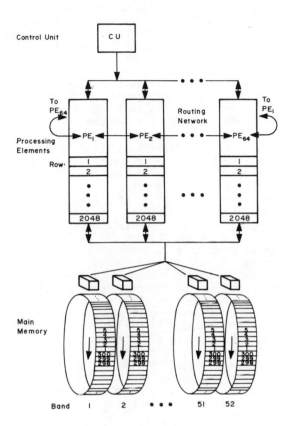

Figure 3.8   Conceptual architecture of Illiac IV

circle with PE 63 adjacent to PE 0, the ROUTE instruction consists of
loading the data, rotating the circle, and storing the data. This data
transfer is very fast since 64 words are transferred simultaneously.
It is general in that all 64 words can be different but the pattern set
by the fact that the routing distance is the same for all PEs is re-
strictive. It does not transfer 64 words randomly distributed in core
to 64 different locations simultaneously.

The primary memory used by Illiac is a disk memory with capacity
approximately 100 times that of core memory. One page (1024 words) of
memory is the minimum amount of data that can be transferred between
core and disk. Although the bandwidth between core and disk is $5. \times 10^8$
bits per second, the average access time to a particular spot on disk
is 20 milliseconds. This relatively long access time (compared to an
80 nanosecond clock time in 64 parallel processors) necessitates careful
planning of disk usage. The number of disk transfers must be kept to a
minimum to avoid waiting for disk accesses.

Since the most important feature of Illiac is its computing power
one of the prime objectives in the design of any Illiac program is to
minimize execution time. The best possible result is a running time
1/64 that possible with only one PE, but due to the architecture of the
machine the degree to which this is achieved is dependent upon the design of the algorithm. First, suppose that it is necessary to code the
trigonometric SIN function for Illiac. If the particular usage makes
it possible to always compute 64 functions simultaneously, one simply
has the same SIN routine running in all PEs on different data, and a
speedup by a factor of 64 is very nearly achieved. (Some time is lost
if there is conditional branching in the original SIN routine which is
changed to enabling and disabling of PEs.) A second approach is to de-
vise a method for utilizing all 64 processors to compute one function
value. No method has been devised for doing this 64 or even 10 times
faster than is possible with one processor. The first approach is both
faster and simpler, but certain algorithms may preclude calculation of
more than one value of SIN simultaneously or may require significant
overhead elsewhere in order to do so.

One misconception is that if all of the PEs are kept "busy" the
machine is running at maximum efficiency. In fact this statement is
not true and one must be very careful in relating the word efficiency
to the use of Illiac. For example, consider the problem of summing
groups of numbers. If it is desired to sum 64 pairs of numbers, keeping 64 different results, each PE forms one sum and the work is done
64 times faster than could be done by one processor. If however, it is
desired to find the sum of one group of 64 numbers, a more complicated method must be used. In order to simplify the explanation somewhat, consider an eight PE machine and the summation of eight numbers,
one in each PE. Figure 3.9 depicts a method whereby this can be done
in three routes and three additions. Since the routes require roughly
equivalent CPU time as the register loads necessary before any operation, the time taken for an 8 PE machine to sum eight numbers is equal
to the time taken for three additions. If this algorithm is extended
to the summation of 64 numbers within a 64 PE machine it takes 6 additions to form the sum. Given that one PE requires 63 additions to sum
64 numbers, the 64 PE machine is 63/6 or 10.5 times faster. Note that
although none of the PEs are ever disabled and all are forming the

STATE OF REGISTERS

OPERATION	PE0	PE1	PE2	PE3	PE4	PE5	PE6	PE7
Initial Conditions	$\$A=I_0$ $\$R=0$	$\$A=I_1$ $\$R=0$	$\$A=I_2$ $\$R=0$	$\$A=I_3$ $\$R=0$	$\$A=I_4$ $\$R=0$	$\$A=I_5$ $\$R=0$	$\$A=I_6$ $\$R=0$	$\$A=I_7$ $\$R=0$
1. Route Contents of $\$A_N$ to $\$R_{N+1}$.	$\$A=I_0$ $\$R=I_7$	$\$A=I_1$ $\$R=I_0$	$\$A=I_2$ $\$R=I_1$	$\$A=I_3$ $\$R=I_2$	$\$A=I_4$ $\$R=I_3$	$\$A=I_5$ $\$R=I_4$	$\$A=I_6$ $\$R=I_5$	$\$A=I_7$ $\$R=I_6$
2. Add $\$A$ to $\$R$ and leave result in $\$A$.	$\$A=I_0+I_7$ $\$R=I_7$	$\$A=I_1+I_0$ $\$R=I_0$	$\$A=I_2+I_1$ $\$R=I_1$	$\$A=I_3+I_2$ $\$R=I_2$	$\$A=I_4+I_3$ $\$R=I_3$	$\$A=I_5+I_4$ $\$R=I_4$	$\$A=I_6+I_5$ $\$R=I_5$	$\$A=I_7+I_6$ $\$R=I_6$
3. Route Contents of $\$A_N$ to $\$R_{N+2}$.	$\$A=I_0+I_7$ $\$R=I_6+I_5$	$\$A=I_1+I_0$ $\$R=I_7+I_6$	$\$A=I_2+I_1$ $\$R=I_0+I_7$	$\$A=I_3+I_2$ $\$R=I_1+I_0$	$\$A=I_4+I_3$ $\$R=I_2+I_1$	$\$A=I_5+I_4$ $\$R=I_3+I_2$	$\$A=I_6+I_5$ $\$R=I_4+I_3$	$\$A=I_7+I_6$ $\$R=I_5+I_4$
4. Add $\$A$ to $\$R$ and leave result in $\$A$.	$\$A=I_0+I_7+$ I_6+I_5 $\$R=I_6+I_5$	$\$A=I_1+I_0+$ I_7+I_6 $\$R=I_7+I_6$	$\$A=I_2+I_1+$ I_0+I_7 $\$R=I_0+I_7$	$\$A=I_3+I_2+$ I_1+I_0 $\$R=I_1+I_0$	$\$A=I_4+I_3+$ I_2+I_1 $\$R=I_2+I_1$	$\$A=I_5+I_4+$ I_3+I_2 $\$R=I_3+I_2$	$\$A=I_6+I_5+$ I_4+I_3 $\$R=I_4+I_3$	$\$A=I_7+I_6+$ I_5+I_4 $\$R=I_5+I_4$
5. Route Contents of $\$A_N$ to $\$R_{N+4}$.	$\$A=I_0+I_7+$ I_6+I_5 $\$R=I_4+I_3+$ I_2+I_1	$\$A=I_1+I_0+$ I_7+I_6 $\$R=I_5+I_4+$ I_3+I_2	$\$A=I_2+I_1+$ I_0+I_7 $\$R=I_6+I_5+$ I_4+I_3	$\$A=I_3+I_2+$ I_1+I_0 $\$R=I_7+I_6+$ I_5+I_4	$\$A=I_4+I_3+$ I_2+I_1 $\$R=I_0+I_7+$ I_6+I_5	$\$A=I_5+I_4+$ I_3+I_2 $\$R=I_1+I_0+$ I_7+I_6	$\$A=I_6+I_5+$ I_4+I_3 $\$R=I_2+I_1+$ I_0+I_7	$\$A=I_7+I_6+$ I_5+I_4 $\$R=I_3+I_2+$ I_1+I_0
6. Add $\$A$ to $\$R$ and leave result in $\$A$.	$\$A=I_0+I_7+$ I_6+I_5+ I_4+I_3+ I_2+I_1 $\$R=I_4+I_3+$ I_2+I_1	$\$A=I_1+I_0+$ I_7+I_6+ I_5+I_4+ I_3+I_2 $\$R=I_5+I_4+$ I_3+I_2	$\$A=I_2+I_1+$ I_0+I_7+ I_6+I_5+ I_4+I_3 $\$R=I_6+I_5+$ I_4+I_3	$\$A=I_3+I_2+$ I_1+I_0+ I_7+I_6+ I_5+I_4 $\$R=I_7+I_6+$ I_5+I_4	$\$A=I_4+I_3+$ I_2+I_1+ I_0+I_7+ I_6+I_5 $\$R=I_0+I_7+$ I_6+I_5	$\$A=I_5+I_4+$ I_3+I_2+ I_1+I_0+ I_7+I_6 $\$R=I_1+I_0+$ I_7+I_6	$\$A=I_6+I_5+$ I_4+I_3+ I_2+I_1+ I_0+I_7 $\$R=I_2+I_1+$ I_0+I_7	$\$A=I_7+I_6+$ I_5+I_4+ I_3+I_2+ I_1+I_0 $\$R=I_3+I_2+$ I_1+I_0

Figure 3.9 Detailed view of rowsum operation

sum, this algorithm does not achieve the factor of 64 speed up. However, the factor of ten speed up that is achieved makes this algorithm usable if data organization requires its use.

The choice of which design approach to take for a particular problem is dependent upon data organization. There is often one approach requiring a very specific data organization which is much faster than any other. It must be decided whether the overhead and execution time involved in data transposition is compensated by decreased overhead and execution time elsewhere in the algorithm.

2. Major Constituents

As the name implies, the main function of the control Unit (CU) is to control lock-step parallel operations of 64 PEs. The CU, as illustrated in Figure 3.10 may be logically partitioned into five functional units that support asynchronous PE computation: a) the Advanced Station (ADVAST), which handles incoming instruction blocks, b) the Instruction Look Ahead (ILA) that, under program command, provides the address of the first program instruction, and requests 8-word instruction blocks, via the memory service unit, from the PEMs to its instruction word storage, c) the Final Station (FINST), which converts instructions into microsequences for the PEs, d) the Memory Service Unit (MSU), which provides memory control for the PEs and memory logic units (MLUs), and, e) the Test Maintenance Unit (TMU) for initialization and testing.

Program execution starts in the CU wherein the stack is used to interpret all instructions. Some serial instructions are completely executed within the CU, others are broadcast to the PEs for synchronous, parallel execution. One view of the CU is that of a small computer complete with a stack, four accumulators and index registers. The CU accumulators can implement many serial instructions including add, subtract, Boolean operations, shifting and bit setting. Additionally, the accumulators may be used for fetching and storing in the processing element memory. The CU also has 64 scratch-pad buffers, called the Advanced Data Buffers (ADB). The CU can selectively enable each of the 64 processors, can control the transfer of information between different processing elements, and can selectively access words anywhere in the PEs primary memory. Accordingly, when the PEs execute instructions in lock step, they perform the same operation on different operands.

Each PE has 6 registers and sufficient logic to execute a full set of instructions under the complete control of the CU. Register R enables information routing to 4 other PEs. As information can be routed between any pair of PEs, no PE is more than 8 steps away from any other. Register X enables independent fetches within each PEM. While Register D contains the mode enable bits for each PE, Registers A, B, and S function as the accumulator, its extension and a scratch register respectively. Operating at the 12.5 megabit clock rate, the PEs can multiply 2 64-bit floating point numbers in 700 nanoseconds. Register-to register adds are accomplished in 550 nanoseconds.

Viewed from the CU, the PEM is a high-speed 128K 64-bit word primary memory. Considered from each PE, the PEM is a 2K 64-bit word

47

local working memory; each PE has direct access to its own column of 2 K words. The function relationship between the CU, PE and PEM is illustrated in Figure 3.11.

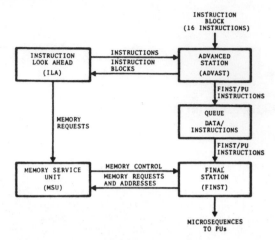

Figure 3.10   Simplified CU block diagram

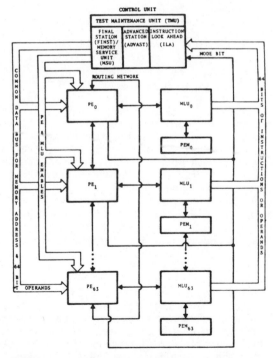

Figure 3.11   Illiac IV functional block diagram

3. Detail Discussion

The Illiac System is represented in detail block diagram form in Figure 3.12. The communication processor (I4CP) communicates over a one mega-baud link with a host computer which provides high-level commands, user programs and the data base for Illiac computation.

A Memory Management Processor (MMP) interprets commands. It controls the I/O subsystem (IOSS) via the descriptor controller (DC) and it controls the Illiac via a register interface in the Test and Maintenance Unit (TMU) of the CU.

User's programs and data bases reach the Illiac via the buffer input/output memory (BIOM) and/or the Illiac disk memory (I4DM), both within IOSS and under control of DC.

The Illiac is an array processor consisting of a single unit (CU) which provides all sequence control for 64 distributed processing units (PU).

1. Array Routing Structure

    The PU array can be viewed as a ring of 64 elements. A user can route data with a ROUTE N instruction. Like a carousel the data moves end around via hardware connections which are +1 or +8 and via paths determined by the hardware to be the fastest.

    The PU array can also be viewed as an 8x8 matrix intraquadrant connected by "x" and "y" data transfer paths. These paths wrap around in both dimensions so that process "routing" can be programmed through any desired PU sequence.

    Consider any element in the matrix. Each PU has four transfer paths to adjacent neighbors. In the "x" dimension PUs are numerically 8 PUs separate.

    The time required for a ROUTE to be accomplished depends upon the number of times a +1 or -1 and/or a +8 or -8 PU shift must be executed to reach the destination. The total time for a "ROUTE" is the number of clock periods (current operation at 80 ns) x 1+4n where "n" is the number of shifts of distance 8 or 1.

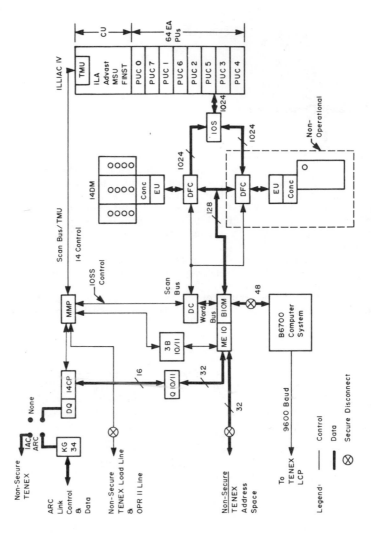

Figure 3.12   Illiac IV system block diagram

2. Control Unit (CU)

The CU consists of five sections which operate semi-indepen-
dently:

   Test Maintenance Unit (TMU)
   Instruction Look-Ahead (ILA)
   Advanced Station (ADVAST)
   Final Station (FINST)
   Memory Service Unit (MSU)

A diagram of the CU is shown in Figure 3.13. The MMP tells
the CU to initiate Illiac processing with a command to register TRI in TMU. The CU return status to the MMP via register
TRO in the TMU.
The user program and data base have already been loaded in
distributed processor element memory (PEM) via IOSS.
ILA fetches 8-word instruction blocks from PEM and places
them in a 64-word content addressable memory which serves as
an instruction word stack (IWS). Instructions are retrieved
by means of an instruction counter in ILA and associative memory which locates the proper 8-word group. IWS can contain
128 instructions.
Instructions from IWS are received in the ADVAST instruction
register (AIR). Instructions can bypass ADVAST (in overlap
mode) or initiate functions such as address arithmetic, loop
control, mode control, interrupt processing and configuration
control. ADVAST contains a 64 word operand stack, four accumulators and combinatorial logic unit. Instructions are output to FINST via the "9th" FINST queue position which is two
registers, the ADVAST to FINST register (AFR) for instructions
and the ADVAST word register (AWR) for data.
FINST has the primary responsibility of decoding instructions
into microsequences (PE enables) and broadcasting these over
a control BUS for lock step synchronous operation of all selected PUs. FINST instructions (ADVAST instructions are executed
in ADVAST) are input from ADVAST into an 8 location instruc-
tion/data queue which acts as a buffer between ADVAST and
FINST. The FINST operand register (FOR) and the FINST instruction register (FIR) drive the diode ROM which creates PE
enables. FOR primarily sets up the second operand for instruction execution although it has other special features. FIR
primarily executes the essence of the FINST instruction.
The MSU arbitrates access between PEM and the IOSS, FINST and
ILA.

3. Processing Unit (PU)

Each PU consists of a processing element (PE), a 2K, 64-bit,
local, three hundred nanosecond PE Memory (PEM) and a memory
logic unit (MLU).

The PE is basically a four register arithmetic unit capable of executing a full repertoire of instructions, for example, fixed or floating point arithmetic in 64-bit or 32-bit mode with options for rounding and normalization.
The PE combines a carry-save adder tree and parallel adder with carry, look-ahead logic to provide either a floating point multiply or a floating point add (with post-normalization) in 720 nanoseconds (9 clocks). A floating point divide (post-normalized) requires 4.5 microseconds (56 clocks). The PE also contains a barrel switch, a leading ones detector and a BOOLE box. Instruction operands can originate from any register, from the common data BUS, from any register in the four adjacent array neighbors or from PEM.
PEM is a bipolar, 300 nanoseconds 2K x 64-bit, local, random access memory.
The MLU contains a PEM data buffer and it controls data transfer between PEM and the PE, IOSS, and CU (FINST and ILA).
A floating point number on the Illiac consists of a 1-bit sign, a 15-bit exponent to the radix 2, and a normalized 48-bit mantissa. The machine thus has about 14 decimal digits of accuracy. A fixed point number has a 1-bit sign and a 48-bit mantissa.

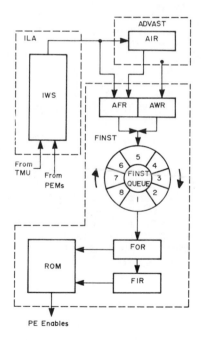

Figure 3.13 Block diagram of control unit

C.   Overlap

Early in 1976 the Institute for Advanced Computation implemented the
overlap feature on the Illiac IV. This allowed the control unit to begin decoding the next instruction while the processing units were completing the execution of the current instruction. Hence the Illiac became a pipeline processor as well as a parallel processor.

1. Introduction

This section will describe two types of overlap, CU and FINST. The term
overlap is sometimes associated with the operation in the I/O but is not
the concern of this discussion.

CU overlap is concerned with processing CU and PU instructions as
fast as possible. To this end, the CU is divided into several units
using the design concept that each unit should be capable of independent
operation with small well defined interfaces between units. This design
philosophy allows for different operations to go on at the same time in
each independent unit. The term CU overlap describes the ability of
these independent units to function in this manner.

FINST overlap refers to the capability of simultaneously processing more than one PU instruction by FINST. Operations such as getting
an operand ready for the next instruction while the present operation is
in progress are typical of this multiprocessing capability.

Both of these overlap processes can be turned off. The mode of
operation when both are disabled is called single instruction mode or
non-overlap. It has the action of processing only one operation throughout the CU at a time.

---

*This section is based on "Overlap in the Illiac IV Control Unit", by
E. Sternberg, IAC Tech Report, 1976.

2. Instruction Flow

Further clarification as to the operation of the individual units is necessary for a full understanding of CU overlap. Four of the five units in the CU are shown in Figure 3.14. The fifth unit, the TMU (Test and Maintenance Unit), does not differ in the two modes of operation, overlap and non-overlap, so it is not shown.

Starting from the bottom up, FINST is the unit that sends the instructions in the form of microsequences, to the PU. By design the PUs are void of control and depend on these microsequences to manipulate the data in the proper fashion to obtain the desired results. The PUs are said to be driven by the CU, in particular FINST. The task for FINST (Final Station) is decoding individual instructions, deciding proper action for the instructions, and issuing microsequences to accomplish the correct actions.

ADVAST's (the advanced station) primary task is to differentiate between two types of instructions. The first type are those destined for the PUs. The second type are those that will operate within the CU. A third type could be considered those instructions that do considerable action in the CU and also reference the PUs. Basically, ADVAST either processes the instruction or passes it on to FINST for processing by the PUs.

ILA (instruction look ahead) has as its function the prefetching of instructions. In an attempt to optimize the instruction processing speed, the unit ILA was established to maintain a significant quantity of instruction in the CU thus negating the need to go to PEM for each new instruction.

MSU (the memory service unit) does what the name implies, correlates and processes memory requests. There are five different requests that can be made of memory and MSU must arbitrate the requests and give them all proper service.

55

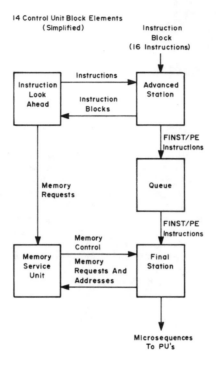

14 Control Unit Block Elements
(Simplified)

Instruction
Block
(16 Instructions)

Instruction
Look
Ahead

Instructions

Instruction
Blocks

Advanced
Station

FINST/PE
Instructions

Memory
Requests

Queue

FINST/PE
Instructions

Memory
Control

Memory
Service
Unit

Memory
Requests And
Addresses

Final
Station

Microsequences
To PU's

Figure 3.14   Illiac IV control unit elements

Important to understanding overlap is understanding the interfaces between the units involved.

ADVAST and ILA share an interface which primarily deals with the obtaining of instructions. ILA is the station where the instructions are stored locally and ADVAST is the station where the individual instructions will first be examined, so in theory their interface is quite simple. A simple handshaking is all that goes on, with ADVAST notifying ILA that it is ready for another instruction and ILA notifying ADVAST when the instruction is ready. Since ADVAST has the only connection with all 64 PEMs in the CU, by means of the CUB (control unit buffer), ADVAST also participates in the block fetching of instructions by ILA in its function of storing quantities of instructions in the CU.

This interface acts differently during overlap operation. ADVAST monitors conditions throughout the CU. These conditions determine when ADVAST goes to ILA for another instruction. In overlap mode this request comes more quickly on the heels of the previous request than in the previous non-overlap mode. ADVAST no longer waits for the rest of the machine to reach an idle state as it did in the non-overlap mode. Thus, as soon as ADVAST decides that it can handle another instruction it requests one from ILA.

Another important interface is the one between ADVAST and FINST. An eight position queue exists as a buffer between the two units. Its purpose is to allow ADVAST to deposit instructions destined for the PUs and return for another instruction to ILA. Meanwhile FINST is free to remove an instruction from the queue as soon as one is available and FINST is ready to process another. Some important control states of the queue are queue full, queue empty and queue not full.

In the non-overlap or single instruction mode the purpose of the queue is defeated because only one instruction is available for processing throughout the CU. ADVAST does not request another instruction from ILA until FINST is finished with the last instruction. Hence, there is no possibility that more than one instruction can exist in the queue at any time. In overlap, however, ADVAST only need deliver the instruction to the queue and it is free to return to ILA for another instruction. Of course, the condition of the queue is important, and ADVAST cannot deliver an instruction to a queue that is already full. Similarly, FINST cannot remove an instruction from a queue that is empty. The purpose of the queue is shown to be a buffer for instruction between the two units allowing for increased independent operation in the overlap mode.

Operation between and within the other units in the CU is not changed in the overlap mode. One additional speed up of the machine will be observed. Previously, after each instruction, ILA provided a delay that would allow settling time for the previous operation so no interference with the next instruction was possible. Overlap mode allows for no such settling time. The next instruction starts as soon as it is determined possible.

3. Finst Overlap

FINST, as noted before, is the section of the control unit that sends
the microsequences to the PUs. The main objective in the design of
the FINST/PU interface is to keep the PUs busy. The result of this
design objective is termed FINST overlap. Basically this is the starting of one instruction before the conclusion of the previous instruction. In order to better understand this concept, refer to Figure 3.15
for a description of FINST/PU instructions.

Every instruction reaching FINST by way of ADVAST is considered
to have two parts. The first part is referred to as the overlap portion. The second section is referred to as the execution portion. As
shown in the four cases across the top of the figure, the combination
of the overlap and execution sections of an instruction can vary. That
is, an instruction can have one clock of overlap and seventy of execution, or ten of overlap and one of execution. Instructions may also be
completed in overlap and have no execution, or contain no overlap and
only execution. The determination is fixed and will be discussed later.
The theory of overlap should then be clear by looking at the bottom half
of Figure 3.15. With clocks being counted as shown on the left, note
that one single clock contains a portion of the execution of one instruction. This is the basis for FINST overlap: the simultaneous processing of more than one instruction.

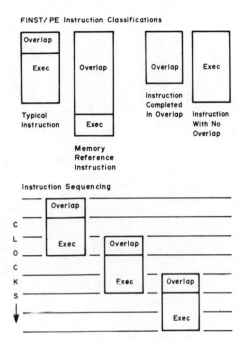

Figure 3.15   FINST/PE instruction classification and sequencing

The description of the FINST/PU instruction in the previous section led the designers to the configuration of FINST shown in Figure 3.16. The FINST hardware is divided into two sections, one dedicated to the processing of the overlap portion of the instruction and the other dedicated to the execution portion of the instruction. There is no duplication of hardware; the execution portion of the instruction cannot be accomplished from the overlap section and vice versa. Each section is dedicated to its portion of the instruction. The flow of instructions through FINST is also fixed. An instruction must always appear in the overlap station before moving on to the execution station.

In a little more detail we see the instructions being deposited in the queue by ADVAST. On a first in first out basis an instruction is removed from the queue and placed in the instruction register of the overlap station (FOR). The instruction is examined for the type of overlap to be accomplished (if any). At the precise time it is determined that it is okay to proceed with the overlapping action the instruction is simultaneously transferred to the read-only-memory address register for the overlap portion of the ROM and sent on to the instruction register for the execution section. The ROM address register (FOAR) will then select the proper word from the ROM to accomplish the desired action for overlap. At the next clock period the enabled condition necessary to accomplish the desired action in the PU will appear in the FINST command register (FCR). A copy of the command register appears in the PU each clock. Meanwhile the instruction register of the execution station (FIR) is decoding the instruction. The next clock will select the address of the word or words in the read-only-memory that are dedicated to the particular instruction decoded. And as in the overlap section, the next clock will load the particular set of enables needed by the PU to perform the instruction.

In examining how FINST overlap works with respect to instruction flow, it will be seen that as soon as the instruction overlap is decoded in FOR and sent to the ROM address register, the overlap station is ready to get another instruction from the queue. In the case of instructions with short overlap portions, this leads to a pipelining effect with instructions in the overlapping station and the execution station.

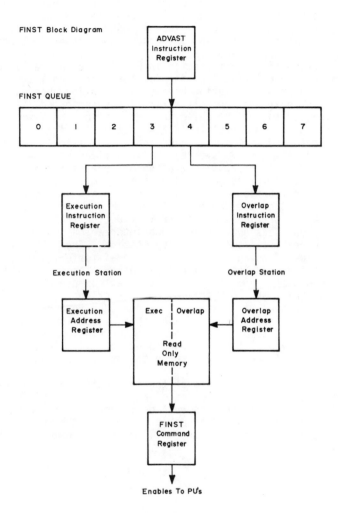

FINST Block Diagram

ADVAST
Instruction
Register

FINST QUEUE

| 0 | 1 | 2 | 3 | 4 | 5 | 6 | 7 |

Execution
Instruction
Register

Overlap
Instruction
Register

Execution Station

Overlap Station

Execution
Address
Register

Exec | Overlap

Read
Only
Memory

Overlap
Address
Register

FINST
Command
Register

Enables To PU's

Figure 3.16   FINST block diagram

   The decision was made to limit the scope of operations that could take place in the overlap station. There are only several types of operations, such as memory references, register transfers, literal transfers and shift count modifications, that go on in overlap. The minor exception overlap is used to get the second operand of an instruction in place before the instruction is executed. Because the action of getting the second operand in place in many cases is similar to other FINST/PU instructions, in most cases those other instructions are also executed in the overlap station.

   The portion of any instruction in FINST done in overlap and the portion in the execution station is predetermined. An instruction does not move from station to station because one station becomes available, it moves to the next station only after it has performed all the tasks it was designated to perform while in that station. A memory reference cannot start in FOR and complete in FIR. It must wait in FOR until the operand has returned from memory and then is permitted to move to FIR.

   The read only-memory is conceptually divided into two sections, one addressed from the execution station and one addressed from the overlap station. No cross addressing is allowed.

   When an instruction enters the execution station, decoded in FIR, and starts addressing the ROM, a state of ROM busy is set up. This state, FIAR busy, precludes any other instruction from being executed from the ROM, but does not prohibit non interfering instructions from generating PU enables from the overlap station. The method for determining if the overlapping instruction is non-interfering will be discussed shortly. An instruction may continue to address the ROM for a considerable time. A divide, for instance, can use 69 clocks in order to accomplish the task. Any following instructions that have completed their overlap portion will wait in FIR until the resources needed to accomplish its desired action are available. Even further overlap at some point will be stopped until the long instruction processing in the execution station completes. Resources do not exist in the PU to store many operands so it makes little sense to get too far ahead in fetching operands.

   So far only the processing of the instruction has been examined. Note, also, that there are a series of registers in FINST that allow the data associated with the instruction to keep in step with the instruction. Therefore, when the enables appear at the PU, the data, if any, associated with these enables will be on the common data bus.

The mechanism mentioned in the previous section which determines when overlap is allowed to proceed, is referred to as the busy bits. For the sake of this mechanism the PU has been divided up into seven areas, each labeled with its own busy bit. Registers A, B, and R all have a busy bit. The mode register has a busy bit M. The address adder has the busy bit Z. The operand select gate, a very important resource in the PU, has the busy bit D. And finally, the LOG (logic unit) and the barrel switch have the busy bit L. These busy bits were selected by careful examination of all PU instructions and the design considerations of FINST and overlap. See Figure 3.17.

Referring back to Figure 3.16, keep in mind there is an instruction processing in the overlap section which requires a portion of the hardware in the PU, and there is an instruction processing in the execution station which requires a portion of the PU hardware. Where both sections require the same hardware, there is a conflict and it is up to the busy bit hardware to resolve it. Solving conflicts is not difficult; the execution station always has priority. If the execution station requires the use of the R register and the overlap station has an identical requirement, the execution gets first use. The overlapping instruction must wait until the executing instruction is finished with the register.

This method of arbitration has the effect of keeping instruction sequences in order and still remaining quite simple. For example, consider an instruction sequence of adding registers A and B and placing the result in memory. The ADD instruction will obtain the two operands in A and B and proceed to add them together. The result of the addition, which takes place in the execution station, will be deposited in the A register. Both A and B will be unavailable to the overlapping station until the results are in A. The next instruction, loading A into memory, takes place in the overlap station. Had the A register not been off limits to the overlapping instruction, some intermediate results not desired would have been placed in memory instead of the final sum, which is correct.

The busy bit hardware is then a mechanism by which the executing instruction notifies the overlapping instruction of those parts of the PU hardware it intends to use during the execution of its instruction. The overlapping instruction then observes the portions of the PU the executing instruction requires and proceeds with overlap only after determining that all the hardware necessary for completing the overlap sequence is available. The overlapping instruction awaits all hardware necessary for the successful conclusion of the overlap portion. If, for example, the overlapping instruction has accounted for all hardware necessary to complete overlap except the R register, and the execution station is processing a divide, the overlapping instruction will begin its overlap as soon as the divide releases the R register, which will come before the instruction in the execution stage is completed.

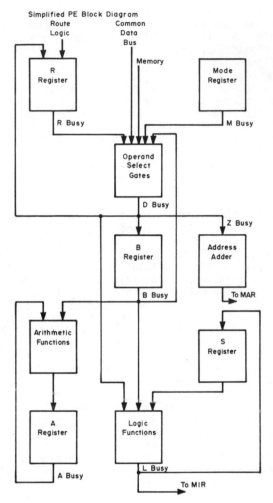

Figure 3.17   Simplified PE block diagram

4. Coding for Overlap Mode

EXAMPLE #1

Perform an arithmetic operation on three arrays stored in PEM, i.e., evaluate the expression:

$$Qj = Aj * Bj * Cj$$

Here,* designates any arithmetic operation of the form: ADRN, MLRN, DVRN, SBRN or a combination of any two of these operations. The following sequence of instructions in assembly language (using the operation ADRN only) worked efficiently in "non-overlap" mode.

```
          LIT(0)      =1,N,0;    %FORM LOOP J FROM O-N
   LOOP:  LDA         A(0);      %LOAD ROW Aj INTO THE ACCUMULATOR A
          ADRN        B(0);      %ADD TO ACCUMULATOR A CONTAINING Aj
                                 %THE CONTENTS OF PEM ROW Bj
          ADRN        C(0);      %ADD TO ACCUMULATOR A CONTAINING THE
                                 %SUM OF Aj + Bj THE CONTENT OF PEM
                                 % ROW Cj
          STA         Q(0);      %STORE THE SUM Aj + Bj + Cj FROM THE
                                 %ACCUMULATOR A TO PEM ROW Qj
          TXLTM(0)    ,LOOP;     %INCREMENT J AND RETURN TO "LOOP" IF
                                 %THE LIMIT N HAS NOT BEEN REACHED
```

In overlap mode however, the times required for memory fetches and for execution of instructions must be considered in order to code the instruction sequence most efficiently. Each PE instruction has a fetching part and may also have an execution part. All arithmetic operations have both. The fetch and execution cycles of the instruction sequence above are tabulated for "non-overlap" in Figure 3.18. The fetch and exexution times are given in clocks, where one clock = 80 milliseconds.

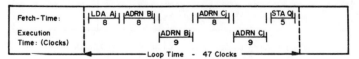

Figure 3.18 Non-overlap timing

65

In Figure 3.19, the memory fetch for "ADRN Cj" is performed while the execution of "ADRN Bj" is taking place, and "ADRN Cj" will be executed as soon as "ADRN Bj" is completed. In this sequence the memory fetch time available during execution of "ADRN CJ" is wasted.

Adding a fetch instruction to this sequence significantly reduces the time needed to perform the loop. To use overlap efficiently, the expression Qj = Aj + Bj + Cj could be coded as follows:

```
          LIT(0)    =1,N,0;     %LOOP J-SETUP
          LDS       A(0);       %PREFETCH
LOOP:     LDA       $S;         %REGISTER TO REGISTER
                                  TRANSFER
          ADRN      B(0);
          ADRN      C(0);
          LDS       A + 1(0);
          STA       Q(0);
          TXLTM(0)  ,LOOP;
```

The fetch and execution cycle chart for the recoded sequence is shown in Figure 3.20. Loop time comparisons for the three cases are shown in Figure 3.21.

The same kind of recoding is advised when dealing with an expression of

$$Qj = Aj * Bj$$

where only one arithmetic instruction is involved in computing Qj.

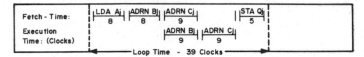

Figure 3.19   Overlap timing

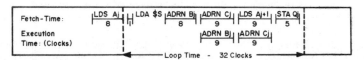

Figure 3.20   Overlap timing, recoded sequence

"Non-Overlap"	Overlap	Overlap, Recoded
47 Clocks	39 Clocks	32 Clocks

Figure 3.21   Loop time comparisons

EXAMPLE #2

Evaluate the expression:

$$Qj = Aj * S * S_1$$

where S and S_1 are scalars (one 64-bit word each) and where * designates any arithmetic expression of the form: ADRN, MLRN, DVRN, SBRN or a combination of any two of these operations.

In Example #1, lines 8 through 11 of the loop which evaluates the array expression of Qj = Aj * Bj * Cj, read as follows:

```
 8)    ADRN    B(0);
 9)    ADRN    C(0);
10)    LDS     A+1(0);
11)    STA     Q(0);
```

However, in investigating the expression Qj = Aj * S * S_1, it became apparent that the storage of S and S_1 is a more important factor in minimizing execution time than is the coding of the loop itself.

In the "scalar" case, it has been determined that moving the LDS A+1(0) between the two ADRN instructions will speed up the loop by two clocks per iteration. This becomes a considerable amount of time when N is large. The complete loop follows:

```
 1)         LIT(0)      =1,N-1,0;
 2)         SLIT(1)     =S;           %FETCH THE SCALAR S
 3)         LOAD(1)     $C1;          %TO THE CU
 4)         SLIT(2)     =S1;          %FETCH THE SCALAR S1
 5)         LOAD(2)     $C2;          %TO THE CU
 6)         LDS         A(0);
 7)LOOP:    LDA         $S;
 8)         ADRN        $C1;
 9)         LDS         A+1(0);
10)         ADRN        $C2;
11)         STA         Q(0);
12)         TXLTM(0)    ,LOOP;
```

Figure 3.22   Example #2 overlap code

Figure 3.23 shows the fetch and execution time in clocks for each instruction in the loop.

Consideration must be given to where to store the scalars S and S_1, since the two LOAD instructions take a much larger amount of time to execute than the actual loop. Experiments have shown that the two LOADs take 81 clocks to execute, which is more than three times longer than the actual loop execution time.

The timing data for the loop in Figure 3.22, expressed as the number of floating point operations per second (FLOPS), with PEM-resident scalars versus the number of rows of A, is graphically displayed.

From Figure 3.24 and Figure 3.25, we see that the Illiac rate of execution approaches $55.2*10^6$ FLOPS asymptotically. For N>>0, there is no significant difference between scalars that are PEM-resident (LOAD) or CU-resident scalars. For N > 0 but small, making the scalars CU-resident is advised.

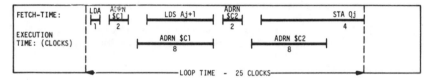

Figure 3.23   Loop times

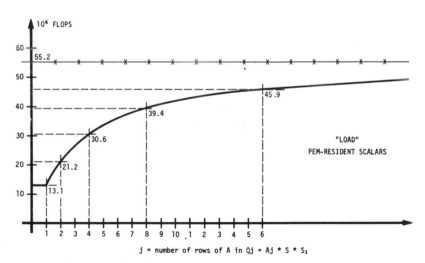

Figure 3.24   PEM resident scalars

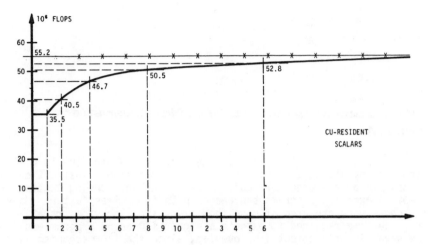

Figure 3.25   CU resident scalars

5. Evaluation of the ILLIAC IV In Non-Overlap and Overlap Modes

Each I4 instruction still takes the same time to execute (the I4 will continue to operate at a "clock rate" of 12.5 MHz.); but instruction sequences can be executed more quickly with overlap. During testing of overlap, I4 executed programs sequenced up to five times faster. Many users' codes were executed at more than twice their previous rate. Clearly the time required to execute a highly I/O bound program would not be significantly affected by overlap, since the I/O mechanism is unaltered.

A number of arithmetic expressions for the Illiac IV have been coded in assembly language in order to analyze the performance of the machine in overlap mode. The following results were produced using the two most common measures of computer performance -- millions of operations per second (mips) and millions of floating point operations per second (megaflops).

PRECISION	MIPS	MEGAFLOPS
64 BIT	140 - 195	40 - 55
32 BIT	250 - 310	70 - 90

These results were for vector lengths which were multiples of 64 and for floating point operations which were rounded and normalized. No routing was involved and all arithmetic operations were done from memory to memory. The sample problems were carefully coded to take advantage of their inherent parallelism.

A 64 x 64 matrix multiply problem was used as a benchmark to evaluate the performance of the Illiac IV, in both non-overlap and overlap modes of execution. This problem was chosen as it utilizes the full parallelism of the Illiac IV. It was found that the most natural method of computing the matrix problem on the Illiac IV was by the "middle product", and not the more usual inner product algorithm:

For I=1, 64 $ROW_I(C) = SUM_K(A_{I,K} * ROW_K(B))$

This algorithm involves a scalar vector product. First a row of A is transferred to the ADB, then elements of this row are broadcast to the PEs, multiplying corresponding rows of B. Accompanying 64 of these products gives a row of C.

The algorithm was coded in both CFD FORTRAN, compiled at NASA Ames, and in ASK (Jobs #1 and #2). In addition to this, two more ASK jobs were coded to exploit the overlap mode of execution. These differed from Job #2 as follows:

Job #3 - The code in the inner loop is reordered to maximize PE overlap. Rows of B are fetched from store ahead of the calculation, using $R as intermediate storage. This allows the memory reference to be overlapped with the ADRN instruction.

Job #4 - Transfer of a row of A to ADB is performed in blocks of eight words during the execution of the inner loop. A buffering technique is used to minimize ADVAST halts when referencing transferred data. Data from the eight word buffer overwrites the previous block as it is being used. It should be noted that this code executes two additional ADVAST instructions during a pass of the inner loop. However, these are effectively free due to overlap.

The results of running Jobs #1 and #2 in both non-overlap and overlap modes show that the overlap mode is three times faster. In addition to this, coding to exploit overlap can give further gains. The results are shown below and compared with similar jobs on a CDC 7600.

ILLIAC EXECUTION TIMES (milliseconds)

	Overlap	Non-Overlap
Job #1	17.2	59.2
Job #2	15.9	37.7
Job #3	12.0	
Job #4	10.0	

CDC 7600 EXECUTION TIMES (milliseconds)

FTN	168
COMPASS	77

Table 3.1   Comparison of Illiac and CDC 7600 Execution Times

D.   Performance

Table 3.2 contains timings for the execution of many commonly used vector operations on the CDC 7600, CDC Star 100, Illiac IV and Cray Cray 1.

Also Figure 3.26 displays performance by the Star 100, Illiac IV and Cray 1 for the operation:

$$V(*)=A(*)*(B(*)+C(*))$$

The units used to measure performance in the tables as well as Figure 3.26 is MFLOPS or millions of floating point operations per second.

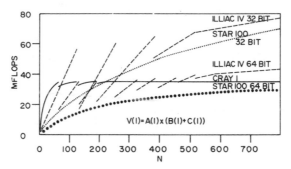

Figure 3.26   Performance of various supercomputers on the operation V=A*(B+C)

This section is based on "Timing Comparison of Several Supercomputers", Appendix D of Optimal Utilization of Supercomputers, Volume II, Report by R&D Associates, RDA-TR-102702-002, February 1977 (J. Levesque, T. Rudy, and G. Wagenbreth).

OPERATION

V(I)=A(I)+B(I)		VECTOR LENGTH					
		5	10	50	100	500	1000
FORTRAN	CDC 7600	1.3	1.5	1.6	1.6	1.6	1.6
RDALIB	CDC 7600	2.55	3.73	5.55	5.75	5.95	6.03
STAR 100	64 BIT	1.7	3.3	13.2	20.8	39.1	43.9
STAR 100	32 BIT	1.8	3.5	15.3	26.6	64.4	78.4
ILLIAC IV	64 BIT	1.45	2.91	14.53	18.13	24.90	25.88
ILLIAC IV	32 BIT	1.45	2.91	14.5	29.1	46.29	49.80
CRAY 1		10.0	14.5	22.9	23.0	23.6	23.6

Table 3.2 Vector operation timings

OPERATION

V(I)=A(I)*B(I)

		VECTOR LENGTH					
		5	10	50	100	500	1000
FORTRAN	CDC 7600	1.4	1.6	1.7	1.8	1.8	1.8
RDALIB	CDC 7600	2.42	3.46	6.3	6.5	6.84	6.88
STAR 100	64 BIT	.8	1.5	6.0	9.7	49.6	66.3
STAR 100	32 BIT	1.0	1.9	9.0	16.4	49.6	66.3
ILLIAC IV	64 BIT	1.45	2.90	14.5	16.25	24.9	25.9
ILLIAC IV	32 BIT	1.45	2.90	14.5	29.0	46.3	49.8
CRAY 1		9.8	14.3	22.7	22.75	23.5	23.5

Table 3.2 Vector operation timings (cont'd.)

OPERATION

		VECTOR LENGTH				
V(I)=(A(I)+51)*S2	5	10	50	100	500	1000
FORTRAN CDC 7600	2.1	2.4	2.7	2.8	2.8	2.8
RDALIB CDC 7600	-	-	10.0	10.6	11.1	11.1
STAR 100 64 BIT	1.1	2.0	8.2	13.2	25.5	28.9
STAR 100 32 BIT	1.3	2.5	11.3	20.3	56.1	71.8
ILLIAC IV 64 BIT	2.40	4.80	24.0	26.55	39.7	41.0
ILLIAC IV 32 BIT	1.47	2.937	14.7	29.37	60.1	67.21
CRAY 1	-	-	59.3	60.2	63.9	64.4

Table 3.2 Vector operation timings (cont'd.)

OPERATION

VECTOR LENGTH

V(I)=(A(I)+B(I))*S1		5	10	50	100	500	1000
FORTRAN	CDC 7600	2.1	2.4	2.6	2.7	2.7	2.7
RDALIB	CDC 7600	-	-	8.9	9.3	9.6	9.7
STAR 100	64 BIT	1.1	2.0	8.2	13.2	25.5	28.9
STAR 100	32 BIT	1.3	2.5	11.3	20.3	56.1	71.8
ILLIAC IV	64 BIT	2.4	4.8	24.04	26.5	39.70	41.0
ILLIAC IV	32 BIT	1.47	2.94	14.7	29.4	60.31	67.45
CRAY 1		-	-	42.8	43.2	45.2	45.5

Table 3.2   Vector operation timings (cont'd.)

OPERATION

VECTOR LENGTH

V(I)=(A(I)*B(I)*S1		5	10	50	100	500	1000
FORTRAN	CDC 7600	2.4	2.6	2.8	2.9	2.9	2.9
RDALIB	CDC 7600	-	-	10.1	10.6	11.1	11.1
STAR 100	64 BIT	.8	1.5	6.0	9.7	19.0	21.6
STAR 100	32 BIT	.9	1.9	8.7	16.0	48.8	65.6
ILLIAC IV	64 BIT	2.3	4.6	23.11	25.47	37.78	38.96
ILLIAC IV	32 BIT	2.15	4.3	21.5	43.0	65.34	68.92
CRAY 1		-	-	43.0	43.0	44.7	44.9

Table 3.2   Vector operation timings   (cont'd.)

OPERATION

$V(I)=A(I)+B(I)+S1$

		VECTOR LENGTH					
		5	10	50	100	500	1000
FORTRAN	CDC 7600	2.0	2.2	2.4	2.5	2.5	2.5
RDALIB	CDC 7600	-	-	9.4	9.9	10.3	10.3
STAR 100	64 BIT	1.0	2.0	8.5	14.5	33.6	40.2
STAR 100	32 BIT	1.0	2.0	9.4	17.2	51.0	67.6
ILLIAC IV	64 BIT	2.4	4.8	24.0	26.84	39.7	41.0
ILLIAC IV	32 BIT	2.15	4.30	21.5	43.03	65.34	68.92
CRAY 1		-	-	43.5	43.5	45.1	45.3

Table 3.2 Vector operation timings (cont'd.)

OPERATION

VECTOR LENGTH

V(I)=A(I)*B(I)*C(I)		5	10	50	100	500	1000
FORTRAN	CDC 7600	2.3	2.6	2.8	2.9	2.9	2.9
RDALIB	CDC 7600	-	-	9.2	9.6	9.9	10.0
STAR 100	64 BIT	.8	1.5	6.0	9.7	19.0	21.6
STAR 100	32 BIT	.9	1.9	8.7	16.0	48.8	65.6
ILLIAC IV	64 BIT	2.31	4.62	23.11	25.21	37.0	38.07
ILLIAC IV	32 BIT	2.15	4.30	21.5	43.03	64.33	67.63
CRAY 1		-	-	33.9	33.9	35.0	35.1

Table 3.2 Vector operation timings (cont'd.)

OPERATION

				VECTOR LENGTH			
V(I)=(A(I)+B(I))*C(I)		5	10	50	100	500	1000
FORTRAN	CDC 7600	2.2	2.4	2.6	2.7	2.7	2.7
RDALIB	CDC 7600	-	-	8.1	8.5	8.7	8.7
STAR 100	64 BIT	.7	1.4	6.1	10.4	23.1	27.3
STAR 100	32 BIT	.8	1.7	7.7	14.4	45.6	62.7
ILLIAC IV	64 BIT	2.40	4.8	24.0	26.27	38.84	40.01
ILLIAC IV	32 BIT	2.23	4.46	22.30	44.58	67.08	70.68
CRAY 1		14.8	21.6	34.2	34.3	35.3	35.3

Table 3.2 Vector operation timings (cont'd.)

OPERATION

			VECTOR LENGTH				
V(I)=A(I)+B(I)+C(I)		5	10	50	100	500	1000
FORTRAN	CDC 7600	2.1	2.3	2.5	2.5	2.5	2.5
RDALIB	CDC 7600	-	-	8.1	8.5	8.7	8.7
STAR 100	64 BIT	1.0	2.0	8.5	14.5	33.6	40.2
STAR 100	32 BIT	1.0	2.0	9.4	17.2	51.0	67.6
ILLIAC IV	64 BIT	2.4	4.80	24.0	26.27	38.8	40.0
ILLIAC IV	32 BIT	2.23	4.46	22.3	44.57	67.0	70.7
CRAY 1		-	-	34.2	34.2	35.2	35.3

Table 3.2   Vector operation timings (cont'd.)

IV.   Programming

Not surprisingly, at this stage of the Illiac IV's evolution, the most serious impediment to the full utilization of the machine's computational power is the lack of applications software. The Illiac is difficult to program; it is even harder to program well.

Part of the difficulty is psychological. Programmers do not naturally think about algorithms suitable for parallel architectures. The mental approach that makes for a good Illiac programmer is a learned skill. More so than in other computer related disciplines, Illiac programming improves with experience. With a regularity bordering on monotony, Illiac programmers with moderate experience would show a piece of their code to an old hand for review and be told that with some minor changes run time performance could be improved by an order of magnitude. Even the old hands continue to improve their skills at a noticeable rate.

A second difficulty is the lack of software tools. To draw a data item from the I4DM main memory into a processing element memory for manipulation can take up to 40 milliseconds due to risk latency, and 40 milliseconds is forever on a machine as fast as the Illiac. So placement of the data on the I4DM can be critical to minimizing run time, since judicious data layout can all but eliminate latency penalties. Placement of the data on the I4DM is under programmer control. But there are no tools available to the programmer to assist in this tedious but critical task.

A third drawback to having satisfactory applications software is the lack of a software library. Code development is dispersed across the world. There is no central repository for application programs. Even the programs developed at IAC get lost in time or become useless through incomplete documentation. Hence new code development efforts are denied the opportunity to use modules from prior codes that might otherwise be applicable.

Another unfortunate circumstance is the undebugged status of the IVTRAN compiler. There are two high level languages in which applicable codes can be written for the Illiac, CFD and GLYPNIR. CFD resembles FORTRAN, GLYPNIR resembles ALGOL. FORTRAN and ALGOL programs do not run directly on the Illiac. Hence an existing FORTRAN program, for example, must be converted into CFD before it can be executed on the Illiac and this conversion effort, for even a moderately sized Fortran program, can be quite time consuming and expensive. Since the world is filled with existing FORTRAN applications programs, a decision was made early on to develop IVTRAN, an Illiac programming language with the feature that an existing FORTRAN program could be converted by machine translation using the IVTRAN compiler into Illiac running code. IVTRAN would even seek opportunities to exploit the parallel architecture of the Illiac.

To a degree the IVTRAN compiler works. Some of the application codes described later in Chapter V were first written in FORTRAN and then converted to Illiac code using the IVTRAN compiler. But the IVTRAN compiler has bugs. Quite frequently its output is gibberish. It has not been released for general use as a practical programming tool.

Finally, the Illiac's status as a one of a kind machine impedes its use for application projects. With no successor machine identified on which Illiac codes would be compatible, the costly code development effort is quite understandably an aversion to program managers. As the Illiac ages this consideration is expected to grow even more serious.

The situation, however, is not all gloom and doom. The Illiac is so fast that the economics often dictate its use despite these problems. Speedup factors for Illiac programs compared with the same programs implemented on conventional computers, where the algorithm is appropriate for parallel implementation, often are 20, 40, 60 or even higher. Illiac time is offered to government agencies at $2500 per hour. Hence, a program need not require very much production running to amortize the cost of code conversion.

This chapter consists of three sections. In the first two the CFD and GLYPNIR languages are described. The third section provides a review of the Illiac languages. ASK, the Illiac assembly language is treated in the Appendix.

A.   The CFD Language

1.   Introduction

To understand the evolution of CFD it is necessary to go back to 1970
and 1971 when the Computational Fluid Dynamics Branch of NASA Ames
Research Center first learned that it would be able to use the Illiac IV.
For a great many years this branch had been coding fluid flow problems in
FORTRAN so that they could be run on the conventional serial machines of
that period (IBM 360 and CDC 6000 series computers). Thus the advent of
the Illiac IV forced the branch to determine how to run the next generation of these fluid flow problems on the Illiac. To do this the branch
first looked closely at how the Illiac hardware performed.
   They wanted to understand the Illiac hardware from the standpoint
of how best to generate code for it. To do this, the branch looked at
the four functional parts of the Illiac IV. Those parts are the control
units, the 64 processing elements, the processing element memories, and
the Illiac main memory. (See Fig. 4.1 for a diagram of the hardware described below.)
   The control unit (CU) contains the instruction stack which interprets all instructions, some of which may be completely executed within
the CU.
   Instructions are partially executed and then broadcast to the 64
processing elements; there the execution is completed by all the processing elements in lock-step. In addition to managing the instruction
stack, the CU may be thought of as a small, self-contained computer.
It has four accumulators which are capable of a full set of shifting,
bit-setting, and Boolean operations, as well as addition and subtraction. Furthermore, these accumulators may be used as index registers
for fetching and storing in the processing elements. The CU also has
64 scratch registers called the Advanced Data Buffer (ADB).

---

*This section is based on "CFD-A FORTRAN-like language for the Illiac
IV", by K. G. Stevens, IAC Newsletter, July, 1977.

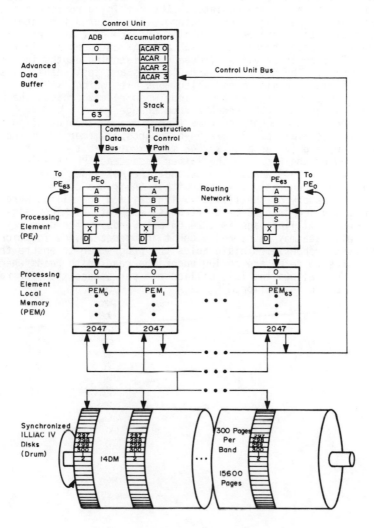

Figure 4.1   Example #2 overlap code

A processing element (PE) has six programmable registers called RGA, RGB, RGS, RGR, RGX, and RGD. RGA is the accumulator and RGB is its extension; RGS is a scratch register. The remaining registers are somewhat peculiar to the Illiac architecture. RGR is used for inter-PE communication of data. Data may be rotated end-around (data from PE 1 going to PE 64) within the 64 RGRs. RGX acts as an index for intra-PE fetching. This register allows independent fetching depths in each of the PE memories. The RGD contains fault bits and test result bits for that PE. It also contains bits called mode bits which, when set, allow the PE to take part in instructions and, when reset, protect the PE memory as well as RGA, RGS, and RGX from change.

The processing element memories (PEMs) may be thought of in two ways: (1) collectively as 131,072 64-bit words of memory from the CU's point of view, and (2) as a 64 x 2048 matrix of 64-bit words from the point of view of the PEs. In the latter case, each PE is able to access its own column of 2048 words. (Note that the RGX indexing permits the PEs to fetch independently any word within their own column.)

The main memory of the Illiac is logically a 16-million word drum. The drum is divided into 52 bands (tracks) each of which contains 300 Illiac pages (an Illiac page is 1024 64-bit words). The drum may be mapped, i.e., data may be stored upon it in predetermined locations and accessed asynchronously. This enables the programmer to ensure that the data he wishes to fetch are coming under the read/write heads when he needs it. This allows the full billion-bit-per-second transfer rate to be realized during execution.

2. History

After examining the Illiac hardware it was determined that if it could
be programmed efficiently it would allow an increase in speed of about
two orders of magnitude over the conventional serial machines the Branch
was using. Moreover, there appeared to be a large class of problems
ideally suited to parallel computation by the Illiac. Once the researcher
understands what is meant by parallel computation, the principal difficulty
is simply that of writing the problem in a language that the machine understands.

It was this problem of language that most concerned the programmers
in 1971. They inspected ASK (the assembly language for the Illiac IV)
but quickly discarded it for general purpose use because of the usual
problems associated with an assembly language. GLYPNIR was also discarded, first because it was more general than the problems required (the
price of that generality was verbose machine code), and second because it
was ALGOL-based rather than FORTRAN-based. Under these circumstances
they decided to develop a new language.

The development of CFD has been governed by three factors: (1) the
architecture and instruction set of the Illiac; (2) the expected nature
of the "average" program; and (3) the ease of writing the translator.
They also tried to have CFD resemble FORTRAN. No attempt was made to hide
the hardware peculiarities from the user; on the contrary, every attempt
was made to give the programmer access and control of all of the Illiac
hardware so that an efficient program could be constructed. This concern
for efficient programming is necessitated by the Illiac's specialized
architecture which increases the speed ratio of good to poor coding.
This ratio of codes that make the machine work well to codes that make
it work poorly can be as great as 50 to 1 for Illiac. This same ratio
for conventional computers is about 5 to 1.

During the very early stages of code development, it became apparent
that trying to debug code on the Illiac IV itself or its hardware simulator, called SSK, was difficult if not impossible. The programmers therefore decided to develop a method by which they could logically debug or
code before ever approaching the Illiac or SSK. To this end they decided to translate CFD into serial FORTRAN so that problems could be
logically debugged on conventional computers using the wide range of
existing FORTRAN debugging tools. This decision then added a fourth
governing factor to the development of CFD; namely, that CFD be trans-
latable into FORTRAN. They also chose to write these two translators (CFD
to Illiac code and CFD to FORTRAN) in FORTRAN so that they would be easy
to write and easy to debug as well as be transportable to a wide class
of machines.

3. The Language

The current version (Version 2.0) of CFD may now be contrasted to
FORTRAN, bearing in mind the hardware for which CFD must generate code.
CFD statements are composed of CFD key words used in conjunction with
the basic elements of the language (constants, variables, and expressions). These statements are written in card format similar to FORTRAN.

Types of Named Quantities

There are four classes of named quantities in CFD: (1) variables,
(2) subprograms, (3) common blocks, and (4) disk areas. Variables may be
divided into three subclasses: (1) scalars, (2) arrays, and (3) vector
aligned arrays. An array may reside in either PE or CU memory and may
be of any length, limited only by the memory size. These arrays, however, may not be used as vectors in vector operations, and may not have
more than one subscript. Vector aligned arrays, on the other hand, must
reside in PE memory, and may have one, two or three subscripts. The
range of the first subscript of a vector aligned array is always 64. All
vector aligned arrays have their first word in the first PE, hence· the
nomenclature "vector aligned."

   There are five categories of CFD statements: (1) specification;
(2) subprogram; (3) input/output; (4) control; and (5) assignment statements. Each statement category is discussed below.

Specification Statements

CFD supports the full range of FORTRAN specification statements; for
example, IMPLICIT, DIMENSION, COMMON, EQUIVALENCE, and explicit statements. There are five types of variables in CFD: CU INTEGER, CU REAL,
CU LOGICAL, PE REAL, and PE INTEGER. Note that the residence of the
variable must be declared. Real and integer variables are similar to
those in FORTRAN. However, CFD logical variables are quite different
from FORTRAN logical variables. FORTRAN logical variables have one
value (either .TRUE. or .FALSE.) while CFD logical variables always
have 64 values, one in each bit of the 64-bit word. In this sense they
are vectors, and when used to control the PEs, each PE receives one bit.
The CFD variable MODE contains the current machine mode bit vector and
is stored in the RGDs.
   In the case of CU variables, a specific CU address must be assigned
by use of an EQUIVALENCE statement. Because there is only one CU, these
variables must be thought of as being in COMMON to all subprograms. The
following are examples of various types of CFD specification statements:

               *IMPLICIT CU LOGICAL(M)

               *CU REAL ALPH

               *PE INTEGER X(*)

               DIMENSION RHO(,64)

               COMMON /CONSV/ EO(,64,2)

               *EQUIVALENCE (I,I), (2MSK), (3,MD), (4,ALPH)

In this example we have the integer variable I residing at CU location 1, while the logical variables MSK and MD reside in CU locations 2
and 3, respectively. X, RHO, and EO are vector aligned arrays of one,
two and three dimensions respectively. The asterisk in column 6 is one
of our concessions to ease of translator writing. All nonassignment
statements must have an asterisk in column 6 to be valid Version-2.0-CFD
statements.

Subprogram Statements

A subprogram may either be a FUNCTION, a SUBROUTINE, or a BLOCK DATA.
The declaration statements for these subprograms are the same as in
FORTRAN. A FUNCTION or a SUBROUTINE is referenced in the usual FORTRAN
manner. The following is an example of a SUBROUTINE statement with one
argument.

                    *SUBROUTINE UPDATE(RHO)

Input/Output Statements

All CFD I/O is between Illiac main memory and the processing element
memories - not printers and card readers - and this I/O is asynchronous
to make use of the overlapping and mapping capabilities of the Illiac.
Since this I/O is asynchronous, CFD also has a WAIT statement which will
halt execution until a previously requested READ or WRITE is completed.
For example:

                    *DISK AREA EOSTAR(4)

                    *READ(3,EO(1,1,2), EOSTAR(1),4)

                    *WAIT 3

In this example the first statement declares that there is a previously mapped area on the Illiac main memory, called EOSTAR, which is
4 Illiac pages long. The second statement requests that four pages be
read beginning with the first page of area EOSTAR into PEM beginning at
EO(1,1,2). This second statement also gives this I/O request the identification number 3. The third statement will stop the program until the
I/O request associated with identification number 3 has been completed.
CFD WRITE statements have the same format as the READ statement.

Control Statements

There are two kinds of program control in Illiac IV: (1) branching
and (2) enabling or disabling PEs. These controls may be used separately or in combination. Branching is the type of control used in serial
computers and determines which statements will be executed next. In
Illiac, however, it is also necessary to specify which PEs will partici-
pate in the execution of a vector statement.
    The following statements are implemented in CFD with their standard
FORTRAN form and meaning.

GO TO (absolute, computed, and assigned)

ASSIGN

CONTINUE

RETURN

STOP

CALL

END

One of the most frequently used control statements is the DO statement, and in CFD it is slightly more general than in FORTRAN. The differences from FORTRAN are: (1) the increment must be a constant, but
may be negative, and (2) the starting and limit values may be a CU
INTEGER variable plus or minus an integer constant. As in FORTRAN, the
index must be greater than zero.

Logical IF statements are implemented in CFD, but arithmetic IF
statements are not. IF statements are of two basic kinds: (1) scalar
IFs having a single true/false result, and (2) vector IFs having 64 true/
false results, one for each PE. Scalar IFs determine the program flow,
and vector IFs define the participating PEs. There are no single-re-
sult, logical variables in CFD, so the variety of scalar IFs is quite
restricted. There are three basic forms: (1) those involving arithmetic
tests between CU integer expressions using only addition and subtraction; (2) those involving quantified logical expressions; and (3) those
testing for I/O request completion. A logical expression in CFD implies
64 true/false results, and "quantifying" reduces it to one true/false
result. The logical quantifiers are .ANY., .ALL., .NOT ANY., and
.NOT ALL.. The following are examples of scalar IF statements:

*IF (INDEX .GT. LIMIT) RETURN

*IF (.NOT ANY. ((A(*) .GT. EPSLON))) STOP

*IF (.COM. 3) GO TO 123

The first statement is true if the CU INTEGER INDEX is greater
than the CU INTEGER LIMIT. The second statement is true if all 64 A's
are less than or equal to EPSLON. The third statement is true if the
I/O request associated with the identification number 3 is completed.

The PEs are controlled in two ways: (1) the instruction stream in
the CU determines the machine instruction to be executed; and (2) the
enabling mode pattern in the PEs determines which PEs will perform the
instruction and which will remain idle. At the CFD level, the enabling
mode controls only vector arithmetic assignment statements and the evaluation of SUBROUTINE arguments that require scratch storage. Vector
arithmetic statements do not alter variables in disabled PEs. The
enabling mode pattern is the logical variable MODE, a reserved symbol,
at all times except when the vector assignment statement following a
vector IF is executed. In that case, the enabling mode is the result
of the vector IF. For example,

*IF((A(*).LT.O.)) A(*) = -A(*)

is one way to replace A(*) by its absolute value. If the sequence

$$\text{MODE} = (-A(*).LT.0.)$$
$$A(*) = -A(*)$$

is used, A(*) is replaced by its absolute value as before, but now the
enabling mode has been set so that only the PEs in which A was negative
will be active in statements following this sequence.

Assignment Statements

In a logical assignment statement a logical variable is assigned the
value of a logical expression. The basic building block of a logical
expression is the "base mode," which may be a logical variable, a logical constant (ON meaning all true and OFF meaning all false), a vector
relation, or any of these preceded by .NOT., which implies logical nega-
tion. A vector relation consists of two vector arithmetic expressions
separated by one of the following: .GT., .LT., .GE., .LE., .EO. or
.NE..
   The logical expression may simply be a base mode, or it may contain
operators having base modes as operands. There are three kinds of operators: (1) bit setting operators, (2) shifting and rotating operators,
and (3) Boolean operators. The two kinds of bit setting operators are
.TURN ON. and .TURN OFF. and are used to turn on (enable) or turn off
(disable) discrete bits of the variable being defined. The bits themselves are specified in a list following the operator. For example:

MASK = ON .TURN OFF. 1,2,.LAST.2

   This statement assigns false to the first two and the last two bits
of MASK while assigning true to the remaining 60 bits. The list may indicate individual PEs or ranges of PEs as may be seen in the following
CFD statements.

MODE = MODE .TURN ON. .FIRST. I-1

MASK = .NOT. MASK .TURN ON. MIN .TO. MAX

   The two kinds of bit shifting operations are "end-off" shifts
(.SHL. and .SHR. for left and right shifts respectively) and "end-
around" shifts (.RTL. and .RTR. for left and right); the end-around
shifts are usually called "rotates" rather than shifts. In the end-off
shifts, vacated bits are set to zero (false).
   The three Boolean operators are .NOT., .AND., and .OR. all of which
have their conventional meaning. The following are typical CFD logical
assignment statements.

MASK = MODE .RTL. I+1

MODE = .NOT. MODE .AND. (A(*) .GT. 1.0)

   There are three kinds of scalar arithmetic statements, all of which
are specific and restricted. The limited vocabulary for CU arithmetic
reflects the absence of the required hardware. The first kind of statement is an arithmetic assignment statement involving only CU INTEGER
variables, integer constants, and the + and - operators. The second
kind of statement involves the transfer of single words of data. No

arithmetic is done, and the data may be REAL or INTEGER and have any residence (CU or PE). The third kind of statement has no FORTRAN equivalent and is required in Illiac to facilitate any necessary juggling between CU and PE memory due to the limited size of CU memory. The TRANSFER statement allows the programmer to move blocks of eight words between CU and PE memory (using special Illiac machine instructions). The following CFD statement causes variable I and the seven CU variables after it to be assigned the first eight values of the PE array TEMP.

$$*TRANSFER \ (8) \ I=A(1)$$

PE arithmetic is vector arithmetic, even when an expression involves only scalars. Expressions must be either REAL or INTEGER, and mixed type expressions are not allowed. The following standard FORTRAN operations are implemented: + ; - ; * ; / ; and **. The order of computation is the same as in FORTRAN. Exponents in CFD must be integer constants in the range 2 through 10 and may not be exponentiated themselves. The variable being defined in a PE arithmetic assignment must be vector aligned, and its first subscript must be * alone. This convention is followed because the enabling mode (MODE) then corresponds directly to the PEs of the defined variable.

When the first subscript contains an *, the subscript possesses some non-FORTRAN qualities. Assume that all PEs are enabled, then the statement

$$A(*) = B(*-1)$$

is equivalent to the FORTRAN statements

$$A(1)=B(64), \ A(2)=B(1), \ A(3)=B(2), \ ..., \ A(64)=B(63)$$

illustrated by the following diagram.

Note that the transfer of data is done in the RGRs and is end-around.

Suppose the central difference of the vector P(*) is needed. Its value, as given by

$$DIFT(*) = P(*+1) - P(*-1)$$

may have no meaning in PEs 1 and 64 unless P is in fact periodic. The difference would not be computed in these PEs if the statement above were preceded by

$$MODE = ON \ .TURN \ OFF. \ 1, \ 64$$

An * in the first subscript implies that the variable is a vector. When the first subscript contains no * the variable is used as a scalar, the same value being used in every PE.

When the first subscript contains an *, the second subscript, if present, may contain an integer vector. This allows each PE to refer to a different position in its memory. Suppose the variable X has been declared a PE INTEGER vector and has been assigned the values 1,0,1,0, ... ,0,1,0. Then, if RHO is a 64 X 64 matrix, RHO(*,X(*)+1) is the saw tooth pattern vector made up of the following variables:

RHO(1,2), RHO(2,1), RHO(3,2), RHO(4,1) ... RHO(64,1)

Note that this integer vector index is stored in and used from RGX. (A complete description of the language may be found in Ref. 2).

4. The Translators

There are two CFD translators in existence. One compiles CFD into relocatable machine code for the Illiac IV and the other translates CFD into standard serial FORTRAN.

Both these translators are written in FORTRAN which allows them to be easily brought up on a wide range of computers. These translators currently run on a PDP 10, an IBM 360/67, an IBM 360/91, and a CDC 7600.

5. The Conclusions

CFD is clearly not a machine independent language. It allows the programmer to use the power of the RGR, RGX, and RGD for intra-PE communication, independent PE indexing, and a wide range of mode control, respectively. It also restricts the user to simple scalar operations because complicated scalar operations are not possible on the Illiac without running at 1/64 its top speed. The machine dependent nature of the CFD language forces the programmer to think parallel, leaving only bookkeeping chores to the compiler. This has allowed the Computational Fluid Dynamics Branch of Ames Research Center (and others) to develop a wide range of application programs which make efficient use of the Illiac IV parallel hardware; for this reason, CFD has met all of its goals.

Although the language can be said to be machine dependent, its dependence is not just on the Illiac IV. Rather, its dependence is on a machine which can execute vector as well as scalar instructions. To this end the Computational Fluid Dynamics Branch is developing a third CFD translator. This translator will translate CFD to CDC 7600 assembly language, which makes optimal use of all the pipelining and overlapping of which the 7600 is capable. Or, as pointed out in Ref. 3 (Feustel, et al.), the Branch will compile CFD for the "vector 7600," which runs from 1 to 5 times faster than the 7600 using FORTRAN.

Thus CFD appears to be a logical extension of FORTRAN which allows for the efficient use of the vector hardware of the Illiac IV and quite probably other parallel and vector machines.

REFERENCES

1. Burroughs Corporation, Illiac IV Systems Characteristics and Programming Manual. NASA Contractor Report 2159, 1972.

2. Computational Fluid Dynamics Branch, CFD -- A FORTRAN-like Language for the Illiac IV, internal paper, NASA Ames Research Center, 1973.

3. Feustel, E.A., et al., Future Trends in Computer Hardware, Proceedings AIAA Computational Fluid Dynamics Conference, July, 1973.

B. The GLYPNIR Language

1. Introduction

GLYPNIR is a language designed for programming the Illiac IV computer. Initial design was begun in early 1968, and a compiler has been available since early 1969. In view of the increasing interest in Illiac IV and in parallel computation in general, this discussion is presented in order to acquaint the reader with GLYPNIR. It will discuss some design goals and sketch pertinent features of the language while omitting as much detail as possible (cf. (13), (14), (17), (18)). It is not claimed that GLYPNIR contains essentially new features which cannot be found elsewhere. Rather, this language is a selection and adaptation of features particularly useful for programming a parallel array type computer. The goal has been to produce a useful, reliable, and efficient programming tool with a high probability of success.

Primary memory consists of 128K 64-bit words divided into 64 2K word modules. Thus, primary memory may be viewed as a two-dimensional structure where each word can be addressed by a pair (a, B) where B specifies a memory module and a specifies an address within that module. A group of 64 words, each in a different module but each having the same address within its module, is called a super word or sword (see Figure 4.2). Each PE is connected to one 2K module and can directly access only its own module. Thus, the PEs can collectively access a sword. Additionally, since each PE has its own index registers, it can index its own module independently of the others. Thus the PEs can collectively access 64 words, one word from each module but with each word at a different address. Any such group of 64 words from distinct modules is called a slice. (Thus a sword is a slice but not vice versa.) Access to other modules must be done through the PE interconnection logic (routing network). Secondary memory consists of special head-per-track disk units with an I/O rate of .5 X 10^9 bits/second (each of two channels) and an average latency of 20 milliseconds. The Illiac IV is supervised by a control computer, currently a PDP-10.

This section is based on "GLYPNIR-A Programming Language for Illiac IV", by D.H. Lawrie, T. Layman, D. Baer and J.M. Randal, Communications of the ACM, Volume 18 Number 3, March 1975, page 157.

It was apparent very early that a language was needed which (1) hides the machine architecture from the users, and (2) results in efficient[1] object code. It was felt that, given limited resources and the requirement for a high probability of succes, GLYPNIR could not attempt to provide both of the above.[2] Since most of the users were contemplating large production codes requiring high efficiency and could afford more programming effort, it was decided to provide an efficient language which would be a considerable improvement in terms of programming effort over assembly language, but which would not compromise efficiency by hiding the machine architecture.

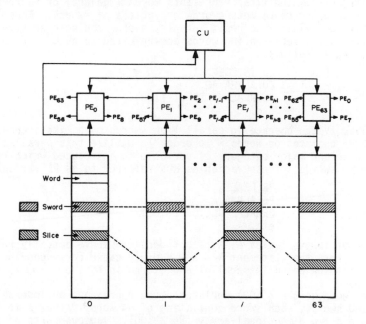

Figure 4.2 Word, sword and slice

---

[1]By efficient is meant that the code generated by the compiler runs "almost" as fast as the same program written directly in assembly language.

[2]A separate language was underway which could satisfy at least (1) above. See (1).

2. Variables

In order to use a machine efficiently, variable types must be provided in the language which represent those entities which the machine recognizes. Traditionally, this has meant providing real (floating), integer (fixed), Boolean (logical), and sometimes other types. In addition to the type, the user can usually specify the size of a variable in terms of the number of bytes, words, etc., and its structure, such as vectors, arrays, and trees.

The variable types available in GLYPNIR can be divided into two major categories. The first represents words (scalars) or vectors of words. The second represents swords or vectors of swords. These can be further subdivided into real, integer, alpha, and pointer type variables. Variables representing words are referred to as CU variables and are declared as follows.

```
CU INTEGER CI
CU ALPHA A2
CU REAL VECTOR Z (100)
etc.
```

Illiac IV can operate in parallel on swords much like a conventional computer operates on words. In order to utilize this parallel capability, a second major category of variable is introduced which represents these swords. These variables are referred to as PE variables:

```
PE REAL X,Y
PE ALPHA A
PE REAL VECTOR Z(100)
etc.
```

Each of the variables A, X, and Y declared above actually refer to a sword. Thus, the statement $X \leftarrow X + Y$ would cause corresponding words of X and Y to be added in parallel and stored in X; i.e. $X_i \leftarrow X_i + Y_i$, $0 \leq i < 63$.

The sword vector Z(100) declared above represents an indexable vector of 100 swords, each sword consisting of 64 words. Thus Z is in some sense a two dimensional array (64 X 100). Various parts of this array can be accessed and processed in parallel. For example, suppose CI is declared as an integer word (CU INTEGER CI). Then Z(CI) references the CI-th sword of Z. Now let I be declared as an integer sword (PE INTEGER I) and initialized such that the value of the ith word is i; i.e. I_0 = 0, I_1 = 1,..., I_{63} = 63. Then the expression Z(I) would reference a slice of Z, i.e., elements (0, 0), (1, 1),..., (63, 63) of this array, as in Figure 4.3. Z(I+36) would reference a different slice consisting of elements (0, 36), (1, 37),..., (63, 99).

In addition to the above variable types there are also Boolean or logical variables declared as follows:

```
BOOLEAN B, TESTRESULT
BOOLEAN VECTOR BUFFERFULL (10)
```

Boolean variables represent 64 separate true/false values. For example, assume X and Y are REAL swords as declared above. Then the Boolean expression $X < Y$ results in 64 separate true/false values, one for each of the 64 pairs of corresponding elements of X and Y. The Boolean assignment statement $B \leftarrow X < Y$ assigns these 64 Boolean results to the Boolean variable B.

GLYPNIR defines a multivalued Boolean result to be TRUE if and only
if all elements of the result are true. It is FALSE if and only if all
the elements are false. Otherwise, the result is mixed. Boolean
quantifiers SOME and EVERY are available for use in Boolean expressions.
For example, SOME B is TRUE if some element of B is true, and EVERY B is
FALSE if some element of B is false.

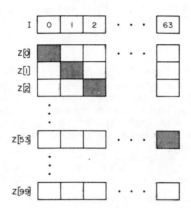

Figure 4.3 Diagonal slice

3.   Storage Control

The primary memory on Illiac IV is quite small relative to the machine speed. For example, it takes Illiac only about 1 millisecond to access the entire primary memory while it would take about 200 milliseconds for a more conventional machine with 256K words of .75 microsecond core. In addition, Illiac has no virtual memory hardware, so the user must segment data for large programs and manipulate these segments himself. Thus, it was considered important to give the programmer a high degree of control over allocation and addressing of primary memory. This was done in several ways.

Block Structure

GLYPNIR is a block-structured language and resembles ALGOL 60 at least in appearance. A GLYPNIR program consists of nested blocks of code and each block may have its own local storage. This helps to minimize the use of storage by allowing the programmer to declare storage areas for vectors, etc., only in that part of the code where they are needed. Block storage also tends to make the program logic more obvious and thus improves its readability.

Packed Storage

Various data types can be packed into 64-bit words. For example, floating-point numbers can be stored one per word in full 64-bit precision or two per word in half precision. Integers may be assigned to arbitrary fields within a word and as many as 32 signed integers can be stored in a single 64-bit word. This packed data is accessed via fields and/or partial word designators. For example, partial word designators used in the expression

    A.(0:20)   A.(21:10) + I

cause the 10-bit field starting at bit 21 of A to be added to I and stored in the first 20 bits of A. (If A is a sword, then this is done simultaneously for each word of the sword.)
Fields can be used to specify a portion of a block of words, where the block of words is addressed by a pointer value. For example, let P be a point variable (see next section) whose value is the machine address of a block of words, and let R be a field declared

    INTEGER FIELD R(2,0,13)

Then the expression P. R refers to the field R of the block pointed at by P, i.e., the 13 bits starting at bit 0 of word 2 of the block. Fields may be of type real, integer, alpha (unsigned integer), or pointer. Real fields are restricted in format to those allowed by the machine. Integer and alpha fields can be of any length but may not cross word boundaries. Pointer fields are explained more fully in the next section.

Pointers, Structures, and Dynamic Storage Allocation

GLYPNIR included facilities which allow creation and modification of user defined data structures. These facilities include dynamic allocation of storage blocks and the ability to declare the manipulate pointers (machine addresses) and fields within these blocks. Perhaps

98

the easiest way to demonstrate these capabilities is to describe how
similar facilities would be used in a conventional (nonparallel) language
and then describe the extensions made for Illiac IV.
First, assume that in our hypothetical language we have pointer type
variables whose values are machine addresses. We might also have vectors of these pointer variables. Let P and PV(3) be examples of
these.
Next, we need a dynamic storage allocator, i.e., a routine which allocates or deallocates blocks of storage at execution time. Assume
ALLOCATE(N) is a procedure or routine which when called allocates N
words of storage and returns a pointer to the first word (word 0) of
this block. For example, the statement P   ALLOCATE(6) would result in
allocation of 6 words of storage and assignment of a pointer to this
block of storage to P. Additionally we need a deallocation procedure,
e.g., FREE(P,N) which would return to the free storage list N words at
location P.
Finally, we need a field specifier, i.e., some notation for specifying
a particular field of an arbitrary data block. For example, we might
allow a field specifier to be declared as follows:
INTEGER FIELD R(2,0,13)
This declares R to be a field of length 13 (consisting of bits 0-12)
in the third word (i.e., word 2) of a block of data. It also implies
that the data in this field represents an integer (or at least it is
to be treated as if it were an integer). Now, if P points to a block
of data, then P. R specifies the field R of that block. Similarly,
if PV(1), PV(2) and PV(3) each point to a block of data, then PV(1),
PV(2) and PV(3) . R each specify field R of each of these blocks.
We would also like to be able to index through a block of data. We can
do this in at least two ways. First, by modifying the pointer; e.g.,
P ← P + I. Second, by indexing the field, e.g., P . (I)R. Thus, if
P points to word 0 of a block, then P + I and P . (I) point to word I
of the block.
Now if we allow fields to contain pointer values, then we can construct
chains of pointers. Assuming PF is a pointer field, then P . PF . R
is the field R of the block pointed at by the field PF of the block
pointed at by P. This can be carried on indefinitely. As an example,
the following program in our fictional language would set up the data
structure shown in Figure 4.4.

```
BEGIN
POINTER VECTOR P(3);
POINTER FIELD PFA(2,0,64), PFB(3,0,64);
INTEGER FIELD INT(0,10,10);
INTEGER N, M;
: (M and N are initialized)
P(0) ← ALLOCATE(N+1);
P(1) ← ALLOCATE(4);
P(2) ← ALLOCATE(M+1);
P(1).PFA   P(0);
P(1).PFB   P(2);
P(0).PFA   P(2)
END
```

The shaded area in Figure 4.4 represents the field which would be referenced by any of the following expressions:

    P(2).(M)INT
or P(1).PFB.(M)INT
or P(1).PFA.PFA (M)INT

In GLYPNIR the above ideas are extended as follows:
1.   There are two kinds of pointers: (a) pointers which can point anywhere in memory; and (b) pointers which can point only within a given memory module.
2.   Pointer variables can represent either a single pointer or a sword of pointers.
3.   There are several kinds of allocation and deallocation statements allowing allocation/deallocation of blocks of words or blocks of swords.
Experience has shown that these facilities are useful even in numerically oriented applications. For example, they are used to allow packing of low precision data, I/O can be performed directly from data areas (without intermediate buffering), and complex relationships between data items can be maintained via pointer link rather than physical movement of the data.

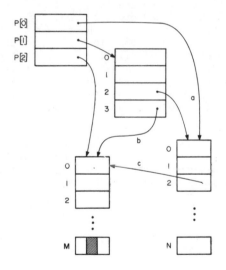

Figure 4.4   Example of pointer structure

4. Control Statements

Control statements resemble those of FORTRAN and ALGOL except they have been extended to facilitate control of parallel calculations. Examples are given below where (BE) is a Boolean expression, and (S) is a statement or block of statements.

```
IF (BE) THEN (S)
IF (BE) THEN (S₁) ELSE (S₂)
FOR ALL (BE) DO (S)
LOOP I ← 11, 12, 13 DO (S)
THRU I DO (S)
FOR ← 11 STEP 12 UNTIL 13 DO (S)
DO (S) UNTIL (BE)
WHILE (BE) DO (S)
GO TO (label)
```

IF Statements and Mode Patterns

One can think of each statement in the language as being executed separately in each PE. For example, take the statement "$X \leftarrow X + 1$" where X is a sword. For each of the 64 elements of X there is a corresponding PE. The above statement causes each (enabled) PE to increment its value of X. Now consider the statement

IF (BE) THEN (S₁) ELSE (S₂)

The (BE) represents 64 Boolean values, one corresponding to each PE. The statement (S₁) is then executed in PEs whose corresponding element of (BE) is true. Then (S₂) is executed in PEs corresponding to false elements of (BE). For example, "IF X < 0 THEN X = -X ELSE X = 0" would cause negative elements of X to be set positive and nonnegative elements to be set to zero. In effect, the statements (S₁) and (S₂) are executed under the control of an enable pattern (mode pattern) generated by the Boolean expression. That is, the Boolean expression causes certain PEs to be disabled before the statements are executed. Since IF statements can be nested, these enable patterns must also be nested and in fact they are kept in an execution-time stack.

Since (S₁) and (S₂) can be any statement including a (go to) statement, we have a problem. "IF (BE) THEN GO TO HERE ELSE GO TO THERE" would imply that some PEs would begin executing a code stream at label HERE while others would begin at THERE; i.e. different PEs would execute different code streams. If we allowed this we would have to provide for all the facilities required to control independent parallel code streams (semaphores, etc.) and we would be providing a capability clearly not supported by the hardware. Instead, we chose to restrict the meaning of (go to) statements in this context. We require that all PEs execute the (go to) if any PE does. Thus, if X < 0 is not FALSE, the statement

```
IF X < 0 THEN BEGIN
             X ← -X;
             GO TO HERE
             END
        ELSE BEGIN
             X ← 0;
             GO TO THERE
             END
```

Since (S_1) and (S_2) can be any statement including a GO TO statement, there is a problem. "IF (BE) THEN GO TO HERE ELSE GO TO THERE" would imply that some PEs would begin executing a code stream at label HERE while others would begin at THERE; i.e., different PEs would execute different code streams. If this were allowed GLYPNIR would have to provide for all the facilities required to control independent parallel code streams (semaphores, etc.) and would be providing a capability clearly not supported by the hardware. Instead, GLYPNIR chose to restrict the meaning of GO TO statements in this context. The requirement is that all PEs execute the GO TO if any PE does. Thus, if X < 0 is not FALSE, the statement

```
IF X < 0 THEN BEGIN
              X ← -X;
              GO TO HERE
           END
         ELSE BEGIN
              X ← 0;
              GO TO THERE
           END
```

would result in "X← -X" followed by an unconditional transfer of control to HERE. The ELSE PART would only be executed if X < 0 is FALSE.

The statement "FOR ALL (BE) DO (S)" is equivalent to "IF (BE) THEN (S)". It is in the language because it is mnemonically somewhat more pleasing to some users than the IF STATEMENT.

Iterative Statements

The iterative control statements (LOOP, THRU, FOR, DO, and WHILE above) cause the specified statement or block of statements to be repeated either until some count is exhausted (LOOP, THRU, FOR) or until some Boolean condition is satisfied (DO, WHILE). The statement "LOOP I ← I1, I2, I3 DO (S)" is similar to a FORTRAN DO loop, except the test for completion (I ← I3) is made before (S) is executed. The controlled variable (I above) must be a CU INTEGER variable and the initial value (I1), increment (I2) and limit (I3) can be arbitrary arithmetic expressions but they must each result in a single value (they may not involve swords or slices). They are converted to integers if necessary. The statement "THRU I DO (S)" causes the statement (S) to be repeated I times. "I" must be a CU variable or a constant (not a sword) and is converted to an integer if necessary.

The statement "FOR I ← I1 STEP I2 UNTIL I3 DO (S)" is similar to the LOOP statement above except that the controlled variable (I), initial value (I1), increment (I2) and limit (I3) may be swords. Thus each PE may execute (S) a different number of times, with different increments, and with different values of the controlled variable, subject to the same restrictions on GO TO statements as apply to IF STATEMENTS. For example, assume I3 is a PE INTEGER (sword) whose ith element has the value i (i.e. $I3_i = i$, $0 < i \le 63$) and Z is a PE REAL VECTOR Z(64) (sword vector). Then the following statements would cause the upper triangular (including the main diagonal) part of Z to be set to zero:

FOR I = 0 STEP 1 UNTIL I3 DO Z(I) ← 0

The statements "DO (S) UNTIL (BE)" and "WHILE (BE) DO (S)" cause
the indicated statement (S) to be repeated UNTIL or WHILE a Boolean
condition is satisfied. For example, assume X is a sword containing
real values > 0. Then the following statement would decrement each
element of X by 1 until it is ≤ 0:

WHILE X > 0 DO X ← X - 1
or DO X ← X - 1 UNTIL X > 0

Note that the UNTIL statement iterates until the Boolean expression
is FALSE, and the WHILE statement iterates while the Boolean expression is TRUE.

5. Example

At this point an example might be helpful. Suppose the memory has a sword C of elements and the program must compute a new sword X, the value of whose elements <u>are</u> the square roots of the corresponding ele- ments of C; i.e., $X_i = \sqrt{C_i}$, $0 \le i \le 63$. It could of course use the built-in function SQRT(C) which would return the required sword. In- stead let it use the iterative formula $X_j = \frac{1}{2}(X_j + C_j/X_j)$ where it will stop iterating when $((X_j)^2 - C_j) < \varepsilon$. In FORTRAN write this as follows:

```
      DO 10 J = 1.N
    9 IF (ABS((X(J)*X(J) - C(J))/C(J)).LE.EPSILN) GO TO 10
      X(J) = (X(J) + C(J)/X(J))*.5
      GO TO 9
   10 CONTINUE
```

In GLYPNIR write this as follows where X and C are PE variables (swords):

```
      L:IF ABS((X*X-C)/C)    UPSILON THEN
            BEGIN
            X - (X+C/X)*.5;
            GO TO L
            END
```

Alternately, we could write

```
      WHILE ABS((X*X-C)/C)    EPSILON DO X ← (X+C/X)*.5
```

These programs would iterate simultaneously on all elements which have not converged, until all elements have converged.

6. Miscellaneous

Subroutines resemble ALGOL procedures in that they can be declared in the block head and they may return values. (They may also be declared and compiled separately.) However, they differ in that they are non-recursive and their arguments are called by value; i.e., the value of the argument is passed to the subroutine. Arguments may be either words, swords, or slices, and typed subroutines may return either word or sword values.

I/O between the Illiac and the outside world is a function of the operating system and control language and will not be discussed here (cf (4)).

Limitations in the scope of this discussion have made it necessary to simplify descriptions of some of the features of the language, and descriptions of other facilities have been omitted entirely, among them: ability to insert in-line assembly code (for optimization of kernals), ability to control hardware register allocation, rather powerful MACRO capabilities, and a number of intrinsic functions having particular relevance to parallel processing. (For a complete, formal description of GLYPNIR, refer to Layman and Baer (17).)

The GLYPNIR compiler was written in Burroughs Extended ALGOL and runs on the Burroughs B6700 computer. It consists of approximately 20,000 ALGOL card images (excluding support systems) and requires approximately 25 K of core for execution. It compiles at a rate of 1200 cards per cpu minute.

Recent experience indicates that unoptimized code generated by the GLYPNIR compiler runs 1.5 to 3 times slower than the same program coded in Illiac IV assembly language (see, for example, (22)). Other experiments on conventional machines indicate this is not unusual (6).

In addition to the compiler, several support packages are provided. These include subroutine and macro libraries, a compiler verification system, and debugging aids. Debugging of user programs can be done on Illiac IV or on the Illiac IV simulator which runs on the Burroughs B6700 computer. A dialect of GLYPNIR which compiles and executes on an IBM 360 is also available and can be used for debugging (7).

7. Discussion

There are two basic problems in compiling code for a parallel computer: (1) detection of parallel operations, and (2) parallel execution of parallel operations.

The first problem involves the automatic analysis of a serially coded algorithm to determine which parts of the code can be done in parallel. Work in this area has been reported in the literature by Muraoka (20), Kuck, Muraoka and Chen (9), and Lamport (11, 12), among others. Alternately, explicit specification of parallelism in the language could be allowed. Techniques for doing this include but are not limited to allowing the programmer to refer to whole vectors or arrays rather than just vector or array elements. This latter idea is not new and is already possible in many languages (e.g. APL, PL/I).

Once there is a set of parallel operations to be performed, it must be decided how to perform them on a given parallel machine. Not all parallel operations can be done in parallel. The problem here lies primarily in the ability of the memory system to access data in parallel and to cause operand pairs to be properly paired. For example, consider a memory system which consists of four separate memory modules, each of which is capable of accessing independent memory addresses. Assume that there is a 3 x 3 matrix stored in these memories as shown in Figure 4.5. Notice that the program can access a row of this matrix (e.g., (A_{00}, A_{01}, A_{02}) in parallel since each element of a row is in a different memory unit. The same is true of a column. However, the diagonal (A_{00}, A_{11}, A_{22}) cannot be accessed in parallel since all these elements lie in the same memory.

Another difficulty is that rows and columns are not in the same order.

Illiac IV hardware is not capable of performing a realignment efficiently unless it consists of a simple uniform shift of the data of distance ± 1 or ± 8.

Thus, we have two problems which must be handled if we are to do a parallel operation in parallel: (a) parallel memory access, and (b) parallel data alignment. Once these problems are solved, there remains only rather simple arithmetic operations between already paired data. Failure to solve either of these problems can cause serious, even complete degradation to serial processing.

On Illiac IV, these problems are solved (at least partially) by using special storage mapping schemes which minimize access conflicts and realignment problems. One of these, called I-skew storage, is illustrated in Figure 4.6. Notice this allows parallel access to rows and columns but not to diagonals, and alignment of rows with columns requires only uniform shifts.

This scheme works well for some problems. Other problems require other schemes. Larger arrays must be sliced or folded in various ways to fit them into these storage mapping schemes while minimizing addressing complexity. A great many schemes have been invented (e.g. see Kraska (8), Millstein (19), Muraoka (21), and Kuck and Sameh (10)), and each scheme is clearly superior to others for some program. The process of selecting and using the right scheme at the right time is not well understood and it is a monumental task for a compiler to assume. And yet it must be done by someone if the compiler is to generate efficient object code. (See also Lawrie (15, 16).)

During the design of the GLYPNIR compiler, these problems and their solutions were not well understood. Experiments with more elegant (and risky) solutions were being undertaken (Abel (1)). GLYPNIR's greatest contribution would be to assure the availability of a language with a compiler capable of producing reliable and efficient object code. To accomplish this, the storage and alignment problems were left to the programmers. This is why programmers using GLYPNIR must explicitly express their parallelism in terms of swords and slices instead of vectors, arrays, etc.

This is clearly not the most desirable solution to the problem. But programmers would rather cope with these problems using GLYPNIR than cope with the same problems using assembly languages.

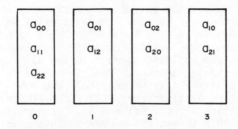

Figure 4.5   A 3x3 matrix stored in a four-unit memory system

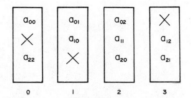

Figure 4.6   One-skew storage

8. Conclusions

From a programmer's point of view, one of the major deficiencies of
GLYPNIR is that it fails to hide the basic 64-wide parallel architecture
of Illiac IV. In effect, the programmer is required to restructure his
data and computation so that the computation can be done in parallel in
"strips" of width 64 or less. Currently, this is done by applications
programmers after much study of their particular application and the
algorithms involved. For the compiler to do this restructuring, i.e.,
to hide the Illiac architecture, would entail generation of code whose
lack of efficiency would violate one of the primary design goals.

In effect, there is a widened gap between the human conceptualiza-
tion of a computation and the macine architecture on which that computation must be performed. Of course, languages exist which allow explicit
specification of parallelism and these might help to bridge this gap.
Unfortunately, no one knows how to translate such languages into efficient machine code, due at least in part to the difficulties of selecting
the proper storage mapping schemes. What is needed is a continuation
and consolidation of three current areas of research: (1) languages
and the representation of algorithms; (2) automatic analysis and modification of computation structures; and (3) "programmable" parallel
architectures. GLYPNIR is not the answer to this problem, but it provides a reliable and useful programming tool in the interim.

References

1. Abel, N., et al. TRANQUIL, a language for an array processing computer. Proc. AFIPS 1969 SJCC, Vol. 34, AFIPS Press, Montvale, N.J., pp. 57-73.
2. Abel, N., et al. Language specifications for a FORTRAN-like higher level language for Illiac IV. Illiac IV Doc. No. 233, *Illiac IV Proj., U. of Illnois at Urbana-Champaign, Urbana, Ill., 1970.
3. Barnes, G.H., et al. The Illiac IV Computer. IEEE TC C-17, 8 (Aug. 1963), 746-757.
4. Bouknight, W.J., et al. The Illiac IV System. Proc. IEEE, 60, 4 (Apr. 1972), 369-388.
5. CFD, a FORTRAN-based language for Illiac IV Computational Fluid Dynamics Branch, Ames Res. Cent., NASA, Moffett Field, Calif.
6. Henriksen, J.C., and Merwin, R.E. Programming language efficiency in real time software systems. Proc. AFIPS 1972, Vol. 40, AFIPS Press, Montvale, N.J., pp. 155-161.
7. Hoffman, R.E. User's manual for GLYPLIT: a program to translate Illiac IV Glypnir to IBM 360 PL/1. Rand Rep. No. R-857-ARPA (Apr. 1972), Rand Corporation, Santa Monica, Calif., 74 pp.
8. Kraska, P. Array storage allocation. M.S. Th., U. of Illinois at Urbana Champaign, Dept of Computer Sci. Rep. No. 344, 1969.
9. Kuck, D., Muraoka, Y., and Chen, S.C. On the number of operations simultaneously executable in FORTRAN-like programs and their resulting speed-up. IEEE TC C-21 (Dec. 1972), 1293-1310.
10. Kuck, D., and Sameh, A. Parallel computation of eigenvalues of real matrices, In Information Processing 71, Vol. II, pp. 1266-1272, North-Holland Pub. Co., Amsterdam-London, 1972.
11. Lamport, L. The coordinate method for the parallel execution of DO loops. Proc. 1973 Sagamore Computer Conf. on Parallel Processing, pp. 1-12.
12. Lamport. L. The parallel execution of DO Loops. Comm. ACM 17, 2 (Feb. 1972), 83-89.
13. Lawrie, D.H., Glypnir: an overview of the language. Illiac IV Doc. No. 230, Illiac IV Prof., U. of Illinois at Urbana-Champaign, Urbana, Ill. 1970.
14. Lawrie, D.H. GLYPNIR programming manual. Illiac IV Doc. No. 232, Illiac IV Proj., U. of Illinois at Urbana-Champaign, Urbana, Ill., 1970.
15. Lawrie, D.H. Memory Systems for Parallel Array Processors. Proc. Eleventh Ann. Allerton Conf. on Circuit and System Theory. Allerton Hse., Monticello, Ill., 1973, pp. 568-576.
16. Lawrie, D.H. Access requirements and design of primary memory for array processors. (To be published).
17. Layman, T., and Baer, D. Glypnir Reference Manual. Illiac IV Doc. No. 263, Illiac IV Proj., U. of Illinois at Urbana-Champaign, Urbana, Ill., 1972, 239 pp.
18. McIntyre, D.E. Illiac IV software development. 1972 WESCON Tech. Papers, Session 1, 1972.
19. Millstein, R.E. Control structures in Illiac IV FORTRAN, Comm. ACM 16, 10 (Oct. 1973). 621-627.
20. Muraoka, Y. Parallelism exposure and exploitation in programs. Ph.D. Th., U. of Illinois at Urbana-champaign, Dept. of Computer Sci. Rep. No. 424, 1971.

21.   Muraoka, Y. Storage allocation algorithms in the TRANQUIL Compiler,
      M.S. Th., U. of Illinois at Urbana-Champaign, Dept. of Computer
      Sci., 1969.
22.   Ogura, M. Sher. M.S., and Erickens, J.H. A study of the efficiency
      of Illiac IV in hydrodynamics calculations. CAC Doc. No. 59,
      Center for Advanced Computation, U. of Illinois at Urbana-Champaign,
      Urbana, Ill., 93 pp., 1972.

      Illiac IV documents are available from: Illiac IV Project.
Documentation.   Institute for Advanced Computation.   Mail Stop 233-14,
NASA Ames Research Center, Motfett Field, CA   94035.

C. Language Review

1. Introduction

This review is a brief examination of some existing programming languages
for the Illiac IV, namely GLYPNIR (1, 2), CFD (3), and IVTRAN (4). A
proposed language, APPLE (5), is also discussed briefly to contrast with
the above languages.[1] In this short overview, the comparison of the
various programming languages is organized from three points of view.
    The first point of view is that programming languages, for Illiac
as for other computers, are tools of problem solving. High-level languages attempt to present the computational facilities of computers in
terms more understandable to the user than machine language. The purpose is to help the user formulate a solution to his problem by providing
him with computational "abstractions" that are "close" to his problem
domain.
    A second and closely related point of view is that programming lan-
guages are tools to implement solutions (programs). Over the past few
years, people have begun to realize the high cost of software production.
Interestingly, it has been found that the major part of this cost is not
due to the initial design and programming efforts, but lies with program testing and debugging and with program maintenance. Even in these
conditions, the reliability and the "quality" of large software systems
is often questionable. Consequently, it is important to look at how
languages can simplify testing and debugging and facilitate program
maintenance.

---

[1]APPLE (5), COCKROACH (6), and TRANQUIL (7) are various languages that
have been proposed for Illiac, but were never implemented. However,
COCKROACH is very similar to CFD, and many of TRANQUIL's features can be
found in IVTRAN. Thus, this overview is limited to CFD, GLYPNIR, and
IVTRAN. As much as possible, only the implemented subset of IVTRAN is
discussed.
This section is based on "A Critical Look at Some Programming Languages
for Illiac IV", by Fred Richard, IAC Newsletter, November/December, 1977.

The third point of view taken in the following sections is that Illiac IV is a unique architecture. Although the development of software for Illiac IV has similarities with the development of software for any other computer, programming the Illiac is much different from programming a classic sequential computer. Because the main advantage of Illiac IV is its speed, Illiac applications are usually applications that cannot be processed within a reasonable amount of time on most other machines. Thus, the major design and programming issues for Illiac IV result from a justified concern for efficiency. A first issue is to isolate, during the design phase, the parallelism inherent to the application, or to reformulate the problem to obtain some parallelism. The second issue is to map this parallelism onto the Illiac IV. The two major difficulties are:

1) Management of the two-level memory hierarchy, i.e., how to lay out the data on the disk memory to provide fast access to portions of the data sets needed at the same time for processing.

2) Management of the CU-PE ensemble, i.e., how to organize program data within this complex to obtain good response time.

Evidently, these two difficulties cannot be resolved independently. However, since most Illiac applications seem to be I/O bound, rather than "CPU" bound, design decisions about the management of the memory hierarchy seem more important for efficiency considerations.

In summary, the following sections provide a comparison of the Illiac IV programming languages both from a usual point of view (language design, implementation, and usage) and from the point of view of producing programs that make efficient use of the Illiac IV resources (management of the memory hierarchy and management of the CU-PE complex). The list of the following sections can be viewed as a list of design issues for parallel machines like Illiac IV.

2. Computational Model Presented to the User

Any programming language defines some abstract machine for its user. The purpose of this abstract machine is to hide (in part or totally) the target machine and provide the user with facilities close to his problem domain, in order to diminish the conceptual distance between the initial problem specifications and the resulting program. Among the languages examined, there are four distinct types of "abstract" machines presented to the user by the four languages considered:

1) APPLE presents generalized array and vector computations. This simple revision of the APL does not require any knowledge of the Illiac to produce a working program (whether efficient or not).

2) IVTRAN presents a FORTRAN machine with some one-dimensional parallel facilities. IVTRAN can be considered in two different ways. Since the IVTRAN compiler accepts standard FORTRAN and attempts to isolate DO loops that can be executed in parallel, IVTRAN can be regarded as a FORTRAN compiler that generates code for the Illiac. Unfortunately, the techniques used by the current compiler to extract parallelism are very restricted, and the code generated for a FORTRAN program is very often code running in one PE at a time. The parallelizing part of the IVTRAN compiler must be considered as a tool to improve programs (see Programming Support Report). On the other hand, IVTRAN can be regarded as a FORTRAN based language with some parallel facilities. The computational model provided by the full IVTRAN language as it is currently implemented is an extension of FORTRAN where some parallel operations can be performed along one dimension of arrays of arbitrary size. IVTRAN requires some knowledge of the Illiac architecture for the allocations of arrays and the alignment of operands.

3) CFD is a FORTRAN-based language which requires the user to know that the Illiac is composed of one CU and 64 PEs, organized in linear order. There is a very clear distinction between control variables and vector aligned variables. However, CFD hides little of the Illiac from the user: the MODE must be manipulated directly, transfers between CU and PE memory must be programmed, and the limited arithmetic capabilities of the CU are reflected in CU arithmetic expressions.

4) GLYPNIR, an ALGOL-like language, requires less detailed knowledge of the Illiac IV than CFD. There are no limitations on CU arithmetic (the programmer, however, should make sure that at least one PE is enabled when such expressions are evaluated). GLYPNIR differs importantly from the other languages in that it presents the Illiac IV as a set of PEs operating simultaneously and does not constrain the user to either a vector or an array approach.

From the point of view of the abstract machines provided by CFD, GLYPNIR, and IVTRAN, three serious criticisms can be made.

First, all three languages fail to abstract more than the CU-PE complex of Illiac. The two-level memory hierarchy is not part of their respective computational models. Management of the disk memory is left entirely to the user and only very low level facilities are provided to transfer data between I4DM and PE memory.

113

Second, CFD and GLYPNIR do not hide enough of the Illiac. They force the user to think directly in terms of Illiac parallelism (e.g., 64 simultaneous operations).

The last criticism applies to more current programming languages besides CFD, GLYPNIR, and IVTRAN. In the case of Illiac languages, none of them provide features that are at the same level of abstraction as the user problem domain. Admittedly, it is difficult to provide, in the same language, a facility like "layers of the atmosphere" to one user and a facility like "particle" to another. However, it is not being too demanding to require some mechanism that would allow each user to define the additional abstractions that fit his problem.

3. Vector and Array Processing

As an APL-like language, APPLE provides very high level capabilities for vector and array processing. Because of the generality and the highly dynamic behavior of some of its features, there are major difficulties in implementing such a language efficiently on Illiac. One should not neglect, however, the importance of such primitives to design large programs. They allow the programmer to concentrate his attention on high level optimizations instead of attempting to organize cleverly very low-level code.

The use of vectors and arrays in IVTRAN, CFD, and GLYPNIR is more primitive, often reflecting the physical limitations of the Illiac, but also allowing the programmer various degrees of control on the use of the machine resources.

PE Variables

The only way to obtain parallelism in IVTRAN and CFD is through the use of arrays. Both IVTRAN and CFD provide arrays of up to three dimensions. Parallelism is obtained by applying the same operation to elements of an array that lie across PEs. Data types are limited to integer and floating point. Furthermore, CFD restricts the first dimension of arrays to be less than or equal to 64.

In GLYPNIR, where the Illiac IV is explicitly presented as a set of 64 processors operating simultaneously, a PE variable defines a collective name for a set of 64 "simple variables" distributed across the PEs. Similarly, a PE vector defines a set of 64 vectors of identical size. The basic data types provided by GLYPNIR are similar to the data types of IVTRAN and CFD, but the ALPHA "type" provides an escape hatch for the representation of other quantities.

PE Variables Memory Allocation

CFD and GLYPNIR PE structures map directly onto the physical memory. A one-dimension 64-element CFD array is equivalent to a GLYPNIR PE variable. A two-dimension CFD array is equivalent to a GLYPNIR PE vector. In CFD, the first dimension of an array lies across PEs. Any other storage structure (e.g., skewed array) that may be needed by the programmer must be implemented on top of the available structures, and each reference to such "application structures" in the text is done by indicating the CFD or GLYPNIR variables (which stand for areas of PE Memory) along with an adequate subscript denotation. The abstraction of the "application structures" is ultimately lost in the program text.

IVTRAN offers a much more powerful scheme for array storage where the programmer can choose which array dimension lies across the PEs and can specify skewing or alignment of other dimensions. There are two problems with IVTRAN array allocation that often force the programmer to restructure his arrays to obtain some efficiency. The first case consists of restructuring an array A (2,30) into B (60) so that all elements lie in one PE row. The second case consists of controlling the allocation of distinct arrays through EQUIVALENCE or DEFINE's to align

them and avoid inefficient routing during computation. Thus,
like GLYPNIR and CFD, IVTRAN often forces the programmer to re-
code his problem in a notation which no longer indicates the
logical structure of the data used in the computation.
A main drawback of all these languages is that they do not provide any facility to pack many data items in various fields of
the same word. Only GLYPNIR enables packing with the ALPHA data
type, but the field manipulations can become tedious.

Array Addressing

The selection of array components in CFD and GLYPNIR reflects
directly the addressing structure of the I4. Each array reference selects one element in each PE. The position of the
elements selected in different PE's may differ if the index
expression includes some quantity local to each PE. This feature is especially important to implement nontrivial algorithms
(see the "diagonal control paradigm" and the "advancing wave
paradigm" described in (8)). However, other accessing methods
must be programmed with additional control structures, e.g.,
proper MODE setting to access a single element, and explicit
loop to iterate overall elements of a two or three dimensional
array.
IVTRAN provides a different approach. First, any array element
can be addressed separately, as in FORTRAN. All mode operations
are hidden from the user. Second, the "*" notation allows references to entire cross-sections (note that an IVTRAN cross-
section is a very restricted form of submatrix) for component-
wise operations; depending on the allocation, cross-section
operations may be parallelized. Finally array references within
a DO FOR ALL loop denote "simultaneous" access to an entire row
of the array. IVTRAN does not allow "local indexing" as in
GLYPNIR and CFD, since the array allocation is supposed to alleviate that need for numerical applications. However, this restriction prevents simultaneous access to array elements that
lie across PEs. when the index set of these elements is not
regular (e.g., not a row, column, or diagonal of a skewed two-
dimensional array), and forbids the implementation of nontrivial
control schemes (see (8)).

Routing

The simultaneous evaluation in many PEs of an expression involving terms that are stored in various PEs requires routing
of the operands. Syntactically, this routing is entirely trans-
parent to the IVTRAN user. The main drawback of this approach
is that it is very difficult to estimate the routing cost of an
IVTRAN program, and thus to be able to modify storage structures
to improve the performance.
In GLYPNIR, the communication of values among PEs is accomplished by specifying a routing expression in an assignment, or
by using an intrinsic function with the appropriate routing expression. When a GLYPNIR assignment contains a routing specification, the expression on the right-hand side of the assignment

is evaluated in the source PEs, although these PEs may not be part of the current MODE setting when the assignment statement is entered. GLYPNIR allows a different routing distance to be specified at each PE, and this provides a great amount of flexibility, but is rather inefficient.

The CFD approach to routing is much more restricted. Routing is implied in an expression like A(*) + B(*+3) where each element of B is transferred 3 PEs to the left before being added to an element of A. Computation is entirely done at the destination PEs. The routing distance must be identical for all elements being routed.

The most important limitation of routing in CFD and GLYPNIR is that only circular transfers (PE's are arranged on a ring) are available. Clever programming seems required to make the PE ensemble look like a square (ends off) of a torus. More elaborate data manipulation functions (e.g., perfect shuffle) require important programming effort.

In summary, two categories of array processing can be distinguished between IVTRAN, on the one hand, and GLYPNIR and CFD on the other. The IVTRAN approach is to provide storage schemes that are as general as possible without indicating precisely the cost of using these structures. GLYPNIR and CFD provide very low level storage structures that reveal entirely the Illiac structure, but for which the implicit computational costs are low and well defined.

Both approaches are flawed because they only provide a fixed set of storage schemes that do not always correspond to the logical structures dealt with by programs. The implementation of a matrix using a skewed storage in GLYPNIR or CFD requires a complex notation to be used every time a row, a column, or a diagonal of the matrix is accessed. Similarly, IVTRAN requires obscure notation if two consecutive elements of a vector have to be stored in the same PE. It is obvious that no language can or should provide all possible structures. At the machine level, there are few possible schemes in addition to the ones provided by the above languages. However, the use of these structures through an entire program leads to obscure notation and represents an important loss of abstraction. It would be preferable to provide a scheme allowing the programmer (1) to define the logical structures in terms of the basic storage structures of the machine, in one part of the program, and (2) to refer to the logical structures through the rest of the program. This hiding mechanism should alleviate much of the program complexity, while retaining control over its efficiency.

4. Scalar Processing

In the context of this discussion, scalar processing means the set of facilities offered by the various languages to perform computations other than component-wise simultaneous operations (parallel processing). A scalar expression evaluates to a single value. The elements of scalar expressions are usually elements of what are called CU variables in CFD and GLYPNIR, although this need not be.

Scalar processing in CFD is limited to the arithmetic capabilities of the Illiac CU. Complex scalar expressions in CFD must be explicitly performed in the PEs. Things are a little bit easier on the programmer in GLYPNIR where arbitrary scalar expressions can be expressed. The only problem is that at least one PE must be enabled to evaluate properly subexpressions involving floating point arithmetic. IVTRAN is even simpler.

An important disadvantage of the IVTRAN language is the provision for numerous type conversions in expressions, which almost defeats the purpose of type and hides the complex transformations that take place during execution. Strong data type checking at compile time, as in GLYPNIR, has been shown to eliminate many programming errors without going through extensive debugging runs, and enforces an explicit notation throughout the program. For these reasons, this approach is preferable.

5. Control Structures

The main drawback of all the languages reviewed is the lack of distinction between control structures that affect the instruction stream (i.e., modifying the instruction fetch by the CU) and control structures that affect the data streams (i.e., modifying or selecting the set of PEs that should execute forthcoming instructions). This is especially true of IVTRAN where IF statements within a DO FOR ALL are interpreted differently from regular IFs. This is also true of some control structures of GLYPNIR. For instance, the GLYPNIR IF statement can be used for two different purposes. On the one hand, it can be used to signify the conditional execution of some statements depending on the single boolean value of some CU expression, as in usual "sequential" programming languages. On the other hand, a GLYPNIR IF statement can be used to signify the execution of a second sequence of statements in a complementary set of PEs. Only one branch is meant to be executed in the first case, while the two branches are executed sequentially in disjoint sets of PEs in the second case. Unfortunately, both cases are handled identically in GLYPNIR and unnecessary mode manipulations occur when the first type of IF is meant.

The distinction is made more clearly in CFD where two kinds of IDs, scalar and vector, are provided. The drawbacks of CFD are the restrictions on the selection expressions and the fact that such IF's can accommodate only a single statement. To restrict the execution of a series of CFD statements to a subset of the PEs, MODE manipulation is required. This feature is also available in GLYPNIR but, fortunately, it can be avoided most often when programming in this language. The problem with an assignment to the pseudo-variable MODE in CFD, as in MODE-SOMEPESONLY, is that it is a highly dynamic feature that modifies the meaning of the statements that follow. This kind of notation is dangerous (for example, it remains in effect when a branch is taken, which complicates debugging) and some other syntactic device (e.g., FOR<PE EXP>DO control structure in GLYPNIR, or indexing with a control vector in APPLE) should be preferred.

Another problem with GLYPNIR and CFD concerns those control structures that indicate iteration over sub-arrays. In many instances (consider the addition of two n x m matrices), the looping statements require the specification of indices and of index sequences unnecessarily. This kind of overspecification reduces further the amount of abstraction available in both languages. The "*" (array cross-section) construct of IVTRAN prevents the need for such overspecifications.

6. Input/Output

Although the management of the memory hierarchy seems to be a critical
factor in the overall performance of an Illiac program, neither GLYPNIR
nor CFD offers facilities beyond BUFFER IN, BUFFER OUT types of statements for data transfer between the disk memory (I4DM) and PE memory.
They only provide access to the primitive facilities of the machine.
IVTRAN provides most of FORTRAN I/O, but at a prohibitive execution
cost.

There are two related aspects to the I/O problem on Illiac. The
first is creating I4DM areas from TENEX files according to a user-supplied map. Within an area, many distinct logical entities may be interleaved, so that all operands required by some iterated step of the program can be loaded in one single I/O request at execution time. The
second aspect consists of the various transfers between I4DM and PE
memory during execution. The efficiency of a program depends on the
relative position of locations addressed by successive requests to the
I4DM. The mapping mechanism that enables the user to distribute data
over the physical disk space requires much knowledge of the program behavior and timing in order to produce a suitable map. Not only do the
current languages fail to include the memory hierarchy of the Illiac in
their computational models, but they also fail to provide the user with
any help. Buffered I/O seems a minimum, with the compiler inserting
I/O requests in the generated code as early as possible. Second, an
estimation of the computation times between successive requests could
enable the compiler to provide an initial map for the user (note that
this may not always be possible). Furthermore, it should be easy for
the user to obtain run-time statistics on program behavior in order to
facilitate improvements of the initial mapping.

This lack of I/O structuring facilities is the major problem of
all languages reviewed. A minor problem is the lack of list directed,
possibly formatted I/O in GLYPNIR and CFD. The only type of I/O statements currently offered by these languages implements transfers between
areas in PE memory and areas in disk memory. It is not possible to produce directly any readable output (program log, intermediate results
for debugging purposes, or simply final results), or to input data in
character form. IVTRAN provides this facility, but very inefficiently.
It should be possible to restrict these features so that most of the
formatting and conversions can be performed by pre- and post-processors
operating on TENEX (which is what users have to do currently to obtain
any readable output).

7. Program Development and Maintenance

IVTRAN appears to be the most sophisticated of the various languages reviewed. Its parallelizing processor does provide some help in convert-
ing a FORTRAN program to a running Illiac program. However, the user
should be warned that the capabilities of the parallelizer are limited
and that usually much program manipulation is required to obtain a program which is at all efficient. Recoding in IVTRAN is strongly recom-
mended. All these operations require a good knowledge of the inner
workings of the IVTRAN compiler. IVTRAN seems to provide a reasonable
debugging package.

Compared to IVTRAN, GLYPNIR offers limited debugging facilities and
run time checks. On the other hand, the compile time evaluation facility and the macro facility of GLYPNIR are important program development
tools that are not provided by any other Illiac language. These facilities assist the development of programs in a systematic fashion, without losing much of the initial abstraction and at no cost in run time
efficiency. As for CFD, no similar facility is provided to support program development or testing.

There are a number of program development and maintenance tools
that are unavailable to the Illiac user, to cite a few: test data selection, program prover utilities, and symbolic dumps, for program validation; program transformation (source to source program "optimization")
and performance prediction utilities, for program enhancement. Although
some of these tools are just being understood and implemented for
"sequential" languages, they are widely recognized as being relevant for
software production. There is no reason why their benefits could not
be exercised in the production of Illiac software.

8.   Closing Remarks

There are three important points that need to be considered seriously before any new language for parallel machines like the Illiac can be proposed.

1)   Software development for the Illiac is not much different from software development for other machines: this means that any new language for Illiac should be designed to be part of a complete programming system including extensive program development tools. Serious restrictions on the language may be required to make these tools possible.

2)   The management of the Illiac memory hierarchy is an important factor of the efficiency of the Illiac applications program: this hierarchy should be manageable in the language itself; the supporting software should facilitate the optimum use of these resources.

3)   There are many ways a given program can be implemented in parallel: a language should not force a user to view problems only in terms of vectors or only in terms of simultaneously executing PEs. No languages of manageable size can provide all desirable facilities to all users. This means that a new language should enable program-defined extensions (abstractions) while leaving the user a good deal of control over the efficiency of the generated code.

References

1.   GLYPNIR Reference Manual by Terry Layman and David Baer. Illiac IV Document No. 263, University of Illinois (December 1972).

2.   GLYPNIR Programming Notes 1-8. IAC Doc. No. PD U8000-0004-A.

3.   CFD: A FORTRAN Based Language for Illiac IV. Computational Fluid Dynamics Branch, Ames Research Center, NASA.

4.   The IVTRAN Manual (Revised Edition). CADO-7051-2811 Massachusetts Computer Associates. (January 1975).

5.   An APPLE Tutorial by Marvin Schaefer. SDC-TM5074/100/100. System Development Corporation (September 1973).

6.   COCKROACH Programming Manual, by N. E. Abel. University of Illinois, June 1970.

7.   TRANQUIL: Status and Prospects by N. E. Abel et al. Illiac Doc. No. 233. University of Illinois (January 1970).

8.   Design of a Linear Programming System for the Illiac IV, by C. E. Pfefferkorn and J. A. Tomlin, Institute for Advanced Computation.

V.   Applications

Historically, the development of applications on the Illiac IV have gone through four phases. The first of these occurred in the period from early 1973 until November 1975. In this phase prior to the Illiac becoming operational a wide variety of application code development projects were undertaken. Many of these were performed by university and private sector personnel under contract to NASA or DARPA. The computational fluid dynamics work performed by the staff of the Ames Research Center CFD Branch is the notable exception. Generally the work was done remotely over the ARPANET communication system. In retrospect the marvel is that not all of these projects failed. The Illiac was not ready; it was down almost all of the time and when it was available, arithmetic errors without diagnostics were rampant.

During this period some programmers divided the Illiac into three sections of 21 processors each and worked the problem three times in parallel. Frequently the intermediate results from the three sections would be compared. If any two agreed, that would be taken as correct and the calculation would proceed. If no two agreed, the program would branch back to the previous checkpoint to try again. The program would be allowed to branch back dozens of times before giving up and aborting.

The machine was clearly designated as experimental. Unfortunately not all of the personnel attempting to develop application codes realized the serious implications of the experimental status. As a result the Illiac developed the reputation of a disaster machine.

To some degree the reputation was deserved. The Goddard Institute for Space Sciences Global Circulation Climate Model implementation (conversion) effort, for example, was undertaken during this period; it was never validated as working. At first direct line for line conversion was attempted. Later a restructuring of the code to better match the Illiac characteristics was tried. At last report, after a major effort, the Illiac version of the code ran to completion but it didn't make weather. Negative atmospheric pressures would occur in the course of the simulation.

To some degree the reputation was not deserved. The conversion of the Fleet Numeric Weather Central Primative Equation Weather Model conversion was another project that was begun and later abandoned. This exercise depended not only on an Illiac advertised as experimental, but also on the IVTRAN compiler that was advertised not yet to have been debugged. The failure of this project is not properly ascribed to the

Illiac, but to impatience to use systems not yet in place. Similar
stories are legion.

This period was very beneficial to the Illiac project, which at
this point had been institutionalized as IAC. The experiences of the
user community were a great help in identifying the glitches of the
Illiac and expedited the advent of its operational status.

Throughout this period IAC provided the services of support representatives. Three people on the IAC staff provided hand holding and
liaison. The burden of successful code development rested with the
contractor organization. Assistance of support representatives was
invoked primarily for trouble shooting.

Remarkably some application code development projects succeeded in
this environment. One of these was the SAM-IV project by the Mathematical Applications Group Incorporated. SAM-IV is a radiation penetra-
tion/transport model. At the time there was a controversy as to whether
Monte Carlo methods could be efficiently programmed on a parallel architecture. Three simultaneous contracts were awarded to explore this
question. Two of the contractors worked on the problem and reported
that Monte Carlo techniques just were not appropriate for a parallel
machine. The third, MAGI, succeeded with SAM-IV. This case exhibits a
phenomenon that continues today, fifteen years after the inception of
the Illiac; namely the unpredictability without major analysis of
whether a particular algorithm will lend itself to parallel implementation.

The second phase of applications development on the Illiac IV
occurred in the period from November 1975 until October 1976. In this
period the Illiac IV was almost exclusively devoted to one application
project. This was the Fixed/Mobile Experiment sponsored by the Tactical Technology Office of the Defense Advanced Research Projects Agency.
This effort was classified to the DOD Secret level, which required that
the Illiac itself be secured. Furthermore, a high speed data link with
encryption had to be established to a remote site. The principal contractor for applications code development was Ensco, Inc., Springfield,
Virginia.

The details of the activity cannot be discussed here but the effort
was ultimately successful and developed confidence in some sectors that
the Illiac could be counted upon for useful work. On the other hand
all other application activities during this period were relegated to a
time available priority, so not much of note can be reported.

The third phase of applications development on the Illiac covered
the period from October 1976 until June 1979. During this period under
the direction of the sponsors, NASA and particularly ARPA, the Institute
for Advanced Computation actively supported applications development.
A Projects Department staffed with applications specialists was established inhouse to provide expertise and project management to various
federal agencies. An Applications Development Department was established in the Washington, D.C. metropolitan area to provide close interaction with various user federal facilities. This turned out to be a
highly successful period for applications on the Illiac.

This period started slowly, with many potential users wary due to
the bad reputation of the Illiac from the pre-1975 days when many
efforts did not go well. Gradually, however, activity picked up. In
1978 dozens of applications projects funded by a wide variety of non-
sponsor federal agencies were underway in diverse application areas.

The interagency funds transfer process brought the Institute substantially more support in this time frame than was provided by either of the sponsor agencies.

June 1979 saw the start of the current phase of Illiac IV applications development. DARPA decided that the success of the phase three period had demonstrated the utility of the Illiac to a wide spectrum of the computational community. Hence DARPA sponsorship was no longer required so the Illiac became a NASA machine. NASA thereupon committed the Illiac to NASA projects, closed the Washington Applications Development Department, reduced the IAC staff from about 115 people to about 85, and began a practice of entertaining no new interagency relationships.

This chapter begins with a summary of the applications projects that were active during 1978 to illustrate the variety of efforts that can effectively exploit this national computational resource, provided that the proper staff and facilities are in place. The sections following this summary section consist of edited articles about specific application projects in the areas of computational fluid dynamics, image processing, mathematics, seismic research, and astronomy.

The application reports of this chapter are certainly not exhaustive. Many articles were considered but not included for lack of space. It is hoped that these examples illustrate the major features of practical Illiac codes.

A. Summary

The unique processing capabilities at the Institute are used by various government agencies for addressing large computation problems and those scientific research efforts which can efficiently employ the computational power and parallel design of the Illiac IV. This section presents an overview of these efforts during 1978.
This section is organized by application areas. These are divided into programs, which are further subdivided into specific projects. The application areas are those broad disciplines which IAC has identified as requiring large scale computing as well as being amenable to parallel processing.
Within these broad application areas, programs are groups of related efforts that require particular expertise. Initially, program areas were developed by using the expertise developed in ongoing projects.

1. Computational Fluid Dynamics

Research in this area is mainly performed by the Computational Fluid Dynamics Branch at the NASA Ames Research Center. In a recent public statement, Harvard Lomax, Chief of the Computational Fluid Dynamics Branch, identified the use of the Illiac IV as crucial to the recent advances in computational fluid dynamics. It is the goal of the CFD Branch to develop computational tools of sufficient strength to assist and to some degree replace the use of wind tunnels in the design of airfoils.

A. TRANSONIC FLOW PROGRAM

AIRCRAFT BUFFET PROJECT - Code developed by the Computational Fluid Dynamics Branch solves the Navier-Stokes equations for 2-dimensional unsteady transonic flow. Results are compared with wind tunnel data with the goal of developing a production code to investigate aircraft buffeting.

TRANSONIC AILERON BUZZ PROJECT - A recently developed viscous-flow airfoil code for the Illiac IV was used to simulate transonic aileron buzz.

126

The thin layer Navier-Stokes equations are solved with the turbulence modeled by a two-layer algebraic eddy viscosity model.   The
results are in essential agreement with the wind tunnel data.
The code uses up to a 64 x 128 grid of points.

3D TRANSONIC FLOW PROJECT - Illiac code developed by the Computation Fluid Dynamics Branch is used to solve the Navier-Stokes
equations in application to three-dimensional transonic flow
problems.   The flow field around complicated surfaces may be calculated.   This code is a research tool suitable for a very large
processor.   Modifications are being made to make the code run
faster and to make it useful for development purposes using
smaller computers.

B.   TURBULENT FLOW PROGRAM

INCOMPRESSIBLE TURBULENCE PROJECT - Turbulence modeling for
three-dimensional incompressible flow is being investigated for
the Navy Department.   The Navier-Stokes equations are solved
using a spectral algorithm.   Flow fields are computed on the
Illiac and then reduced on the CDC 7600.

SIMULATION OF TURBULENCE PROJECT - Turbulence and transition
phenomena were simulated by solving the compressible Navier-
Stokes equations for several three dimensional geometrics including a circular jet.   The mean velocity profile and turbulent
intensities in the resulting turbulent jet are in agreement with
those observed in subsonic jets.   More detailed comparisons with
experimentally measured shear stresses and temporal correlations
are planned.   These classes of codes use Fast Fourier Transforms
and finite difference methods on grids as large as 128 x 64 x 64
and make heavy use of the Illiac IV disk system (I4DM).

TURBULENT CHANNEL FLOW PROJECT - Code is being written to
solve the Navier-Stokes equations for 3-dimensional unsteady
incompressible flow.   Small-scale turbulence is taken into consideration.   Comparison is made with experimental measurements
in order to understand the physics of turbulent flows near a
boundary.

2D TURBULENCE SIMULATIONS PROJECT   - Illiac code developed
by the Computational Fluid Dynamics Branch is being used to
solve the Navier-Stokes equations in application to two-dimensional flow.   The flow over simple surfaces is calculated to
develop a model for turbulence.

3D TURBULENCE PROJECT - Vortex methods are used to solve the
Navier-Stokes equations.   Boundary layer turbulence simulations
for 3-dimensional incompressible unsteady flow are computed.
Comparison is made to measurements of actual fluid flow in order
to develop the method of solution and to understand the physics
of the problem.

3D TRANSONIC FLOW PROJECT - Illiac code developed by the Computation Fluid Dynamics Branch is used to solve the Navier-Stokes equations in application to three-dimensional transonic flow problems. The flow field around complicated surfaces may be calculated. This code is a research tool suitable for a very large processor. Modifications are being made to make the code run faster and to make it useful for development purposes using smaller computers.

VISCOUS SEPARATED FLOW PROJECT - A code which uses an implicit method for solving the three dimensional Reynolds averaged Navier-Stokes equations was developed for the Illiac IV. The calculations compare well with experimental profiles. The code currently uses a 40 x 40 x 40 grid. It is being modified to simulate the flow around a wing using an 88 x 40 x 48 grid. This code is a path finder on the way to engineering use of the three dimensional Navier-Stokes solutions for developing airfoils.

C.   VEHICLE MODELLING PROGRAM

AXI-SYMMETRIC WAKE PROJECT - The Galileo Project involves entry into the Jovian atmosphere. This problem is being studied for the Ames Thermal Protection Branch. Compressible, supersonic flow behind the initial shock wave of an entry vehicle is being calculated and compared to experimental measurements to determine entry conditions.

SPACE SHUTTLE PROJECT - Euler's equation with chemical non-equilibrium is solved in two and three dimensions by the finite volume method with three separate codes. Supersonic and hypersonic fluid flow simulations about the Space Shuttle Orbiter are calculated. The results will complement the experiments that Ames Research Center will place on the early Shuttle flights, and the code may possibly be used to process Shuttle data.

2.   On-Orbit Satellite Support

TERRA PROJECT - There has been a continued thrust within IAC to support projects concerning satellite tracking and geodetic parameter estimation. Recently the Navel Surface Weapons Center funded IAC for the implementation of a program to form matrices of preprocessed satellite observation data, an essential step in determining accurate geodetic parameters.

3.   Physics/Chemistry/Mathematics

A.   CHEMISTRY PROGRAM

MOLECULAR DYNAMICS PROJECT - Under the auspices of the Computational Fluid Dynamics Branch at Ames, Drs. Chris Jesshope and James Craige with the University of Reading, England, have just completed a three dimensional molecular dynamics simulation model for the Illiac IV. The model is able to simulate from 8 to 10 thousand particles, and the code will be made available for general use.

One motivation behind the development of this code is the comparison of the power of various machines. It is hoped that the same program will be developed for the IBM 360/195, CDC 7600 and the CRAY so that an accurate comparison can be made. This will help to assess the power of the different architectures of these machines for this application.

B. MATHEMATICS PROGRAM

RATIONAL COMPUTATION PROJECT - Dr. Newman at the University of California at Santa Barbara under funding from the Air Force Office of Scientific Research has been using the Illiac to invert exactly matrices with integral coefficients. The method uses modular arithmetic and the Chinese Remainder Theorem to express the answer using rational numbers.

NUMBER THEORETIC FUNCTIONS PROJECT - Dr. Lehmer of U.C., Berkley continues to use the Illiac for the evaluation of functions with number theoretic importance.

C. OPERATIONS RESEARCH PROGRAM

MULTI-STAGE GAMES PROJECT - A proposal for developing methods for solving multi-stage games and dynamic programming problems on the Illiac was funded by the Office of Naval Research. This research is currently underway.
A consulting project for the U.S. Army Military Personnel Center was carried out to enhance their "Objective Force Model" and was completed successfully.

4. Seismic

The seismic applications area was formed to apply the Institute's unique computational resources to large seismic models. The I4TRES code, which simulates near-field radiation from earthquake sources, was implemented on the Illiac IV and successfully completed all acceptance tests early in 1978. One model use is to discriminate between natural and nuclear events in support of the nuclear test ban treaty. Another is the assessment of hazards associated with earthquakes. In all of these areas, there is an acute need for accurate numerical simulation of earthquake induced ground motions. Major support for this application area is provided by the Nuclear Monitoring Research Office of DARPA.

A. SEISMIC APPLICATIONS SYSTEM DEVELOPMENT PROGRAM

ACTION PROJECT (A finite element earthquake simulation program.) - The Institute continues with its design work on ACTION. Contact with current and potential users consistently identifies three primary requirements for a seismic simulation code. These are large size, flexibility and low run cost. These requirements will be incorporated in the ACTION system. The finite element philisophy underlying this system and the modularity of the code will make this code well suited to the user's needs.

B.   SEISMIC APPLICATIONS SYSTEM ENHANCEMENT PROGRAM

I4TRES ENHANCEMENT PROJECT - In order to allow the I4TRES
code solve a wide range of problems, the seismic fault
mechanism was expanded to include non-uniform pre-stress and
unilateral rupture. These alterations were designed, programmed
and debugged during 1978. Toward the end of 1978, design plans
were underway to expand the code to include multiple materials.

C.   SEISMIC APPLICATIONS SYSTEMS MAINTENANCE PROGRAM

I4TRES MAINTENANCE PROJECT - The most recent development
work has been centered largely on developing an algorithmic
definition of the I4TRES code to permit orderly and efficient in-
clusion of proposed modifications. Additionally, work has gone
forward on providing an improved results scanner for more efficient monitoring of the output of production runs.

D.   SEISMIC APPLICATIONS PRODUCTION PROGRAM

SSS PRODUCTION PROJECT - The I4TRES system was employed
for the Air Force Geophysics Laboratory in cooperation with
Systems, Science and Software, Inc. These runs were aimed, in
part, at determining the effects of an elastic material behavior
in the region immediately surrounding the rupture surface.

NRC PRODUCTION PROJECT - Illiac runs are planned for a
recently funded Nuclear Regulatory Commission study. These
runs are intended to assess seismic hazards at the San Onofre
Nuclear Power Plant using the I4TRES system.

E.   SEISMIC APPLICATIONS SCIENCE PROGRAM

MADARIAGA COMPARISON PROJECT - I4TRES runs were completed
during 1978 to validate the published results of R. Madariaga
for a circular fault.

5.   Signal/Image Processing

IAC made substantial progress in 1978 in developing image
and signal processing capabilities. The results of this effort
are apparent in the variety and extent of the image processing
tasks currently underway. In the past, most of the effort has
been directed toward LANDSAT processing; however, in the past
year, a number of applications involving digital cartography
were begun at the Institute.

A.   IMAGE PROCESSING PROGRAM

LANDSAT (EXPERIMENTAL NASA EARTH RESOURCES SATELLITE)- Much
of the effort in this area centered on the software system
created for processing LANDSAT images called EDITOR. An IAC

version of this system was established and user documentation
compiled, published, and distributed under an arrangement with
Ames Research Center. A second associated project was completed
for the United Stated Geological Survey Geography Program that
analyzed alternatives for data movement of LANDSAT image data
within the IAC computer environment.

Due to the establishment of the EDITOR command system at IAC,
there has been a marked increase in the planned use of the IAC
for LANDSAT processing. For example, the U.S. Department of
Agriculture substantially increased its use during 1978. USDA
currently has plans to process over 30 scenes by the middle of
1979.

The USGS Geography Program has also increased its Illiac IV
use. In 1978, a program was completed to classify the land cover
of a large region of the Alaskan coast. In addition, USGS is in
the process of classifying ground cover in Northern California
for use by the Land Information and Analysis Division.

Ames Research Center has also extended its use of the Illiac
IV and EDITOR for land use analysis. A number of projects were
begun in 1978. Among them is a project to categorize and measure
forest use and potential forest use in the State of California.
A second project being undertaken for Ames by Humbolat State
College requires applying the LANDSAT analysis programs to other
agricultural analysis within the State of California. The State
of Hawaii is also using the system. Land use classification has
been made of the Island of Maui and the work is continuing. The
State of Idaho has recently completed an analysis of agricultural
acreage in the Snake River region.

Besides providing raw computational resources, IAC is directly involved with the complete processing of LANDSAT data. Ames
Research Center has requested production support of the California
Forest Inventory Project. Under this project, IAC personnel
will convert over 60 formatted images from the Jet Propulsion
Laboratory into EDITOR format and will manage the running of this
large production effort.

B. SIGNAL PROCESSING PROGRAM

SASE PROJECT - In support of DARPA's Tactical Technology
Office (TTO), IAC developed a high-speed secure link between IAC
and ARPA Research Center at Moffett Field and used this link
successfully for secure processing on the Illiac IV in a prior
year. In 1978, IAC achieved a major success using the Illiac
and this link.

Besides providing the Illiac IV and operators, IAC also
provided software support which included:

- Improving the reliability of the LINK;
- Improving file handling software to transfer variable
  length files on the PDP-10, a medium-sized computer
  at the ARC computing center; and
- Developing a graphic subsystem for the ARC system.

SAR PROJECT (Synthetic Aperture Radar) - IAC has supported a continued effort in the area of SAR processing. IAC was funded through an Applications Notice to NASA Headquarters to support Lockheed in developing an on-board analogue processor for SAR data. They intend to use an algorithm called QSARP and IAC is currently testing the effects of round-off on this algorithm.

C. DIGITAL CARTOGRAPHY PROGRAM

TEXTURE MEASUREMENT PROJECT - In 1978, IAC developed a parallel implementation of an image texture measurement process denoted as MAXMIN. The Engineer Topographic Laboratories will use this algorithm to detect locations on stereo photographs which would be appropriate for extraction of topographic eleva- tion data. After test and verification, this code was applied to over 30 production images with the results delivered to the ETL analysts. This texture measurement process is being continued with the development of a second algorithm known as a grey scale spatial dependency matrix technique. This technique provides a different way to characterize a scene's texture information.

RELAXATION SMOOTHING PROJECT - A second project is also being undertaken for the Engineer Topographic Laboratories. This is a major effort to develop a relaxation-based smoothing technique that will improve the quality of elevation data extracted from stereo pair photography.

VECTOR TO RASTER CONVERSION PROJECT - A major cartographic effort of a different type is currently under study for the National Ocean Survey of the National Oceanic and Atmospheric Administration (NOAA/NOS). One of their most demanding product- ion tasks is the creation of map overlay transparencies. A fis- cal year 78 qualitative analysis of this process indicated a high probability that the Illiac IV would provide an effective and economical alternative to serial processors in the conversion of NOAA/NOS digital data bases (which are vector in nature) to a format suitable for recording on a raster plotter device. An extensive quantitative analysis is currently underway to find optimum techniques by which this process could be implemented on a production basis.

AUTOMATED INFORMATION SYSTEM PROJECT - National Oceanic and Atmospheric Administration, National Ocean Survey (NOAA/ NOS) is moving in the direction of automating the production of NOS mapping and charting products. IAC has delivered to NOAA/NOS a qualitative assessment and proposal in support of this activity. The proposal has been funded for IAC to produce a system specification for their Automated Information System (AIS). This effort will involve system design, hardware, and software specification, the validation of the hardware configuration and the establishment of the operating environment for a system which generates NOS nautical charts. The objective will be to specify and deliver production work stations which fulfill NOAA/NOS's

requirements. There will be 10 nautical chart work stations and
one geodetic control diagram work station (for the National Geodetic Survey).

FILTERING TECHNIQUES PROJECT - A project for the U.S. Geological Survey Topographic Division investigated the use of
convolutional and Fourier transform filters to smooth topographic
elevation data.

NGS/READJUSTMENT PROJECT - The National Geodetic Survey
has funded a design study to determine the feasibility of
using the Illiac for their 1983 readjustment of the North American Geodetic Network. The object is to employ all the available
surveying information with appropriate weights to obtain more
accurate estimates of the monument positions using a least
squares fit. This problem represents the largest set of nonlinear equations for which a solution has ever been attempted.

6. Weather/Climate Simulation

STRATOSPHERIC MODEL PROJECT - Using the ARPANET, Dr. Fred
Alyea of MIT has been developing a dynamic atmospheric model
incorporating chemistry and heat exchange. The model stretches
from the ground to 72 kilometers, but the primary interest is the
stratosphere. The Jovian stratospheric model is ready to operate
since it uses no dynamics. The fully dynamic model is in the
final testing stages and may use as many as 200 Illiac hours a
year when it gets into production.

TRAJCAL PROJECT - IAC finished a system design for putting
the trajectory part of a model which calibrates the disposition of effluents in the atmosphere on the Illiac IV for
AFTAC (Air Force Technical Applications Center). This is a
post-facto trajectory mode intended primarily for use in calculating the transport, diffusion, and disposition of effluents on
a regional/continental scale. The Illiac code would be based on
a version of this model currently running on a 360/75 at Patrick
Air Force Base in Florida.

B.   Computational Fluid Dynamics

Aircraft and aerospace vehicles have become increasingly large and
complex. Both the difficulty and the cost of evaluating new aerodynamic designs are rising exponentially. If this trend persists, it could
require many years of wind tunnel testing to develop the next major
aerospace vehicle beyond the Space Shuttle. The plot in Figure 6.1 shows
the enormous increase in development time over the history of manned
flight.

In contrast, the cost of computer simulated fluid flow analysis
has been decreasing by a factor of 10 about every five years. These
trends have had an enormous impact upon computational fluid dynamics.
Computational physics can replace or supplement the wind tunnel for
engineering design and test purposes when the physics of the problem
is well enough known to be represented by an accurate mathematical
model, and when the computational resources are available to obtain a
numeric solution in a practical amount of time at a competitive cost.

In general, the objectives of computational aerodynamics are to
decrease the time and cost required for the design of new aerospace
vehicles and eventually to provide more accurate simulations of flight
aerodynamics than can be obtained from ground based experimental test
facilities. In assessing the relative roles of computer and wind-tunnel
simulation facilities, it is important to recognize that their inherent
limitations, tabulated below, are complementary:

Wind Tunnel	Computer
Model Size	Speed
Velocity	Storage
Density	Accuracy of equations
Temperature	of motion
Wall interference	
Support interference	
Aeroelastic distortions	
Atmosphere	
Stream-uniformity	

134

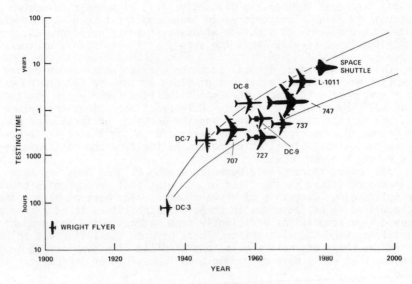

Figure 5.1 Wind tunnel testing time

The uses of any wind tunnel are restricted by the size of the model that can be placed in it and by its maximum pressure and velocity of flow (Reynolds number). Wall and support interference limit the accuracy of such simulations, particularly in transonic wind tunnels. Artificial aeroelastic distortions of model wings induced by high dynamic pressures further significantly limit high-Reynolds-number transonic tunnels. The temperature range and the type of atmosphere restrict the ability to simulate atmospheric entry aerodynamics; stream non-uniformities greatly limit the accuracy of simulations of the flight boundary-layer transition.

On the other hand, typical computer simulations - in which the governing Navier-Stokes equations of fluid motion are integrated over a large number of grid points throughout the flow field - are limited principally by speed and storage. More exact approximations become possible as both computing power and the accuracy of turbulence models are increased. Some progress has been made on the Illiac IV in over-coming these limitations, which determine the time and cost required to simulate a given flow.

The Computational Fluid Dynamics Branch at NASA Ames has made major contributions to the field of computational aerodynamics under the outstanding leadership of Harvard Lomax. The work of this branch has explored recent advances in computer capabilities to obtain aero-dynamic flow simulations efficiently from methods quite independent of traditional wind-tunnel testing. Their work on the Illiac has helped extend the scope of these simulations of fluid flow dynamics to include problems that would have otherwise been impossible or impractical to solve.

1. Parallel Computation of Unsteady, 3-D, Chemically Reacting, Nonequilibrium Flow Using a Time-Split Finite-Volume Method on the ILLIAC IV

The system of unsteady, three-dimensional, partial differential equations used to simulate the inviscid flow of air in chemical nonequilibrium is approximated by a set of factored, finite-volume difference operators where the effect of chemical production is also contained in the factorization. The method is similar to that of Rizzi and Bailey (NASA SP-347, 1975, pp. 1327-1349), except for the emphasis on vector-matrix reformulation designed to be suitable for the special architecture of modern advanced computers (e.g., the Illiac IV, CDC 7600, or STAR). The systematic application of the operators yields a second-order accurate numerical algorithm. The method is programmed in the vector FORTRAN-like language called CFD: all results for the examples given were obtained from the Illiac. The problem described is a numerical simulation of the flow in the high temperature stagnation region of a reentering Space Shuttle orbiter flying at large angles of attack ($40°$). Capability for treating arbitrary geometry in a flow containing subsonic, sonic, and supersonic regions is demonstrated by this method. The air chemistry is described by a five-reaction model which includes the three dissociation reactions for N_2, O_2, and NO and the two rearrangment reactions involving NO. The vector-matrix formulation and the unique disk-memory mapping results in extremely efficient data management for the architecture of the Illiac and makes maximum use of the Illiac's "data crunching" capability. Comparative running times are given for the Illiac IV and the CDC 7600.

INTRODUCTION

The new generation of very fast, special purpose vector computers (e.g., Illiac IV, CDC STAR, CDC 7600, TI ASC, CRAY 1, and IBM 370/195) has made possible the numerical simulation of complicated flow fields, including chemical reactions, about geometrically complex bodies[1]. The need for these solutions results partly from the continuing interest and usefulness of more sophisticated atmospheric entry vehicles such as the space shuttle. To obtain such results, the split finite-volume method discussed in this paper is

---

Based on an article by Walter A. Reinhardt in the IAC Newsletter, October, 1977.

a viable numerical method. The equations that are approximated
using this scheme are quite general and, with the exception of
the easily modifiable chemical reaction model, are applicable for
studies of combustion, pollution, and other chemically reacting
flow phenomena, where convective transport effects dominate the
influence of radiative, viscous, and other transport mechanisms.
The resulting numerical simulations are particularly valuable to
the vehicle designer (2,3,4,5) as a source of information for estima-
ting heat transfer rates, boundary layer effects (6) (e.g., the influence of flow separation and entropy layer "swallowing"), surface-
material corrosion, as well as the aerodynamic loads acting on
the spacecraft during atmospheric entry. Wind-tunnel tests alone
cannot provide such information (3,4). The effect of chemical
reactions greatly complicates the scaling of such data to what
happens in full scale actual flight.

The shock perturbed flow about a shuttle orbiter flying at a
large scale angle-of-attack during atmospheric entry is interlaced
with embedded discontinuities that enclose non-reacting or reacting regions, depending on the altitude and velocity along the
flight trajectory. The flow field itself contains a large variety
of possible flow phenomena. To numerically simulate these flows
requires several varied methods. Within the nose region, there
exists subsonic flow (in the stagnation region), transonic flow,
and supersonic flow. Here the numerical simulations (7,8,9,10,11)
generally involve marching the unsteady fluid flow equations in
time, starting with an initially specified estimated flow field.
The marching continues until unsteady effects are no longer observed.

The flow field on the exit boundary of this soluation (i.e.,
on the "data surface") serves as the initial condition for numerical methods that approximates the steady representations of the
flow equations. As long as the exit boundary lies in supersonic
flow, the problem is hyperbolic in the direction of the flow. The
coordinate in this direction is time-like; the data surface can
then be marched step-wise down the body either as a generalized
coordinate (12,13,14) surface, as a plane, (15,16) or by method-of-
characteristics (17). Still other methods solve this flow using the
unsteady flow equations similarly as in the noise region (18,19).
Canopy shocks, induced by body curvature, and cross-flow shocks
that result from strong cross flow at large angles of attack, are
also found in the numerical simulations. (15,20,21) The intersection of the bow and wing shocks, besides introducing subsonic flow
pockets at the wing leading edge, yields a variety of complicated
flow discontinuity effects such as multiple shocks and slip surfaces. These have also been investigated in numerical simulations
(15,20).

The subjects of this paper is the finite-volume method first
proposed by MacCormack, Warming and Paullay (22,23) and generalized
by Rizzi, ibid Schiff, 24 Hung, (25) and Diewert (26). The method
is quite flexible and has been employed by Rizzi ibid in the calculation of the supersonic flow as well as the subsonic flow regions
about the space shuttle. The method has also been used in inviscid
studies of jet counterflow (24) as well as the two-dimensional vis-

cous studies of separated transonic flow over an airfoil (26) and of separated supersonic flow over a compression corner (25).

The method is based on the integral conservation-law representations of the fluid flow equations. "Finite-volume" denotes the partitioning of the entire flow region into arrays of topological hexahedra that are the computational elements. The calculation procedure of Rizzi and Bailey (8) involves calculating the fluxes through the hexahedra faces and the chemical production within these elements. In applying the method to special purpose advanced computers, a valuable adjunct is "time-splitting", that is, factoring the three-dimensional spatial differencing operator into three one-dimensional operators. This method remains second-order accurate, but improves operational efficiency on conventional computers (7,8) and has especially profound effects on Illliac IV efficiencies. This occurs because either data arrays or their transposes are equally accessible within the Illiac's main memory disk storage and thus data transfer is equally optimal, regardless of data order requirements of the operator being executed.

Another "splitting" discussed here is that of separating the species convection from chemical production. In this case the production terms are contained within a separate operator that is also one-dimensional. Several advantages occur. The chemical effects can be "advanced" with a smaller time step than that used for convection (several applications of the chemical production operator are still required, however so that the aggregate step is that of the convection); and, depending on whether the chemistry is "stiff"(27,28) implicit or explicit numerical algorithms can be used without penalty to the accuracy of the overall method.

The computation of chemically-reacting, three-dimensional flows, even with the simplest chemical models, seriously strains the capability of other than the new generation of vector computers. These computers achieve their rapidity principally through special hardware features (overlap, parallelism, or pipeline), but to take greatest advantage of their computational capability requires careful use of vector-matrix formalism and programming in a vector language.

MATHEMATICAL FORMULATION

In this paper the basic equations will be introduced first. Then the procedure for approximating these equations using the finite-volume method will be described. The generality of the equations and discussion will be relaxed when the coordinate system, which has proved valuable for solving the flow in the nose region of the shuttle at large angles of attack, is introduced. The discussion becomes more specific when the Illiac IV architecture is described and we point out the procedure for solving the flow on the Illiac. Finally, several results are presented to demonstrate the viability of the method as well as of parallel processing.

CONSERVATION EQUATIONS

The unsteady equations of fluid dynamics, which govern the flow of a multicomponent reacting mixture of gases, are described in vector integral conservation-law form by the representation

$$\frac{d}{dt} \iiint_{vol(t)} U d\tau + \oiint_{s(t)} H \cdot \vec{ds} = \Omega \tag{1}$$

where the column vectors U and Ω and the second-order tensor H, whose elements are flux vectors, are defined as

$$U = \rho \begin{bmatrix} 1 \\ u \\ v \\ w \\ e_T \\ c_\ell \\ \cdot \\ \cdot \\ \cdot \end{bmatrix} \qquad H(U) = \rho \begin{bmatrix} \vec{q} \\ u\vec{q} + (p/\rho)\ \hat{i}_x \\ v\vec{q} + (p/\rho)\ \hat{i}_y \\ w\vec{q} + (p/\rho)\ \hat{i}_z \\ h_T\ \vec{q} \\ c_\ell\ \vec{q} \\ \cdot \\ \cdot \\ \cdot \end{bmatrix} - U\vec{\lambda} \ ,$$

$$\Omega = \rho \begin{bmatrix} 0 \\ 0 \\ 0 \\ 0 \\ 0 \\ \omega_\ell \\ \cdot \\ \cdot \\ \cdot \end{bmatrix} \qquad\qquad \ell = 1, 2, \ldots, S$$

for flow velocity $\hat{q} = u \, \hat{i}_x + v \, \hat{i}_y + w \, \hat{i}_x$, total specific internal energy $e_T = e + q^2/2$ and total enthalpy $h_T = e_T + p/\rho$, pressure ρ, density ρ, concentration (mass fraction) c_ℓ, and chemical production ω_ℓ. The explicit formulation for the ω_ℓ will not be given here. The relation used for this study, which depends on a chemical reaction model to be defined, is a conventional expression which can be found in a number of references (e.g., see ref. 31 or 32). The equations given above refer, respectively, to conservation of mass, of the three components of momentum, of energy, and of species within an unsteady volume region enclosed by surfaces which move with a velocity $\vec{\lambda}$.

The above equations are made complete with the addition of a state relation for pressures $p(e,\rho,c_\ell)$. The Lighthill model is introduced where the translational and molecular rotation modes are assumed to be fully equilibrated while the molecular vibrational mode is assumed half-excited (16). The following equation for pressure results

$$p = (\gamma-1)\rho(e - \sum_{\ell=1}^{S} c_\ell \, h_\ell^\circ) \qquad (2a)$$

where $e = e_T - (U^2 + v^2 + w^2)/2$ is the internal energy per unit mass and h_ℓ is the heat-of-formation corresponding to the species c_ℓ. The ratio for specific heats is $\gamma = c_p/c_v$, and the sound velocity, needed in subsequent expressions, is given by

$$a = \sqrt{\gamma p/\rho} \qquad (2b)$$

The model air mixture is assumed to contain the molecular species (oxygen (O_2), nitrogen (N_2), and nitric oxide (NO)) and the atomic species (oxygen (O), and nitrogen (N)). The production terms are based on a relatively simple chemical reaction model given in the table.

Table I: Chemical Reaction Model

1	$O_2 + M \rightleftharpoons 2O + M$
2	$N_2 + M \rightleftharpoons 2N + M$
3	$NO + M \rightleftharpoons N + O + M$
4	$NO + O \rightleftharpoons N + O_2$
5	$NO + N \rightleftharpoons O + N_2$

It includes those reactions that most significantly affect the enthalpy. The reaction rates used in this study, which appear explicitly in the chemical production terms ω_ℓ, equation 1, are the same as used by Davy and Reinhardt (16). Using the above reaction model, the specific heat ratio may now be written explicitly:

$$\gamma = \left[4(c_{O_2} + c_{N_2} + c_{NO}) + \frac{5}{2}(c_O + c_N) \right] \bigg/ \left[3(c_{O_2} + c_{N_2} + c_{NO}) + \frac{3}{2}(c_O + c_N) \right] \tag{2c}$$

SPLIT FINITE-DIFFERENCE OPERATORS

Finate-difference approximations to the gas dynamic conservation-law equations described in the previous section are used to advance the flow in time from specified initial data. The finite-difference operators to be defined here approximate equation 1 for the labeled computational cell illustrated in Figure 5.2. If the solution is known at time

$$t \left(= \sum_{\ell=1}^{n} \Delta t_\ell \right)$$

inside the topological hexahedron i,j,k with volume $\Delta t_{i,j,k}$ and bounded by the six sides $\Delta \vec{s}_i$, $\Delta \vec{s}_{i+1}$, $\Delta \vec{s}_j$, $\Delta \vec{s}_{j+1}$, $\Delta \vec{s}_k$, and $\Delta \vec{s}_{k+1}$, then it can be determined at time $t + \Delta t$ from the time split sequence denoted by

$$U^{n+1/3} = L_j U^n \tag{3a}$$

$$U^{n+2/3} = L_k U^{n+1/3} \tag{3b}$$

$$U^{n+1} = L_i U^{n+2/3} \tag{3c}$$

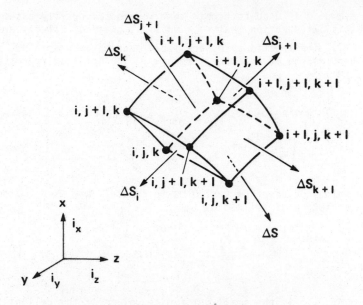

Figure 5.2   A typical computation cell i, j, k

The symbol U is used to denote that we are temporarily assuming for this illustration that $\omega_\ell = 0$ (i.e., chemical effects are frozen). The fractional powers imply that three fractional steps are required to advance one time step. The operator representation $U^{n+1/3} = L_j U^n$ denotes

$$\tilde{U}_j^{n+1/3} = U_j^n - \frac{\Delta t}{\Delta \tau_j} \left(H_j^n \cdot \Delta \vec{s}_{j+1} + H_{j-1}^n \cdot \Delta \vec{s}_j \right) \tag{4a}$$

$$U_j^{n+1/3} = 0.5 \left[U_j^n + \tilde{U}_j^{n+1/3} - \frac{\Delta t}{\Delta \tau_j} \left(\tilde{H}_{j+1}^{n+1/3} \cdot \Delta \vec{s}_{j+1} + \tilde{H}_j^{n+1/3} \cdot \Delta \vec{s}_j \right) \right] \tag{4b}$$

Mean values of the flow variables in the cell are used in the above representation as defined by

$$U_{i,j,k}^n = \iiint_{vol(t)_{i,j,k}} U d\tau \bigg/ \Delta \tau_{i,j,k} \tag{5}$$

where $\Delta \tau_{i,j,k}$ is the small but finite volume of the cell at that time step. Also, the flux vector

$$\tilde{H}_j^{n+1/3} \quad \text{denotes} \quad H \left(\tilde{U}_j^{n+1/3} \right).$$

In equation 4 the subscripts i and k, which do not vary, are implied but are not written, to simplify notation. The operational relation for L_k appears identical to that for L_j except for the replacement of k with j and appropriate modification of the fractional power denoting substep, and similarly for L_i. This notation exemplifies the one-dimensional character of the operators, and it is this essence that characterizes "splitting".

The condition on Δt necessary for the stability of the above method is that the numerical domain of dependence must include the physical one (8,20,22,23). Stability conditions can be determined analytically for each operator. For L_j we have

$$\Delta t_j \leq \min \left\{ \frac{\Delta \tau_j}{|\vec{q} \cdot \Delta \vec{s}_j| + a|\Delta \vec{s}_j|} \right\}_{\text{for all } i,j,k} \tag{6}$$

Similar relations are used to obtain Δt_k and Δt_j. The operator sequence denoted by equation 3 is then stable if

$$\Delta t \leq \min \left(\Delta t_i, \ \Delta t_j, \ \Delta t_k \right) \tag{7}$$

This discussion of time-splitting has been brief; additional detail can be obtained by referring to the original sources (see 8, 22, or 23).

Chemical production effects were not considered in the above development; as a result the symbol Ω does not appear in these relations. The species concentrations may, however, still be contained in the vector U (see Eq. 1). Therefore, given an initial non-uniform distribution of the species c_ℓ, the above relations allow an accurate simulation of the convection of c_ℓ through the flow field. To account for chemical production another operator, denoted L_p, is introduced. Consistent with the notation above we define $U^{n+1} = L_p \ U^{n+1}$ to denote the set of operations

$$\tilde{U}^{n+1} = U^{n+1} + \frac{\Delta t_f}{\Delta \tau} \ \Omega$$

$$\tag{8}$$

$$U^{n+1} = 0.5 \left[U^{n+1} + \tilde{U}^{n+1} + \frac{\Delta t_f}{\Delta \tau} \ \tilde{\Omega} \right]$$

where, similarly as before $\tilde{\Omega} \equiv \Omega \ (\tilde{U}^{n+1})$. Accuracy requirements may necessitate that the time step Δt_f for chemistry be different from the Δt found by equation 7. For the simulation of shuttle flows $\Delta t_f = 0.5 \ t$ gave satisfactory results, but small values can be used. The L_p is successively applied

$$L_{chem} = \prod_{\ell=1}^{N} L_{p_\ell} ; \quad N = \Delta t / \Delta t_f$$

until the aggregate chemistry step matches that used for the convection, that is,

$$\Delta t = \sum_{n=1}^{N} \Delta t_f \ .$$

One advantage of splitting the chemistry is that implicit operators may be exchanged with the explicit method given above. This may be necessary if the system of equations becomes "stiff" (27,28). Then methods similar to those described by Lomax and Bailey (27) may be applied.

The sequence of operations $U^{n+1} = L_{chem} L_i K_k U^n$ represents a complete time step that properly accounts for chemical production as well as convection. This sequence of operations, however, is only accurate to first order in Δt. Second-order accuracy is achieved by reversing the operator order during the next time step. The proper second-order sequence, therefore, is given by the two time-step sequence

$$U^{n+2} = L_j L_k L_i \left(\prod_{\ell=1}^{2N} L_{P_\ell} \right) L_i L_k L_j U^n \qquad (9)$$

COMPUTATIONAL CELL NETWORK

To apply the finite-difference operators require that the entire flow region be divided into a network of small topological hexahedra. For the nose region flow field of the shuttle orbiter discussed here, the coordinate surfaces are cones, shells and planes. The cones are arbitrarily positioned and translated in the manner displayed in Figure 5.3. Translation of the cone is accounted for by the coordinate X of its apex measured along the body axis, rotation by the angle ψ between its axis and the free stream and, lastly, dilation by its vertex angle ω. Each of these conical surfaces is then divided by rays from the apex into equally spaced angular increments. The planes formed by the ray of one cone and the corresponding ray of the next (see Fig. 5.4.) delineate a system of contiguous pyramidal columns. All that is needed to specify the ray i,k are its two angles $\theta_{i,k}$ and $\phi_{i,k}$, made with the z and x axes, and its intersection x_i with the body axis. The columns are partitioned into small hexahedra by a sequence of shells that coincide with the body and shock and divide the distance ξ along each ray into J equal segments. The cells compose

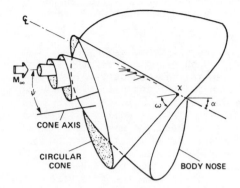

Figure 5.3   Mesh geometry determined by a series of nested cones

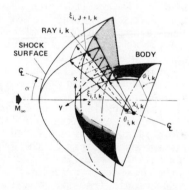

Figure 5.4   Partitioning the shock layer into finite volumes

a nonorthogonal mesh network floating in time that fills the time-dependent shock layer. The other boundaries are the pitch plane of symmetry and a down-stream boundary immersed in supersonic flow. The mesh network is quite general and allows a wide range of flow regions and computational spaces to be studied.

INITIAL AND BOUNDARY CONDITIONS

Because the governing equations are hyperbolic and the subsonic region is bounded by supersonic flow, the time-dependent method is well posed as an initial-boundary-value problem. To commence the calculation, an initial approximation must be specified for the complete field.

Our initial flow field is built up as follows (7,8). A shock surface, axisymmetric about the wind direction and positioned at an estimated standoff distance, is generated by a quadratic function of the latitudinal angle θ. The slope of this surface can thus be determined at any given point, and the flow properties there are then calculated from the free-stream conditions by use of the Rankine-Hugoniot shock relations. On the body, pressure is derived from a Newtonian formula, and the entropy there is set to the same value as that of the streamline which has passed through a normal shock (the stagnation streamline). With these two properties, the density and velocity components can be found by using the equation-of-state and integrated steady-energy relation (the species are assumed constant at their free-steam values throughout the field). Finally, the flow properties within the shock layer are specified by linearly interpolating between the shock and body values along each pyramidal column of cells.

This procedure yields a satisfactory set of initial conditions for perfect gas flow over a broad range of Mach numbers and for angles of attack approaching 45°. For nonequilibrium flow, however, the transients generated from the impulse start of the estimated flow fields with frozen species composition can cause difficulties. A more satisfactory initial condition in this case is a perfect gas solution after most unsteady effects have decayed.

For the inviscid calculations presented here, three distinct types of boundaries are encountered at the edges of the overall mesh: entrance, exit, and streamline boundaries. Along the entrance boundary the dependent variables U (in eq. 1), are held constant at their supersonic free-stream values, while at the exit they are calculated using one-sided differences. Across cell faces coincident with a streamline boundary, such as an impervious body, no transport is allowed. The only variable actually needed at such a cell face is the pressure, which can be expressed in terms of the interior mesh values of pressure and the derivative of pressure normal to the face. This derivative, $\partial p / \partial n \big|_{body}$ is

obtained from the momentum equation normal to the streamline

$$\left.\frac{\partial p}{\partial n}\right|_{body} = \rho\left(u^2 F_{xx} + v^2 F_{yy} + w^2 F_{zz} + 2uv F_{xy} + 2uw F_{xz} + 2vw F_{yz}\right)\bigg/ \sqrt{F_x^2 + F_y^2 + F_z^2}$$

where the body is the surface $F(x,y,z)=0$ and the subscripts indicate partial differentiation with respect to that variable.

The bow shock-wave itself is treated as an interior feature of the flow field (8) and is not assigned any special attention within the different operators L_i, L_j, and L_k. After every iteration the mesh is readjusted to maintain alignment with the shock. The conservation form of the difference operators will then implicitly satisfy the Rankine-Hugoniot shock-wave "jump" relations and, in addition, accurately determine the solution in the vicinity of the shock. To maintain alignment, the mesh surface coincident with the shock must move with the unsteady shock itself. This is accomplished within an operator called L_{BSHK}.

The velocity of each cell segment of this mesh surface is obtained from the simultaneous solution of the shock jump relations for a moving discontinuity and a local characteristic relation, which is valid in the plane defined by the free-stream velocity and the shock normal direction (see Ref. 8). An iteration procedure yields the shock velocity λ for each ray i,k shown in Figure 5.4. The shock-mesh surface is then moved by the increment $\lambda \Delta t$ computed for each ray. Coordinates are assigned new values to maintain equal spacing of the shells between the shock and body surface, and values of the variables, U, are then found by interpolation.

OPERATIONS ON THE ILLIAC IV
Discussed below are considerations unique to vector machines for selecting and programming a method as well as assessing the machine and running the code. The arithmetic units and replication features of advanced computers (Illiac, CDC 7600, CDC STAR, CRAY 1, TI ASC, and 370/195) have such high cycle frequencies that most often machine speed is controlled not by cycle time for an operation, but by time for data transfer to and from a massive bulk storage area. Thus a numerical method designed for minimizing arithmetic operations without considering data transfer may yield very inefficient vector computer programs.

The disk memory (I4DM) and PEM have features that lead to very efficient array operations on the Illiac. The entire data base required for a problem is stored in the I4DM; selected portions of these data are then transferred to or from PEM, which can be considered as the "working" storage area where data are actually modified. (Problems not requiring the large data base of the blunt-body program discussed here may be designed to operate within PEM and hence use the I4DM only for data output, e.g., see (16). We denote the massive data stored in I4DM by the symbol $M(I,J)$. This symbol refers to the two-page blocks of data stored

in the I4DM that are conceptually labeled I and J. As pointed
out earlier, a page is the smallest unit of data transferred and
assigns 16 words to each PE. Data assignment within these I4DM
blocks is such that for each mesh point, the conservative dependent variables U (eq. 1) are sequentially stored first (10 variables). In addition, also stored are the coordinates (3), surface
area (9), volume (1), and the shock velocity along a ray (1) for
a total of 24 variables (eight additional locations are reserved
for species variables in studies involving more complicated
chemistry models). The mesh points in the meridianal direction
are stored along the PEs and the subscripts I and J of the array
M(I,J) in I4DM refer, respectively, to cones and to shells. We
denote by B the actual array of data transferred as it appears
stored in the PEM. Ideally, B should be large because of the
rapidity of data transfer on the Illiac (half-million bits per
second). For example, we may have $B(*,L,I) = M(I,3)$ or just as
easily, we might get $B(*,L,J) = M^t(J,4)$; that is (see Figure 5.5)
B contains all of the variables for the computations involving the
third shell or the fourth cone (M^t designates the matrix transpose
f M(I,J). The asterisk denotes the vector row alignment along
the PEs; L denotes variable type (e.g., p, u, v, w, etc.). The
array M(I,J) need not be square. The advantage of the data transfer flexibility on the Illiac should now be apparent; PEM storage
is really a "buffer" area and data stored depend only on operator
requirements. The operator L_j, equation 3a, involves data only
on a cone; L_k, equation 3b, involves data on a ring which may be
on a cone or shell (see Fig. 5.5); and L_i considers data on a shell.
The chemistry operator L_{CHEM}, equation L_{REMESH}, designating the
reinterpolation of data after the advancement of the unsteady
shock-wave surface, has a cone preference. Finding the shock-wave
velocity L_{BSHK} involves only the single shell that is the shock
surface.
     The actual sequence of operations implemented during each
step is illustrated on the flow chart in Figure 5.6. The looping
about the operators shown in the block diagram denotes that the
entire sequence of cones or shells is processed by the loop. Each
two-step sequence requires three complete passes through the en=
tire data base stored in the I4DM. The operator L_t appearing in
the last cone processing loop in Figure 5.6 denotes the sequence
of operations (eqs. 6 and 7) required to find the time increment
t which is needed in the difference equations (eqs. 4 and 8) and
in L_{BSHK} (see discussion on Initial and Boundary Conditions).

RESULTS
Results from two entirely different calculations are discussed
here to demonstrate the variability of the method as well as of
paralle processing. The first is a perfect gas calculation
(i.e., with frozen chemistry and specific heat ratio Y = 1.4) for

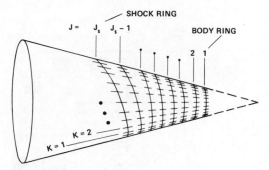

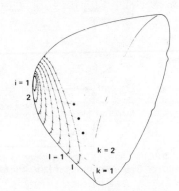

Figure 5.5a   The cone coordinate surface

Figure 5.5b   The shell coordinate surface

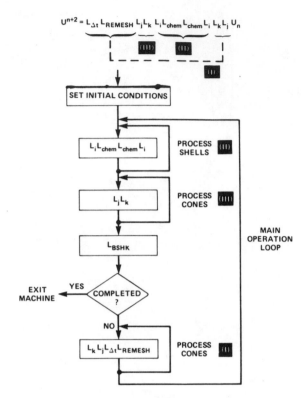

Figure 5.6   Program flow chart

a flight Mach number of 22.0 and angle-of-attack of 40.2°. The second is a chemical nonequilibrium calculation for a trajectory point corresponding to a Mach number of 21.7, an altitude of about 65.1 km, and an angle of attack of 30° (free-stream conditions are: P_∞ (pressure) = 106.2 dynes/cm^2, ρ_∞ (density) = 1.55 x 10^{-7} g/cm^3, V_∞ (velocity) = 6.544 km/sec). Several parameters from the perfect gas calculation will be used to illustrate the convergence to steady state. Several contours of selected variables will be presented from the nonequilibrium solution to illustrate features about the flow.

As discussed in the previous section, the calculation starts with a specified set of initial conditions. The entire flow field is then marched in time until the solution becomes steady. Steady state is determined by monitoring the fractional total enthalpy given by $^e H_T = |H_\infty - (h+q^2/2 /H_\infty$ where $H_\infty = Y_\infty P_\infty /(Y_\infty - 1)\rho_\infty$.

This difference is a measure of deviation from steady flow and is computed for each point in the entire flow field. Displayed in Figure 5.7 are two curves; the upper curve denotes the total number of mesh points with $^e H_T$ greater than one percent, while the lower curve similarly denotes the number of points greater than 10 percent. The perfect gas calculations used a coarse grid network of 2295 points: 9 shells, 15 cones, and 17 meridianal planes (i.e., 17 enabled PEs). These results are preliminary and were for comparison with results obtained on the CDC 7600. The grid network, however, is easily refined. We see in Figure 5.7 that the number of points that satisfy the one and ten percent error criteria increases to a maximum and then decreases. After 579 steps all points have an error less than ten percent; after 800 steps, 289 points still have an enthalpy error between one and ten percent.

The shock distance measured from the body on the lee-side ray and on the wind-side ray is shown in Figure 5.8. Also shown is the standoff distance on the innermost cone whose axis points in the wind direction (see Fig. 5.3). On this cone there is negligible variation of the shock distance around the cone. This distance, therefore, approximates what is normally referred to as the stagnation stream line "shock stand-off distance." We observe that the shock-wave locations in the windward region, where pressures are highest, decay most rapidly to a constant value (i.e., within about 100 steps). In contrast the lee-side shock-wave location on the outermost cone, where the flow has expanded most greatly with considerably lower pressures, shows the slowest convergence rate. Here the shock-wave position oscillates with decaying amplitude to the final constant value. Even though the shock-wave position is constant everywhere after about 600 steps, the flow within the shock may still have pockets with errors of between one and ten percent (Figure 5.7.).

Displayed in Figure 5.9 are the shock-wave positions relative to the body surface and contours of molecular oxygen, nitrogen, and nitric oxide and of temperature. Within each frame, the inner

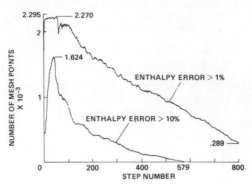

Figure 5.7 Enthalpy error measure

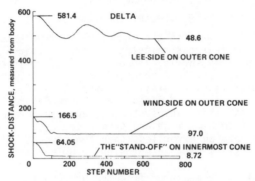

Figure 5.8 Shock-wave location

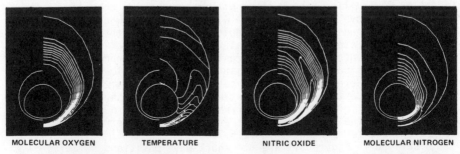

MOLECULAR OXYGEN   TEMPERATURE   NITRIC OXIDE   MOLECULAR NITROGEN

Figure 5.9 Contours on axis normal plane 1.6 m from nose

closed curve represents the body and the outer curves are the
shock. The left-half set of curves shows the body and shock
positions properly scaled relative to each other. In the right
set of curves, the shock perturbed region is expanded five times
so that contour features can be seen. The plots are on the last
coordinate surface after the cones are entirely opened to become
an axis normal plane located 1.6 meters from the shuttle orbiter
nose. The grid network is also more refined, which explains the
smooth contours.

The molecular oxygen contours are easiest to explain; their
positions are principally caused by the dissociation reaction,
equation 1 in Table 1. Approximately 100 percent dissociation
of O_2 occurs and on the windward symmetry plane this dissociation
occurs near the shock wave. In the lee side, however, where the
flow is cooler and the shock-wave strength is considerably less,
the dissociation is not as abrupt and occurs somewhat more uni-
formly throughout the field. This explanation is simplistic
because convection effects also play an important role in the
lee-side oxygen concentration field.

The temperature relaxation observed on the windward symmetry
plane is due principally to oxygen dissocation. (The contour
closest to the windward shock has a temperature of about $8000^{\circ}K$;
each adjacent contour represents an 8-percent change of this
temperature.) The field away from this region is complex, depending on convection as well as on the chemical effects. The
nitric oxide contours show a complex interplay of production,
destruction, and convection of this species as evidenced by the
closed contour lines. The maximum concentration of NO within the
field, however, does not exceed around five percent of the
mixture.

The molecular nitrogen contours (each level corresponds to
about a three percent change of the free-stream concentration)
show very little dissociation but do not show a coupling effect
with the nitric oxide as expected (see chemical reaction model
in Table 5.1).

CONCLUSIONS
The present numerical method permits an efficient and accurate
calculation of three-dimensional reacting flow. The method itself
was developed originally (7) using FORTRAN language on a serial
computer (i.e., IBM 360/67) and allowed relatively efficient
studies of perfect gas blunt-body flows. The current design, using
CFD language (29), yields the most efficient computer codes for
either the CDC 7600 or the Illiac IV. The Illiac results require
the least computational time (i.e., about 1/5 the CDC 7600 time).
The method uses a time-splitting of the convection differencing
operator to achieve efficient data management between random
access and disk access storage on the Illiac. The efficient
calculation of the effects of the chemical reactions is achieved
by an additional splitting of chemical production from convection. The demonstration reported in this paper continues the
successful series of applications (22,8,13,24,25, and 26) of
the finite-volume method for solving complicated multi-
dimensional fluid flow problems.

References

1, F.R. Bailey, Computational Aerodynamics -- Illiac IV and Beyond. Meeting IEEE Computer Society, Compcon Spring, Feb. 28 - Mar. 3, 1977, San Francisco, Calif.

2. J.A. Lordi, R.J. Vidal, and C.B. Johnson, Chemical Nonequilibrium Effects on the Inviscid Flow in the Windward Plane of Symmetry of Two Simplified Shuttle Configurations. NASA TN D-7189, March 1973.

3. W.D. Goodrich, C.P. Li, C.K. Houston, R.M. Meyers, and L. Olmedo, Scaling of Orbiter Aerothermodynamic Data through Numerical Flow Field Simulations. NASA SP-347, March 1975.

4. W.D. Goodrich, C.P. Li, C.K. Houston, P. Chiu, and L. Olmedo, Numerical Computations of Orbiter Flow Fields and Heating Rates. AIAA Paper No. 76-359, July 1976.

5. J.V. Rakich, and M.J. Lanfranco, Numerical Computation of Space Shuttle Heating and Surface Streamlines. AIAA Paper No. 76-464, July 1976.

6. J.C. Adams, Jr., W.R. Martindale, A.W. Mayne, Jr., and E.O. Marchand, Real Gas Effects on Hypersonic Laminar Boundary-Layer Parameters Including Effects of Entropy-Layer Swallowing. AIAA Paper No. 76-358, July 1976.

7. A.W. Rizzi, and M. Inouye, Time-Split Finite-Volume Method for Three-Dimensional Blunt Body Flow. AIAA J., 11, No. 11, (1973), pp. 1478-1485.

8. A.W. Rizzi, and H.E. Bailey, Reacting Nonequilibrium Flow Around the Space Shuttle Using a Time-Split Method. Aerodynamic Analysis Requiring Advanced Computers, Part II, NASA SP-347 (1975), pp. 1327-1349.

9. C.P. Li, Time-Dependent Solutions of Non-equilibrium Airflow Past a Blunt Body. J. Spacecraft and Rockets, 9, No. 8, Aug. 1972, pp. 571-572.

10. G. Moretti, and G. Bleich, Three-Dimensional Flow Around Blunt Bodies. AIAA J., vol. 5, no. 10, Oct. 1967, pp. 1557-1562.

11. R.W. Barnwell, A Time-Dependent Method for Calculating Supersonic Angle-of-Attack Flow About Axisymmetric Blunt Bodies with Sharp Shoulders and Smooth Nonaxisymmetric Blunt Bodies. NASA TN D-6283, 1971.

12. A.W. Rizzi, A. Klavins, and R.W. MacCormack, A Generalized Hyperbolic Marching Technique for Three-Dimensional Supersonic Flow with Shocks. Proc. Fourth Int. Conf. on Numerical Methods in Fluid Dynamics, ed. R.D. Richtmyer, Lecture Notes in Physics, 35, Springer-Verlag, 1975, pp. 341-346.

13. A.W. Rizzi, and H.E. Bailey, A Generalized Hyperbolic Marching Method for Chemically Reacting 3-D Supersonic Flow Using a Splitting Technique. Proc. AIAA 2nd Computational Fluid Dynamics Conference (June 1975) pp. 38-46.

14. A. Rizzi, and H. Bailey, Finite-Volume Solution of the Euler Equations for Steady Three-Dimensional Transonic Flow. 5th Conference on Numerical Methods in Fluid Dynamics, Enschede, Holland (June 1976).

15. P. Kutler, W.A. Reinhardt, and R.F. Warming, Multishocked, Three-Dimensional Supersonic Flowfields with Real Gas Effects. AIAA J., vol. 11, no. 5, pp. 657-664 (May 1973).

16. W.C. Davy, and W.A. Reinhardt, Computation of Shuttle Nonequilibrium Flow Fields on a Parallel Processor. Aerodynamic Analyses Requiring Advanced Computers, Part II, NASA SP-347 (1975) pp. 1351-1376.

17. J.V. Rakich, Three-Dimensional Flow Calculations by the Method of Characteristics. AIAA J., vol. 5, no. 10, 1967, pp. 1906-1908.

18. A.W. Rizzi, Transonic Solutions of the Euler Equations by the Finite-Volume Method. Proc. Symposium Transsonicum II, eds. K. Oswatitsch and D. Rues, Springer-Verlag (1976) pp. 567-574.

19. J.E. Daywitt, and D.A. Anderson, Analysis of a Time-Dependent Finite-Difference Technique for Shock Interaction and Blunt-Body Flows. Engineering Research Institute, Iowa State U., ERI Project 101 (May 1974).

20. P. Kutler, Computation of Three-Dimensional, Inviscid Supersonic Flows. Progress in Numerical Fluid Dynamics, Lecture Notes in Physics, vol. 41 (ed. H.J. Wirz), pp. 287-374 (1975).

21. J. Daywitt, D. Anderson, P. Kutler, Supersonic Flow About Circular Cones at Large Angles of Attack; A Floating Discontinuity Approach. AIAA Paper 77-86 (Jan. 1977).

22. R.W. MacCormack, and A.J. Paullay, Computational Efficiency Achieved by Time Splitting of Finite Difference Operators. AIAA Paper 72-154, 1972.

23. R.W. MacCormack, and R.F. Warming, Survey of Computational Methods for Three-Dimensional Supersonic Inviscid Flows with Shocks. "Advances in Numerical Fluid Dynamics" AGARD Lecture Series 64, Brussels, Belgium (Feb. 1973).

24. Lewis B. Schiff, The Axisymmetric Jet Counterflow Problem. AIAA Paper no. 76-325 (July 1976). AIAA 9th Fluid and Plasma Dynamics Conference, San Diego, Calif., July 14-16, 1976.

25. George S. Deiwert, Computation of Separated Transonic Turbulent Flows. AIAA Paper no. 75-829 (June 1975).

26. C.M. Hung, and R.W. MacCormack, Numerical Solutions of Supersonic and Hypersonic Laminar Flows over a Two-Dimensional Compression Corner. AIAA Paper no. 75-2, Jan. 1975.

27. H. Lomax, and H.E. Bailey, A Critical Analysis of Various Numerical Integration Methods for Computing the Flow of a Gas in Chemical Nonequilibrium. NASA TN D-4109, 1967.

28. Robert J. Gelinas, Stiff Systems of Kinetic Equations -- A Practitioner's View. J. Comp. Physics, 9, no. 2, (Apr. 1972), pp. 222-236.

29. K.G. Stevens, Jr., CFD -- A Fortran-like Language for the ILLIAC IV. ACM SIGPLAN Notices, 10, no. 3. March 1975, pp. 72-76.

30. Computational Fluid Dynamics Branch: CFD A Fortran-Based Language for Illiac IV. C.F.D. Branch, 202-1, NASA-Ames Research Center, Moffett Field, Calif. 94035.

31. W.G. Vincenti, and C.H. Kruger, Jr., Introduction to Physical Gas Dynamics. John Wiley and Sons, Inc., New York, 1965.

32. J.F. Clarke, and M. McChesney, The Dynamics of Real Gases. Butterworths Inc. (1964).

2. An Illiac Program for the Numerical Simulation of Homogeneous Incompressible Turbulence

SUMMARY

An algorithm and Illiac computer program, developed for the simulation of homogeneous incompressible turbulence in the presence of an applied mean strain, are described. The turbulence field is represented spatially by a truncated triple Fourier series (spectral method) and followed in time using a fourth-order Runge-Kutta algorithm. Several transformations are applied to the numerical problem to enhance the basic algorithm. These include:

1. Transformation of variables suggested by Taylor's sudden-distortion theory

2. Implicit viscous diffusion by use of an integrating factor

3. Implicit pressure calculation suggested by Taylor's sudden-distortion theory

4. Inexpensive control of aliasing by random and phased coordinate shifts

INTRODUCTION

The primary difficulty in the numerical simulation of homogeneous turbulence is that the nonlinearity of the equations of fluid motion excites a large range of scales (i.e., a large ratio of largest to smallest scale) of motion in both space and time. The computer resource required for a complete simulation is proportional to the product, over all space-time dimensions, of the range of computed scales of each dimension. These scale ranges increase with Reynolds number (R), and their product increases so rapidly, in three space dimensions, that only the weakest experimentally studied turbulence can be simulated completely on today's computers.

This section is reprinted from a paper in the IAC Newsletter, July 1978, Robert Rogallo.

The overall range of scales continues to increase indefinitely with Reynolds number. (Fig. 5.10) However, at a sufficiently high Reynolds number, the scales of motion can be grouped, in order of decreasing scale, into three distinct ranges: the energy-containing range, the "inertial" range, and the dissipation range (Fig. 5.11). Further increases in Reynolds number increase only the inertial range. The range of energy-containing scales, which determine the features of turbulence of engineering interest, is bounded as R, and the motion in these scales becomes independent of the motion at similar scales. At somewhat lower R, the inertial and dissipation ranges merge, but still do not affect the energy-containing range. At sufficiently low R, dissipation occurs in the energy-containing range itself. This physical description of the scale dependence upon Reynolds number is encouraging because it indicates that, in principle, only the energy-containing scales of motion need to be included in a high Reynolds number turbulence simulation. The difficulty is that, mathematically, all the scales are coupled through the nonlinear terms in the governing equations and, although we know that physically (i.e., statistically) the energy-containing range is uncoupled from the smaller scales, we do not know how to uncouple it mathematically.

The range of statistically interdependent scales increases with the anisotropy of the motion and, because most flows of engineering interest are anisotropic, it is important to determine the nature and magnitude of the additional computational difficulty posed by anisotropy.

THE NUMERICAL SIMULATION

The computational tool presented here is an unsteady incompressible Navier-Stokes code that runs on the Illiac IV computer. The program computes the evolution in time from an arbitrary homogeneous turbulence field in the presence of a single class of spatially-linear mean flows. The simulation is a spectral decomposition similar to that of Orszag (1) but differing in detail. The primary purpose of this report is to present the simulation algorithm in detail sufficient to allow its use by others. The program can be used as presented to study weak (low Reynolds number) turbulence for which typical results are presented. The magnitude of the computation (Fig. 5.12) requires a computer at least as fast as a CDC-7600.

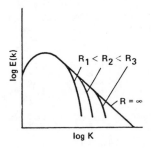

Figure 5.10   Scales of motion R_1, R_2, R_3

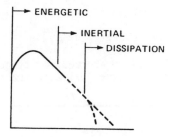

Figure 5.11   Scales of motion: energetic, inertial, dissipation

NUMBER OF MESH CELLS	262144	$(=64^3)$
DEPENDENT VARIABLES	786432	$(=3 \cdot 64^3)$
DATA BASE	2.62×10^6	$(=10 \cdot 64^3)$
FFT'S PER STEP	376832	$(=4 \cdot 23 \cdot 64^2)$
COMPUTER TIME PER STEP	20 sec	(REAL TIME)
COMPUTER TIME PER RUN	10 to 30 min	(REAL TIME)

ALGORITHM

| SPATIAL RESOLUTION | SPECTRAL (ALIAS-DAMPED) |
| TEMPORAL RESOLUTION | RUNGE-KUTTA (FOURTH-ORDER) |

Figure 5.12   Simulation program

THE EQUATIONS OF MOTION

The equations governing the flow of a viscous constant-density fluid are the familiar Navier-Stokes equations:

$$u_t+(uu)_x+(vu)_y+(wu)_z+p_x=\nu(u_{xx}+u_{yy}+u_{zz})$$

$$v_t+(uv)_x+(vv)_y+(wv)_z+p_y=\nu(v_{xx}+v_{yy}+v_{zz})$$

$$w_t+(uw)_x+(vw)_y+(ww)_z+p_z=\nu(w_{xx}+w_{yy}+w_{zz})$$

$$u_x+v_y+w_z=0$$

Where (u,v,w) is the velocity vector, p is the pressure-density ratio, ν is the kinematic viscosity, and subscripts denote differentiation.

We wish to simulate numerically the effect of a simple class of imposed strains on a homogeneous field of turbulence. The strain field is given by:

$$(\bar{u},\bar{v},\bar{w}) = [xa(t),yb(t),zc(t)]$$

Where $a + b + c = 0$ as required by continuity. It is convenient to introduce the following transformation of the dependent variables:

$$u=ax+A^{1/2}\hat{u}$$

$$v=by+B^{1/2}\hat{v}$$

$$w=cz+C^{1/2}\hat{w}$$

$$p=-\tfrac{1}{2}\left[(\tfrac{da}{dt}+a^2)x^2+(\tfrac{db}{dt}+b^2)y^2+(\tfrac{dc}{dt}+c^2)z^2+\hat{p}\right]$$

Where $a(t)$, $b(t)$, and $c(t)$ are the arbitrary time-dependent strain rates imposed, and the resulting inverse square strains are:

$$A(t) = e^{-2\int_0^t a\,dt}$$

$$B(t) = e^{-2\int_0^t b\,dt}$$

$$C(t) = e^{-2\int_0^t c\,dt}$$

It follows from the continuity condition that material volumes are invariant, (i.e., ABC=1). Explicit spatial dependence of the resulting system of equations is eliminated by the following transformation of independent variables;

$$\hat{x} = A^{1/2}x$$
$$\hat{y} = B^{1/2}y$$
$$\hat{z} = C^{1/2}z$$

The equations of motion for the transformed turbulence field are then:

$$\hat{u}_t + A(\hat{u}\hat{u})_{\hat{x}} + B(\hat{v}\hat{u})_{\hat{y}} + C(\hat{w}\hat{u})_{\hat{z}} + \hat{p}_{\hat{x}} =$$

$$\nu(A\hat{u}_{\hat{x}\hat{x}} + B\hat{u}_{\hat{y}\hat{y}} + C\hat{u}_{\hat{z}\hat{z}})$$

$$\hat{v}_t + A(\hat{u}\hat{v})_{\hat{x}} + B(\hat{v}\hat{v})_{\hat{y}} + C(\hat{w}\hat{v})_{\hat{z}} + \hat{p}_{\hat{y}} =$$

$$\nu(A\hat{v}_{\hat{x}\hat{x}} + B\hat{v}_{\hat{y}\hat{y}} + C\hat{v}_{\hat{z}\hat{z}})$$

$$\hat{w}_t + A(\hat{u}\hat{w})_{\hat{x}} + B(\hat{v}\hat{w})_{\hat{y}} + C(\hat{w}\hat{w})_{\hat{z}} + \hat{p}_{\hat{z}} =$$

$$\nu(A\hat{w}_{\hat{x}\hat{x}} + B\hat{w}_{\hat{y}\hat{y}} + C\hat{w}_{\hat{z}\hat{z}})$$

$$A\hat{u}_{\hat{x}} + B\hat{v}_{\hat{y}} + C\hat{w}_{\hat{z}} = 0$$

The above transformations seem to be the natural ones for the study of the effect of uniform imposed strain on a homogeneous turbulent field, regardless of the rate at which the strain is imposed. A more general set of transformations can be used when the mean strain-rate matrix is not diagonal, and also when the mean vorticity is nonzero.

NUMERICAL APPROXIMATION

We wish to simulate a spatially homogeneous turbulence field in an infinite space, and this suggests that we represent the field spatially as a Fourier series. The resulting field is periodic in all three space dimensions, with correspondingly periodic spatial correlations. However, if these correlations decay to negligible magnitude within the period, (e.g., if the integral scale is much smaller than half the period), the error due to the finite period should be small. In practice, this requirement is difficult to satisfy with the resolution allowed by today's computers.

In this section we develop the equations in more detail and describe the integration process as programmed.

Let $\tau_{11} = \hat{u}\hat{u}$, $\tau_{12} = \hat{v}\hat{v}$, $\tau_{13} = \hat{u}\hat{w}$, etc., tilde $\sim$ denote the three-dimensional Fourier transform, and k_1, k_2, k_3 be wave numbers in the x, y, and z directions, respectively. The equations (5) in wave space are then:

$$\tilde{u}_t + ik_1 A\tilde{\tau}_{11} + ik_2 B\tilde{\tau}_{12} + ik_3 C\tilde{\tau}_{13} + ik_1\tilde{p} =$$

$$-\nu(Ak_1^2 + Bk_2^2 + Ck_3^2)\tilde{u}$$

$$\tilde{v}_t + ik_1 A\tilde{\tau}_{12} + ik_2 B\tilde{\tau}_{22} + ik_3 C\tilde{\tau}_{23} + ik_2\tilde{p} =$$

$$-\nu(Ak_1^2 + Bk_2^2 + Ck_3^2)\tilde{v}$$

$$\tilde{w}_t + ik_1 A\tilde{\tau}_{13} + ik_2 B\tilde{\tau}_{23} + ik_3 C\tilde{\tau}_{33} + ik_3\tilde{p} =$$

$$-\nu(Ak_1^2 + Bk_2^2 + Ck_3^2)\tilde{w}$$

$$ik_1 A\tilde{u} + ik_2 B\tilde{v} + ik_3 C\tilde{w} = 0$$

The linear terms are combined by multiplying the equations by the integrating factor

$$F(\underline{k},t) = e^{\nu k_1^2 \int_0^t A\,dt}\, e^{\nu k_2^2 \int_0^t B\,dt}\, e^{\nu k_3^2 \int_0^t C\,dt}.$$

giving

$$\frac{d}{dt}(F\tilde{u}) + F\{ik_1 A\tilde{\tau}_{11} + ik_2 B\tilde{\tau}_{12} + ik_3 C\tilde{\tau}_{13} + ik_1 \tilde{p}\} = 0$$

$$\frac{d}{dt}(F\tilde{v}) + F\{ik_1 A\tilde{\tau}_{12} + ik_2 B\tilde{\tau}_{22} + ik_3 C\tilde{\tau}_{23} + ik_2 \tilde{p}\} = 0$$

$$\frac{d}{dt}(F\tilde{w}) + F\{ik_1 A\tilde{\tau}_{13} + ik_2 B\tilde{\tau}_{23} + ik_3 C\tilde{\tau}_{33} + ik_3 \tilde{p}\} = 0$$

$$ik_1 A(F\tilde{u}) + ik_2 B(F\tilde{v}) + ik_3 C(F\tilde{w}) = 0$$

Now multiply the first equation by ik_1, the second by ik_2, etc., to obtain (Let $U = ik_1 u$, $V = ik_2 v$, $W = ik_3 w$)

$$\frac{d}{dt}(F\tilde{U}) = F\{k_1^2 A\tilde{\tau}_{11} + k_1 k_2 B\tilde{\tau}_{12} + k_1 k_3 C\tilde{\tau}_{13}\} + k_1^2 F\tilde{p}$$

$$\frac{d}{dt}(F\tilde{V}) = F\{k_1 k_2 A\tilde{\tau}_{12} + k_2^2 B\tilde{\tau}_{22} + k_2 k_3 C\tilde{\tau}_{23}\} + k_2^2 F\tilde{p}$$

$$\frac{d}{dt}(F\tilde{W}) = F\{k_1 k_3 A\tilde{\tau}_{13} + k_2 k_3 B\tilde{\tau}_{23} + k_3^2 C\tilde{\tau}_{33}\} + k_3^2 F\tilde{p}$$

$$A(F\tilde{U}) + B(F\tilde{V}) + C(F\tilde{W}) = 0$$

(The purpose of this transformation of dependent variables is discussed later on; note that k_1, k_2, $k_3 = 0$ are special cases.)

The usual procedure for the computation of p requires the time differentiation of the continuity condition. However, we want the algorithm to handle impulsive strains correctly (jumps in A, B, and C), that is, according to Taylor's sudden distortion theory, so we need to avoid the differentiation. We thus define a potential $\tilde{\phi}$ as:

$$\tilde{\phi} = -F^{-1} \int_0^t F\tilde{p}\ dt$$

and absorb it into the time-advanced variables. Then

$$\frac{d\tilde{X}}{dt} = F\{k_1^2 A\tilde{\tau}_{11} + k_1 k_2 B\tilde{\tau}_{12} + k_1 k_3 C\tilde{\tau}_{13}\}$$

$$\frac{d\tilde{Y}}{dt} = F\{k_1 k_2 A\tilde{\tau}_{12} + k_2^2 B\tilde{\tau}_{22} + k_2 k_3 C\tilde{\tau}_{23}\}$$

$$\frac{d\tilde{Z}}{dt} = F\{k_1 k_2 A\tilde{\tau}_{13} + k_2 k_3 B\tilde{\tau}_{23} + k_3^2 C\tilde{\tau}_{33}\}$$

and the continuity condition becomes

$$\tilde{\phi} = F^{-1}\left(\frac{A\tilde{X} + B\tilde{Y} + C\tilde{Z}}{Ak_1^2 + Bk_2^2 + Ck_3^2}\right)$$

where

$$F^{-1}\tilde{X} = \tilde{U} + k_1^2\tilde{\phi}$$

$$F^{-1}\tilde{Y} = \tilde{V} + k_2^2\tilde{\phi}$$

$$F^{-1}\tilde{Z} = \tilde{W} + k_3^2\tilde{\phi}$$

The t's are functions of $\tilde{u}$, $\tilde{v}$, $\tilde{w}$ only, so that, if u, v, w are known at the beginning of a time step and satisfy the continuity condiition, we may advance $\tilde{X}$, $\tilde{Y}$, $\tilde{Z}$. However, to form (12) advanced values of $\tilde{u}$, $\tilde{v}$, $\tilde{w}$ this requires the solution (11) for $\tilde{\phi}$ at the advanced time. This is done using the continuity condition at the advanced time, and does not require its time differentiation.

At the beginning of a step t=0, and we have

$$ F = 1, \quad \tilde{\phi} = 0, \quad \tilde{X} = \tilde{U}, \quad \tilde{Y} = \tilde{V}, \quad \tilde{Z} = \tilde{W} $$

The equations for X, Y, and Z are integrated over the time step, and the final values are used in equations (11) and (12) to produce final values of U, V, and W. The origin of time is then shifted to the final time giving the proper initialization for the next time step.

Spatial differentiation is a point operator in wave space but multiplication (e.g., $\tilde{t}_{12} = \tilde{\tilde{u}}\tilde{\tilde{v}}$) is not, and the most efficient means of forming the Fourier transform of a product from the transforms of its terms is to return to physical space by inverting the transforms, form the product, and then transform the result back to wave space. Unfortunately, the transformation of the product back to wave space introduces an error due to spectral truncation.

The truncation errors are most easily demonstrated in one spatial dimension. The representation of the product of two Fourier series a,b (in complex form) as a Fourier series c is given by the (infinite) convolution sum

$$ c_k = \sum_{s=-\infty}^{+\infty} a_{k-s} b_s $$

However, the process of inverting finite transforms $\tilde{a}$ and $\tilde{b}$, forming the product ab, and then taking its finite transform reresults instead in two sums:

$$ \tilde{c}_k = \sum_s \tilde{a}_{k-s} \tilde{b}_s + \sum_s \tilde{a}_{k\pm M-s} \tilde{b}_s $$

The first sum represents a contribution (incomplete due to truncation) to ab correctly attributed to wave number k. The second sum also represents a contribution to ab, but it is actually a contribution not to k, but to k±m, wave numbers beyond those allowed by the length (M) of the finite transforms used. This is the "aliasing" error. Now it may be argued that because aliasing errors do not account for all of the truncation error, suppression of the aliasing error is not cost effective so far as accuracy is concerned. However, in the algorithm used here, the aliased terms can lead to nonlinear instability, and their control is essential.

Now to consider the effect of a shift of the physical coordinate system. In wave space this amounts to multiplication of $e^{ik\Delta}$, where Δ is the amount of coordinate shift. If we use $e^{ik\Delta}$ to shift a_k, b_k prior to inverting them to physical space, form the product ab on the shifted grid, transform back to wave space, and finally shift coordinates back with $e^{-ik\Delta}$ we obtain

$$\tilde{c}_k = \sum_s \tilde{a}_{k-s}\tilde{b}_s + e^{\pm iM\Delta} \sum_s \tilde{a}_{k\pm M-s}\tilde{b}_s$$

The first (alias-free) sum is invariant under these shifts, but the second sum, the aliased one which we wish to suppress, has a phase dependency on Δ and can be eliminated. For example, if two evaluations are made, one with $e^{\pm iM\Delta} = 1$ and the other with $e^{\pm iM\Delta} = -1$, the alias-free result is one-half their sum. The second sum (which is multiplied by the phase factor) itself vanishes identically for $|\ k\ | < N$, $(N \leq M/3)$ if modes of $\tilde{a}$ and $\tilde{b}$ outside of this range are nulled prior to inversion, and transforms of length M are retained. Thus two independent procedures are available for alias suppression.

The extension of these procedures to three dimensional gives for each $\tilde{c}_k$ eight terms, seven of which represent aliasing errors. The aliased terms are classified according to the number of dimensions in which aliasing has occurred.

We then have

$$[\underline{k} = (k_1, k_2, k_3), \Theta_n = e^{\pm ik_n \Delta_n}]$$

$$\check{c}_{\underline{k}} = S_o \qquad \text{(alias-free)}$$

$$+ \Theta_1 S_1 + \Theta_2 S_2 + \Theta_3 S_3 \qquad \text{(singly-aliased)}$$

$$+ \Theta_1 \Theta_2 S_4 + \Theta_2 \Theta_3 S_5 + \Theta_3 \Theta_1 S_6 \qquad \text{(doubly-aliased)}$$

$$+ \Theta_1 \Theta_2 \Theta_3 S_7 \qquad \text{(triply-aliased)}$$

All of the aliased sums $(S_1, \ldots S_7)$ vanish if modes having any $k_i > N_i$ are nulled. The doubly and triply aliased sums $(S_4, \ldots, S_7)$ vanish if modes having any two $k_i > N_i$ are nulled. The triply aliased sum (S_7) vanished if modes having all three $k_i > N_i$ are nulled. Alternatively one can evaluate the convolution eight times using the eight combinations of Θ_x, Θ_y, Θ_z, $= \pm 1$ and sum to eliminate the aliased terms. Note that suppression by the latter means requires eight evaluations to eliminate all of the aliased terms. One can also, as suggested by Orszag (1) remove $S_4, \ldots S_7$ by truncation and the remaining single aliases by coordinate shift with two evaluations. We are faced with the choice between losing information (truncation) or losing computational speed (multiple evaluations).

We have, following Orszag, eliminated doubly and triply aliased sums by truncation, though the truncation used here differs slightly from that of Orszag who nulls modes having $\underline{k} \cdot \underline{k} > 2(M/3)^2$. We have not exactly eliminated the remaining single aliases, due to the computational cost of the double evaluations required. Instead, we have used the fact that the Runge-Kutta algorithm requires pairs of evaluations at each half step and that by using a shifted grid for the second evaluation we reduce the total alias error for the pair by a factor of Δt^2. The possibility of nonlinear instability is further reduced by ensuring that the Θ_j for the first evaluation in a pair are not correlated with those of other pairs. This is easily accomplished by the use of a uniform-random-number generator during computation of the phase factors.

DATA MANAGEMENT

In large simulations the high-speed random-acess memory of the
computer cannot hold the entire data base of the problem (in the
present code it holds 6% of it). In this case, the high-speed
memory may only be able to hold a few lines of the mesh (e.g., all
values of k_1 for a few k_2, k_3 values), and it is convenient to
transform and take derivatives only along those lines. In general,
separate passes over the data base are required for each spatial
dimension. The directional order in which operations are performed then determines the required number of passes over the data base.
We will demonstrate how this number may be reduced in a spectral
algorithm.

Consider the evaluation in wave space of $(uu)_x$ and $(uu)_y$,
which is required in equation (5). The transforms of u and v are
inverted in the x, y, and z directions, each direction requiring
a separate pass over the data base. On the last (z) pass of this
sequence we also form, in physical space, the uv product and then
transform back to wave space in the z direction. In principle,
there remain only the x and y transforms and the multiplications
by ik_x and ik_y to form the derivatives in the x and y directions.
The problem is that, under our constraints, transforms and derivatives can only be taken in the direction of the grid lines held
in fast memory. Under these constraints we must either perform
three transforms and two derivatives in two passes, or two transforms and two derivations in three passes. If the constraint on
the derivative is absent, the results can be obtained in two transforms and two derivatives in two passes. This constraint can be
removed only if four lines of the mesh can be held simultaneously
in fast memory (so that all eight real numbers representing wave
number $\underline{k}$ are present). The Illiac fast memory is sufficiently
large to accommodate four mesh lines, but not within a single
processing element (PE), so that differentiation would require
communication across the PEs. We have instead used a slightly
altered set of dependent variables that avoids this problem alto-
gether.

If the $\hat{x}$ momentum equation is differentiated with respect to
$\hat{x}$, and the $\hat{y}$ momentum equation with respect to $\hat{y}$, and the $\widehat{uv}$ stress
terms appears as $(\widehat{uv})_{\hat{x}\hat{y}}$ in both equations, and its evaluation under
the constraints. But two extra integrations (of $\hat{u}_{\hat{x}}$ and $\hat{v}_{\hat{y}}$) are then
required to form $\hat{u}$ and $\hat{v}$ in physical space; however since integration and differentiation cost far less than either a transform or
an I/O pass, this method is quite efficient. To avoid loss, upon
differentiation, of information in a Fourier mode having a null
wave number we simply do not multiply that mode by its wave number
(i.e., zero) and similarly, when we integrate it we do not divide
by its wave number. What this amounts to is that, instead of the
usual spectral dependent variables

$$\tilde{u}(k_1,k_2,k_3)$$

$$\tilde{v}(k_1,k_2,k_3)$$

$$\tilde{w}(k_1,k_2,k_3)$$

we use

$$\tilde{u}(0,k_2,k_3) \quad , \quad ik_1\tilde{u}(k_1,k_2,k_3) \quad , \quad k_1 \neq 0$$

$$\tilde{v}(k_1,0,k_3) \quad , \quad ik_2\tilde{v}(k_1,k_2,k_3) \quad , \quad k_2 \neq 0$$

$$\tilde{w}(k_1,k_2,0) \quad , \quad ik_3\tilde{w}(k_1,k_2,k_3) \quad , \quad k_3 \neq 0$$

Use of these variables simplifies the continuity condition and minimizes the number of transforms and passes over the data base.

APPENDIX

THE ILLIAC PROGRAM

The fourth-order Runge-Kutta algorithm is used to integrate the system of equations (10-12). The strain inverses A,B,C, and the integrating factor F are considered known. The bulk of the computation is the evaluation of the right side of (10), which is done in subroutines PHASE 1, PHASE 2, and PHASE 3. The dependent variables $\dot{X}, \dot{Y}, \tilde{Z}$ are then advanced in STEP and the continuity condition (11), is used by PRESSR to recover the physical velocities (12). These five subprograms are called sequentially by the control routine LOOP which is responsible for data management and step control.

The functions of processes called by these routines are given by in-line comments in the listing.

Data Structure and Flow
The data base resides on disk and consists of two blocks. The first block of data holds the velocity field at the beginning of Runge-Kutta step (three words/node) and a predicted velocity accumulator field (three words/node) in which the right side of (10) is evaluated, requiring both sequential and nonsequential page accesses from the disk.

Each prediction within the Runge-Kutta process requires two complete passes through the data base, one bringing (x,y) planes into core (PHASE 1, PHASE 3, STEP, and PRESSR) for operators in the y direction, and one bringing in (x,z) planes (PHASE 2) for operators in the x and z directions. In the latter pass, only the working space data block is required, allowing the (x,z) planes to be handled by a triple buffered scheme.

Listing of Program
The program is coded for execution in 32-bit precision on the Illiac computer. The routines listed in the full paper, which are coded in the CFD language, cover the major algorithmic steps of the computation. Some of the lower level routines are coded in assembly language (ASK) for efficiency, and others had to be hand coded because of the restrictions placed on 32-bit operation by the CFD language.

REFERENCE

Orszag, S.A.: Numerical Methods for the Simulation of Turbulence. Physics of Fluids Supplement II, 1969, p. 250.

(Note: A discussion of the physics has been omitted from this condensation. To obtain copies of the completed paper, order NASA TM-73,203.)

3. TRIOIL IV, a Three Dimensional Hydrodynamics Code for the ILLIAC IV Computer

In most cases, an understanding of the complex phenomena involved in the numerical simulation of hydrodynamic studies can be accurately described using one- and two-dimensional codes. Many times, however, situations arise in which the phenomena are clearly three-dimensional. Unfortunately, the length of time and number of cells required for the solution of such problems is not practical on most present day computers. Development of the Illiac IV has provided the opportunity to attain the speed, economy and mesh sizes needed to realistically treat these problems. A project was, therefore, initiated to reconfigure the TRIOIL code to make optimum use of the unique features of the Illiac IV computer. The resulting version of the code, TRIOIL IV, is operational and has been used to calculate a three-dimensional blast wave problem. The basic logic of the code, its utilization of the Illiac IV and comparisons with other computers are discussed.

This section is based on a report by L.L. Reed and D.R. Henderson; System, Science and Software Corp., La Jolla, California, (SSS - IR - 76-2807) Dec. 1975.

173

DESCRIPTION OF TRIOIL IV

The TRIOIL IV code treats two materials and permits variable zone size in each of the three dimensions. The current version is capable of processing a 64 x 70 x 70 grid (313,600 zones). Either reflective or transmitted boundary conditions may be specified. In mixed cells, the energy is partitioned in proportion to the mass of each constituent cell. The Tillotson (1) equation of state form is incorporated and can be used for describing a wide range of material properties.

TRIOIL IV incorporates a unidirectional, explicit technique (splitting)(2) for solving the hydrodynamic equations in an Eulerian formulation. The splitting technique is a series of one-dimensional passes over the computational grid performed in such a manner as to arrive at a three-dimensional solution without the use of "look ahead" for mass transport. The look ahead feature is used in many current 2-D and 3-D Eulerian codes.

The three hydrodynamic conservation equations for inviscid flow are

$$\frac{\partial \rho}{\partial t} + \nabla \cdot \rho \vec{u} = 0 \qquad \text{Conservation of mass}$$

$$\frac{\partial \rho \vec{u}}{\partial t} + \nabla \cdot \rho \vec{u}\vec{u} = -\nabla P \qquad \text{Conservation of momentum}$$

and

$$\frac{\partial \rho E}{\partial t} + \nabla \cdot \rho \vec{u}E = -\nabla \cdot P\vec{u} \qquad \text{Conservation of energy}$$

where

ρ = density

$\vec{u}$ = velocity

P = pressure

E = specific total energy

t = time .

In the TRIOIL code, these equations are solved in two phases. Terms involving pressure forces are treated in Phase 1 (PH1) and transport terms are treated in Phase 2 (PH2). The Phase 1 processing is completed for all three coordinate directions before proceeding to Phase 2. Detailed descriptions of the Eulerian finite difference equations are described in (3).

In the splitting technique used in TRIOIL IV, the conservation equations are identical to those of TRIOIL. However, in the TRIOIL IV code, both Phase 1 and Phase 2 are completed for a given coordinate direction before proceeding to another coordinate direction. A complete computation cycle consists of three calculational sweeps over the grid; one for each coordinate direction. The direction of the sweeps are permuted to account for the six possible combinations of the three coordinate directions. This is done to avoid preferential mass flow which would occur if the calculations were performed in the same coordinate sequence each cycle.

The parallel processing characteristic of the Illiac IV makes it undesirable to halt the normal flow of calculations for the handling of individual cells as is usually the case in the treatment of boundary conditions. In order to avoid this problem in the TRIOIL IV code, boundary cells are placed at the ends of the normal computational grid. These cells are initialized at the beginning of each calculational cycle in a manner which causes the interface between the boundary cell and the adjacent cell to receive the appropriate boundary conditions (transmittive or reflective).

A typical TRIOIL IV cycle is outlined in Figure 5.13. After the initial grid generation, a slab of data (e.g., x-y) is read in from disk. In this slab, PH1 and PH2 are carried out for one direction, say, the x-direction. This process is then repeated for the other y-direction in the slab and the resulting data are written back onto the disk. This same procedure is then followed until all (x-y) slabs have been processed (Figure 5.14).

Next, the data are read in and processed a slab at a time in an orthogonal direction (e.g., x-z) with the appropriate equations being solved for the z-direction. At the end of the cycle, the new timestep is calculated and the next cycle is initiated with a different permutation of the x, y and z directions.

The unique feature of the Illiac IV, which requires special programming considerations, is that 64 processing elements (PEs) are used in parallel processing mode. For simplicity, the code was organized so that one coordinate direction (the x-direction) would always lie "across" the PEs. That is, difference equations involving shifting information from one PE to another apply only to the x-direction. Equations involving the y and z-directions use the standard serial type of difference equations. For instance, "UBAR", the average velocity at a cell interface is represented in the y and z directions in the following manner:

$$UBAR = (U[LOC] + \dot{U}[LOC + N])/2$$

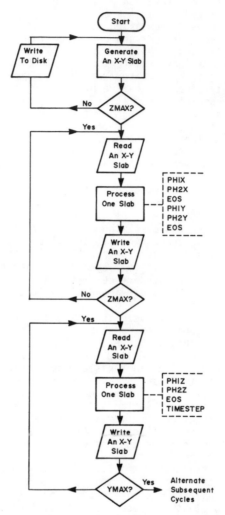

Figure 5.13   Flowchart of a typical cycle of TRIOIL IV

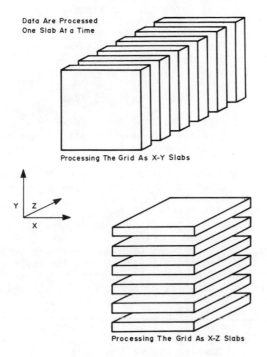

Figure 5.14   Grid subdivisions

where "U(LOC)" represents the velocity of the cell center, and "U(LOC+N)" represents the velocity at the center of the neighboring cell. However, due to the parallel processing feature of the Illiac IV computer, information contained in adjacent PEs is not directly available. It must therefore be shifted into the appropriate PE, when performing calculations in the x-direction. This requires an additional set of equations for the x-direction. The same velocity calculation as mentioned above would be represented in the x-direction as:

UBAR = (U(LOC) + RTL(1, ,U(LOC)))/2 ,

where "RTL" indicates a shift of data to the left adjacent PE. This technique eliminated the need for either skewing the storage or performing a matrix inversion to change coordinate directions during processing.

As described above, the TRIOIL IV code alternately processes a series of x-y planes and x-z planes. The data for these planes are arranged on the I4DM disks so that the y-direction lies sequentially along disk "pages" (1 page equals 1024 words) and the z-direction lies across the disk bands (1 disk equals 4 bands). This is best illustrated in Figure 5.15. For simplicity, the necessary page delays between bands have not been included. Each page on the disk contains all values of x for any given value of y or z. The ability to read either along or across bands allows the TRIOIL IV code to utilize common in-core storage for both the y and z planes, the main storage vector being dimensioned to the larger of the two directions.

Each cycle requires a total of one read and one write per plane. In a typical cycle, an x-y plane would be read in from the first band, processed and written back out to the same band. The next band (or x-y plane) would then be read in and the process continued until the last band has been processed and written out. For the second half of the cycle, the first x-z plane is read across the bands and into the storage vector previously utilized by the x-y plane. This plane is then processed and written out to the same storage area or disk. The heads are then positioned one page down and the rest of the x-z planes are serially processed in the same manner completing a full cycle.

It is interesting to compare disk reading time with computing time. The time needed to read and write information (I/O) on the disk per cycle depends on the average access time, 20 msec per read or write, and the number of x-y and x-z planes needed for the calculation. Assuming a 64 x N x N grid, the disk I/O time T_D per cycle is roughly

$$T_D = 20 \text{ msec} \times 4N$$

The computational time needed per cycle T_C is the number of cells (64 x N x N) times the processing time per cell T_P in ms

$$T_C = T_P \times 64 \times N^2$$

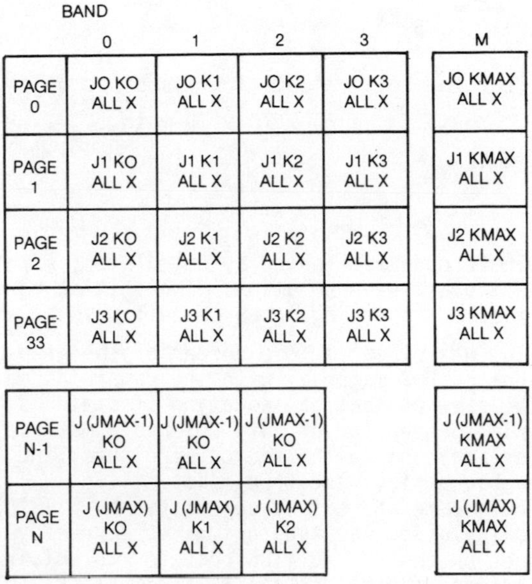

BAND

	0	1	2	3	M
PAGE 0	JO KO ALL X	JO K1 ALL X	JO K2 ALL X	JO K3 ALL X	JO KMAX ALL X
PAGE 1	J1 KO ALL X	J1 K1 ALL X	J1 K2 ALL X	J1 K3 ALL X	J1 KMAX ALL X
PAGE 2	J2 KO ALL X	J2 K1 ALL X	J2 K2 ALL X	J2 K3 ALL X	J2 KMAX ALL X
PAGE 33	J3 KO ALL X	J3 K1 ALL X	J3 K2 ALL X	J3 K3 ALL X	J3 KMAX ALL X
PAGE N-1	J (JMAX-1) KO ALL X	J (JMAX-1) KO ALL X	J (JMAX-1) KO ALL X		J (JMAX-1) KMAX ALL X
PAGE N	J (JMAX) KO ALL X	J (JMAX) K1 ALL X	J (JMAX) K2 ALL X		J (JMAX) KMAX ALL X

Figure 5.15   Organization on disk of data for TRIOIL IV calculation on the Illiac

Then the ratio of T_D to T_C is

$$\frac{T_D}{T_C} = \frac{80}{T_p 64 N}$$

T_p, for the test calculation discussed below, was 0.14 msec per cell. Thus, for a 64 x 70 x 70 mesh, $T_D/T_C = 0.13$.

TEST PROBLEM

The TRIOIL IV code was tested by calculating a point source three-dimensional blast wave solution. The initial conditions are tabulated in Table 5.1. A single source cell with an energy density of 10^{15} erg/gm was placed in one corner of the grid. The source cell was designated DOT material with the remaining material designated as X. The same perfect gas equation of state was used to define the material properties of both DOT and X materials. The three boundaries adjacent to the source were specified as reflective and the outer boundaries were transmissive.

Both in-core and out-of-core options in TRIOIL IV were used. A third calculation was made using the current version of the TRIOIL code on the UNIVAC 1108 computer to obtain a timing comparison between serial and parallel computers.

Results of the TRIOIL IV calculation are compared with the analytic solution in Figure 5.16 in the form of peak shock pressure vs. time. As shown in Figure 5.16, the finite source zone leads to a lower pressure than the analytic solution at early times. As time progresses, the pressure calculated overshoots and by the end of the calculation, good agreement with the analytic solution is obtained. A tabulated comparison of peak pressure vs. time is given in Table 5.2. The difference in the values for peak pressure at 2.473 μs is assumed to be due to the increased accuracy of the 64-bit Illiac IV vs. the 36-bit UNIVAC 1108.

Parameter	ILLIAC In-Core	ILLIAC Out-of-Core	UNIVAC 1108
Density	1.0 g/cm^3	1.0 g/cm^3	1.0 g/cm^3
Specific energy of source	10^{15} erg/g	10^{15} erg/g	10^{15} erg/g
Gamma of gas	1.4	1.4	1.4
x of all cells	1.0 cm	1.0 cm	1.0 cm
y of all cells	1.0 cm	1.0 cm	1.0 cm
z of all cells	1.0 cm	1.0 cm	1.0 cm
Number of active x partitions	62	62	16
Number of active y partitions	10	8	10
Number of active z partitions	10	8	10

Table 5.1   Tabulated data

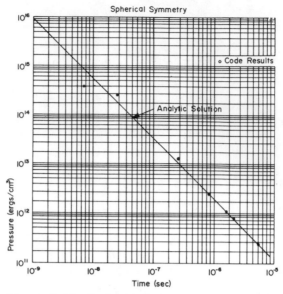

Figure 5.16   Peak shock pressure versus time

Time (sec)	Peak Pressure (erg/cm^3)	
	UNIVAC 1108	ILLIAC IV
2.70×10^{-8}	2.935×10^{14}	2.935×10^{14}
2.95×10^{-7}	1.305×10^{13}	1.246×10^{13}
8.78×10^{-7}	2.519×10^{12}	2.509×10^{12}
1.61×10^{-6}	1.180×10^{12}	1.217×10^{12}
2.47×10^{-6}	7.683×10^{11}	7.916×10^{11}

Table 5.2   Tabulated comparison of peak pressure vs time

TIMING COMPARISON BETWEEN ILLIAC IV AND UNIVAC 1108

Some timing studies were performed to compare speeds of the TRIOIL computations on the UNIVAC 1108 computer with the two Illiac IV versions of the code. The results are as follows:

Code/Computer	Processing Time per Cell
TRIOIL/UNIVAC	7.5 msec/cell
In-core/Illiac IV	0.14 msec/cell
Out-of-core/Illiac IV	0.35 msec/cell

The gains in processing time are truly impressive. Of course a problem must contain 64 cells in at least one direction in order to realize the full capability of the Illiac IV. The out-of-core Illiac IV code will approach the speed of the in-core version as the number of cells increases.

References

1. J. H. Tillotson, "Metallic Equations of State for Hyper-velocity Impact (U)," General Dynamics Corporation (July 1962).

2. W. E. Johnson, unpublished notes on splitting in hydro-dynamics calculations (U).

3. W. E. Johnson, "Development and Application of Computer Programs to Hypervelocity Impact (U), Systems," Science and Software, Report 3SR-353, (December 1970). (U)

4. "System Guide for the Illiac IV User," Institute for Advanced Computation, IAC Doc. No. SG-I1000-0000-D, (March 1974). (U)

C.   Image Processing

Digital image processing research is particularly well suited
to the architecture of the Illiac IV. A wide variety of algorithms have been experimentally implemented in the areas of multispectral classification, line detection, enhancement, skeletonizing, shape detection, transform coding, and others. The
Illiac is not well suited to production processing of images
since many image processing activities are data intensive
rather than compute intensive. Moving large images from tape
onto the I4DM is a relatively slow process. The Illiac, however, has been useful in the development of parallel algorithms
for hardwiring into special purpose image processing systems.

1. Image Line Detection on the ILLIAC by Hough Transform

Five years ago Duda and Hart reported (1) the use of the Hough transformation to detect lines and curves in digital pictures. They suggested an alternative parameterization to that used by Hough ten years previously as reported by Rosenfeld (2). Extending the Hough transform for angle and shape detection, texture classification, template orientation and other applications is discussed in (3). Briefly, the Hough transform replaces the original problem of finding colinear points by a mathematically equivalent problem of finding concurrent lines. Suppose we have a set of N points (x_i, y_i), = 1, 2...,N . The lines through a given one of these points (x_i, y_i) are given by

$$P = x_i \cos \theta + y_i \sin \theta \qquad (1)$$

where θ specifies the angle of the normal to the line with respect to the x axis, and P is the distance of the line from the origin as shown in Figure 5.17. Note that the range of P is both positive and negative, but bounded by the format size. Concurrent lines are characterized by the same P, θ parameter values. Quantizing P and θ into suitable increments allows the generation of a two dimensional histogram of all of the P, θ values associated with the N points; for each (x_i, y_i) and for each θ increment, equation 1 indicates a specific P value. If the accumulated count of P, O occurrences - the histogram- is termed $H(P,\theta)$, then high values of H indicate a high number of colinear points. An example $H(P,\theta)$ is shown in Figure 5.18. The left half of this H display reports line counts with P ranging from 0 (top) to 63 (bottom) and θ ranging from 6° (left) to 180° (right); the right half shows counts for P between -1 (top) and -64 (bottom). The ten lines correspond to the ten *'s in H.

185

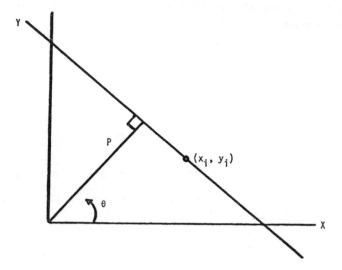

Figure 5.17   Hough transform geometry

```
00001000010000100001000010000100
00001000010000100001000010000100
00001000010000100001000010000100
00001000010000100001000010000100
00001000010000100001000010000100
11111111111111111111111111111111
00001000010000100001000010000100
00001000010000100001000010000100
00001000010000100001000010000100
00001000010000100001000010000100
00001000010000100001000010000100
00001000010000100001000010000100
00001000010000100001000010000100
00001000010000100001000010000100
00001000010000100001000010000100
00001000010000100001000010000100
00001000010000100001000010000100
00001000010000100001000010000100
11111111111111111111111111111111
00001000010000100001000010000100
00001000010000100001000010000100
00001000010000100001000010000100
00001000010000100001000010000100
00001000010000100001000010000100
00001000010000100001000010000100
11111111111111111111111111111111
00001000010000100001000010000100
00001000010001000010000100001001
00001000010000100001000010000100
00001000010000100001000010000100
00001000010000100001000010000100
11111111111111111111111111111111
```

Figure 5.18a   Grid pattern input

```
0000000000000001232233432322000  0000000000000001232344333221
0000000000000011432233332221000  0000000000000012123344332231
1000000000000011422333332111000  0000000000000122223443333441
3210010001001114323233221 10000  0000000000000011223322333 3*
42100000111224*111222222210000   0000000000000021223323333211
32110001001134111223432111000    0000000000000011123443222 1
22110111111234111233332210000    0000000000000011123333323 1
13221111112232111323222110000    0000000000000011222332441
43311011111231111233321110000    0000000000000001112332333*
333211111122311122333220000000   0000000000000001112333211
432122111123211132332111000000   00000000000000001112333221
123222221222111122333211000000   0000000000000000011232231
133322222332111333321000000000   0000000000000000011123333441
433321222222111333232110000000   00000000000000000011223333*
332333222322211433421110000000   00000000000000000011233211
423332223321111434211100000000   00000000000000000011.33221
123333333322214323211000000000   00000000000000000011132231
13334232232234*122221000000000   0000000000000000001123441
332324333222341133221000000000   000000000000000000111333*
433323343222341133210000000000   00000000000000000000113211
323244323322321333210000000000   0000000000000000000112321
123432444323311433100000000000   000000000000000000012331
132334443332211432100000000000   0000000000000000000002341
333333333333321431100000000000   00000000000000000000001133*
433313433232334*121000000000000  0000000000000000000000001111
423332333333341121000000000000   00000000000000000000000011221
123333344332341310000000000000   00000000000000000000000001231
133333322433221410000000000000   0000000000000000000000000141
432323333342311310000000000000   000000000000000000000000002*
323221233324421200000000000000   000000000000000000000000000001
423232222233334*000000000000000  00000000000000000000000000001
122223232232323000000000000000   000000000000000000000000000000
021212222222230000000000000000   000000000000000000000000000000
022220022122220000000000000000   000000000000000000000000000000
001122112222100000000000000000   000000000000000000000000000000
001112211111100000000000000000   000000000000000000000000000000
000111111111100000000000000000   000000000000000000000000000000
000110111100000000000000000000   000000000000000000000000000000
000011010100000000000000000000   000000000000000000000000000000
000001101000000000000000000000   000000000000000000000000000000
000000000000000000000000000000   000000000000000000000000000000
000000000000000000000000000000   000000000000000000000000000000
000000000000000000000000000000   000000000000000000000000000000
000000000000000000000000000000   000000000000000000000000000000
000000000000000000000000000000   000000000000000000000000000000
000000000000000000000000000000   000000000000000000000000000000
000000000000000000000000000000   000000000000000000000000000000
000000000000000000000000000000   000000000000000000000000000000
000000000000000000000000000000   000000000000000000000000000000
000000000000000000000000000000   000000000000000000000000000000
000000000000000000000000000000   000000000000000000000000000000
000000000000000000000000000000   000000000000000000000000000000
000000000000000000000000000000   000000000000000000000000000000
000000000000000000000000000000   000000000000000000000000000000
000000000000000000000000000000   000000000000000000000000000000
000000000000000000000000000000   000000000000000000000000000000
000000000000000000000000000000   000000000000000000000000000000
```

Figure 5.18b   Hough transform of grid pattern

In practice, then, a digital image can be subjected to a derivative and threshold operation to generate a set of N candidate line and edge elements. Then the Hough histogram is generated and thresholded. The surviving P, θ pairs indicate image lines that can be used to eliminate spurious line and edge candidate elements, and fill in gaps of the detected lines and edges.

As Duda and Hart point out, a similar method can be used to find just the lines through a given point, just the lines of a given direction, and by extension to higher dimensions for H, any arbitrary type curve.

This technique seems not to have found wide popularity in the digital image processing community. Perhaps, as suggested by a more recent paper by Duda and Hart, this is due to run time considerations, particularly for large image formats and for higher H dimensionality. If so, perhaps the economics should be reconsidered since the advent of faster computers.

The Hough transform is an efficient, effective detector of lines since the computational effort grows linearly with N rather than as N^2 for considering all pairs of figure points. Since lines and edges occur in most digital images and since these lines and edges convey so much of the image content, it is important that such an efficient detector be more fully exploited. This is particularly true in light of the growing importance of parallel processors since the Hough transform exhibits substantial parallelism.

This algorithm has been experimentally implemented on the Illiac IV as part of the continuing effort to explore the benefits of a parallel computer architecture for a wide range of general digital image processing operations.

References

1.   Richard O. Duda and Peter E. Hart, Use of the Hough
     Transformation to Detect Lines and Curves in Pictures,
     Comm. of ACM, January 1972 (Vol. 15 No. 1) page 11.

2.   A. Rosefeld, Picture Processing by Computer, Academic
     Press, New York, 1969.

3.   R. M. Hord, Extending the Hough Transform, Automatic
     Image Pattern Recognition Symposium, U. of Md.,
     May 23-24, 1977.

2. Use of ILLIAC IV in Analysis of LANDSAT Satellite Data

1. INTRODUCTION

The data from the LANDSAT Multi-spectral Scanner (MSS) satellite is available for analysis as a collection of picture elements (pixels) in frames containing about 7.5 million pixels.
In the area of the continental United States, each pixel corresponds to about 1.14 acres and each frame to about 8.5 million
acres. Each pixel has four component channels, one for each of
the four bands of spectral data collected. Each of these components is stored as an eight-bit integer with a value from 0
to 127, and represents an intensity in a particular frequency
band. These frequency bands are: green (5000-6000 angstroms),
red (6000-7000 angstroms), far-red (7000-8000 angstroms) and
near-infrared (8000-11000 angstroms). Each frame is placed on
a single tape and portions of these tapes are read and analyzed
using the EDITOR system (6).

EDITOR is an interactive file management and image pro-
cessing system. It was developed by the Center for Advanced
Computation (CAC) of the University of Illinois for, and with
the aid of, the Statistical Reporting Service of the United
States Department of Agriculture (USDA/SRS), the Geological
Survey of the United States Department of Interior (USDI/USGS),
and the Ames Research Center of the National Aeronautical and
Space Administration (NASA/AMES).

The EDITOR system is currently available at two ARPANET
hosts: Bolt, Beranek, and Newman (BBN) and at I4-TENEX.
While EDITOR can read portions of LANDSAT frames from tape to
disk at BBN, interactive user access to magnetic tape is not
implemented at I4-TENEX. At IAC, entire frames must be read
from tape and portions deleted from the disk before data analysts can proceed.

The preparation of the data in the form suitable for the
EDITOR system consists of reformatting of the tapes received
from Goddard Space Flight Center and, optionally, a skew cor-

This Section is reprinted from a paper in the IAC Newsletter by
Martin Ozga, September, 1977.

rection process with a rotation to a north-south orientation. Skew correction is not really necessary for analysis, but it is helpful when checking data against maps. These preprocessing steps will not be described further here since they in no way currently involve the use of the Illiac IV.

For data analysis, two of the procedures, clustering and classification, are often done on large data sets for which the computation time on TENEX becomes prohibitive. These programs have been made available on the Illiac IV. As will be seen, the computations required for clustering and classification are quite parallel and thus well-suited for Illiac use; processing turns out to be only a short job on the Illiac IV. For the convenience of users, EDITOR provides a program to create PIF's and handle the transfer of files over the ARPA network to I4-TENEX and then submit jobs to the Illiac IV. For I4-TENEX users, of course, only the PIF creation is necessary. This facility saves the user the problem of worrying about the proper Illiac disk format required for each program and saves wasted runs which might be caused by improper control sequences.

2.   DATA ANALYSIS

The analysis of LANDSAT MSS data generally consists of looking at small areas of data, identifying characteristics of pixels representing areas with particular ground covers or usages, and then applying these characteristics to large areas to obtain some sort of picture of the distribution of ground covers in these larger areas. Some users may want to estimate acreages devoted to various crops such as corn, soybeans, etc. Other users may be interested in maps of various agricultural uses, of forest lands, or urban areas and urban densities.

The first step in analysis is to perform a cluster analysis on the smaller areas of data. This cluster analysis, as will be seen, divides the data into a collection of classes and assigns each pixel to some class. Also, and what is more important for further analysis, a statistics file is generated giving the means and variance-covariance matrix (for the four channels) for each of these classes based on the pixels which fall into the classes.

To give meaning to these classes, it is necessary to find areas of data about which something is known. Thus, accurate information should be available for small areas of land known as "ground truth areas". To use this information in connection with LANDSAT data requires that all ground truth data be registered very accurately to the LANDSAT data. All this is achieved through digitization and registration procedures available within EDITOR, descriptions which are beyond the scope of this article (6). Once registration is complete, it is possible to identify certain pixels as belonging to particular fields and thus to identify those pixels with known ground covers. When clustering is done, one can check the assignments of pixels to classes and the assignment of these same pixels to ground cover and thus obtain a correspondence. Unfortunately, in practice, things do not work out so easily due to problems in distinguishing certain ground covers. These problems include variations in spectral characteristics of the same ground cover over a large area, general noise in the data, and seasonal variations in spectral characteristics -- corn and trees are confused during many parts of the year.

No matter what method is used to assign categories to ground covers, it should be emphasized that this process is probably the most difficult and also the most important in the analysis of LANDSAT data. From the clustering a collection of statistics for the various categories is obtained. If possible, several categories are selected for the ground covers of interest to allow for variation in the data for those covers. Finally pixels in a large area are assigned to those categories using the statistics. This is referred to as the classification of the data into the categories. Due to memory size limitations on the ILLIAC IV, a maximum of 64 categories may be used for classification. While this is enough or more than enough for most applications, it still means that care must be taken in the selection of categories corresponding to the various ground covers.

Since the number of categories allowed is limited to 64, it is necessary to combine or pool categories which represent the same ground cover and which are "close" to each other. What constitutes "close" is a matter of some dispute and seems to vary with the type of ground cover under consideration. The EDITOR system provides a statistics file editor to compute the distance between categories, pool categories, print listings of statistics files, and assemble the statistics files needed for classification.

Before the final classification of the large area is performed, it is prudent to classify smaller areas about which something is known to check the accuracy of the final classification. These small areas may be the same areas used for clustering framing areas or they may be different test areas, if any are available.

If the accuracy of classification is not sufficiently high (what constitutes "sufficiently high" varies from application to application), more work must be done on the statistics. This would mean using more categories for ground covers with which the worst problems are experienced, pooling different categories than before, etc. It might even be necessary to do additional cluster analyses on areas not previously used to get more or different categories for various ground covers.

Once a statistics file is obtained which seems to yield classification with sufficient accuracy, the entire large area is classified using the Illiac IV. This large area would typically correspond to at least one or more counties and might even be an entire frame for certain applications.

For any sort of estimate on land usage or ground cover, an aggregation is made of the classified data by category (and hence by ground cover or land usage using the user-supplied category assignment) and by areas within the frame. These areas may correspond to such things as political or geographic boundaries. To obtain the mapping of pixels into these areas, a further digitizing and registration procedure is needed using subsystems of the EDITOR system. The estimates given may be simple sums of the pixels in the categories or may be arrived at using a more complex statistical process.

In summary then, it is seen that analysis of LANDSAT data is a process involving many steps. The clustering and classi- fication steps lend themselves well to Illiac IV processing as will be seen. However, for the results of clustering and clas- sification to be meaningful, a great deal of manual interpreta- tion, with the assistance of various interactive programs in the EDITOR system, is needed.

3. ILLIAC IV IMPLEMENTATIONS

3.1 Clustering

The clustering technique used is taken from LARSYS (1,2) as developed at the Laboratory for Applications of Remote Sensing (LARS) at Purdue University and applied to Illiac IV by CAC.

The clustering algorithm can be divided into the following four steps:

Step 1 -- Initialization

Let $X_1, \ldots X_N$ be the N(four-channel) pixels in the area to be clustered, each pixel represented by a four-dimensional integer vector $X_k = (S_{k1}, X_{k2}, X_{k3}, X_{k4})$. If the number of categories desired from the cluster is C, let M_1, ---, M_C be the C initial mode centers of these categories to be computed, where each M_i is a vector, $M_i = (m_{i1}, m_{i2}, m_{i3}, m_{i4})$. Then, let $S = s_1, s_2, s_3, s_4)$ be the sample mean of the N pixels.

$$s_j = \frac{1}{N} \sum_{k=1}^{N} X_{kj} \qquad j = 1, 2, 3, 4$$

and the sample variance for each dimension

$$\sigma_j^2 = \frac{1}{N-1} \sum_{k=1}^{N} (X_{kj} - S_j)^2 \qquad j = 1, 2, 3, 4$$

Next, consider the real line intervals

$$\gamma_j = [s_j - \sigma_j] \text{ for } j = 1, 2, 3, 4.$$

The Cartesian product $X_iY_1 \cdot X_kY_2 \cdot X_kY_3 \cdot X_kY_4$ for all X_k defines a rectangular parallelepiped in the observation space which should contain most vectors. The C initial category mean values $M_i = (m_{i1}, m_{i2}, m_{i3}, m_{i4})$ are chosen along the diagonal of this parallelepiped as follows:

$$M_i = S + \gamma[2 \frac{i-1}{C-1} - 1] \qquad i = 1, 3, ..., C$$

Step 2 -- Category Assignment

The square of the Euclidean distance is determined from each pixel $X_1.$ to each category mean M_i as

$$d^2_{ki} = \sum_{j=1}^{4} (X_{kj} - M_{ij})^2$$

and pixel K is assigned to the category i giving the smallest value of d^2_{ki}.

Step 3 -- Category Migration

If Step 2 did not change the assignment of any of the N pixels (and the first time through Step 2 it always changes the assignment of all pixels), go to Step 4. Otherwise, replace the old category mean values by the mean of all the pixels currently assigned to that category. Then return to Step 2, Category Assignment.

Step 4 -- Variance-Covariance Calculation

The mean values for each category will have been calculated as part of Step 2. To complete the statistical description of the categories, the variance-covariance matrix for each category is calculated (the variances are the diagonal elements of this matrix and the covariances are the off-diagonal elements). An element of the matrix is calculated as

$$c_{ij1} = \frac{1}{P_{i-1}} \sum_{k=1}^{P} (X_{kj} - m_{ij})(X_{k1} - m_{i1})$$

where M_i (m_{i2}, m_{i3}, m_{i4}) is the mean for the category i being considered, P_i is the number of pixels found to be in that category, the $X_k = (X_{k1}, X_{k2}, X_{k3}, X_{k4})$ are the pixels which are determined to be in the category and j and i are the two channel values.

The data is presented to the Illiac IV as a two row header containing various information about the data file followed by the pixels. The pixels are each stored in 32 bits and thus two per PE. The file is seen by the Illiac IV as shown in Figure 5.19.

Now since the pixels each take up 32 bits, by doing some shifting it is easy to get each pixel into either the inner or outer part of the word and thus process separate pixels in parallel in each half of the PE using 32-bit mode.

The first step is to convert each channel value into a floating point value so that all further computation may be done in (32-bit) floating point. The memory row used by the original data then is used to store the category of the pixel and four additional rows are used to store the floating point values, so we have data in a PE as shown in Figure 5.20.

Of course, the classes for all pixels (as was true for the original data) would all be stored together and then would come the floating point values in a separate area of memory.

The summing required for calculation of mean values proceeds first in parallel down the PE's for all rows. Next, the sums in the inner and outer parts of each PE are added and finally the entire sum is computed by routing and adding (as is well known, only 6 routes are needed since $2^6 = 64$). The summing, where necessary, is done separately for each PE.

The category assignment (Step 3) is, of course, easily done in parallel for 128 pixels at a time since in this phase the pixels are handled quite independently.

Finally, when the process converges, the output clustered and statistics files are created. The output clustered file has 16 bits for each pixel (only eight of these are used, the other eight are to maintain compatibility with files created by the classification programs). The creation of this file requires several routing steps in order to combine two rows of categories into one.

Since clustering is an iterative process, the current implementation on the ILLIAC IV is core-contained. This means that the maximum number of pixels which may be processed is 40704.

PE
0
1
2
3
4
59
60
61
62
63
2 Row Header
n Rows of Data
pixel 0
pixel 1
an ILLIAC IV Word
Bits
0
31 32
63

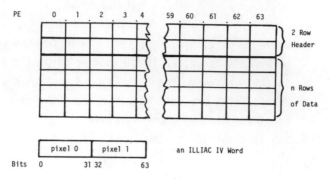

Figure 5.19 Pixel data file

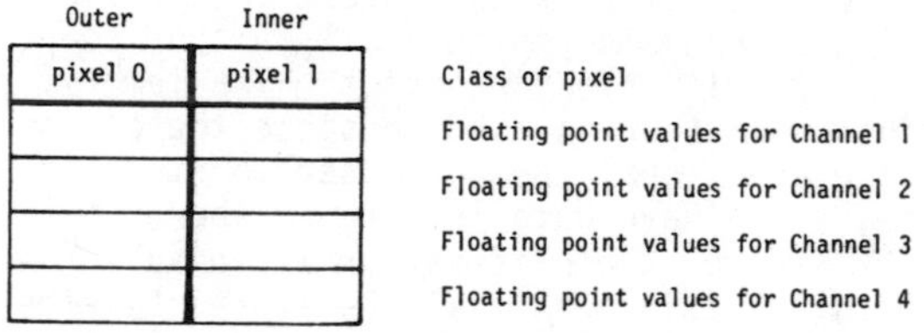

Outer
Inner
pixel 0
pixel 1
Class of pixel
Floating point values for Channel 1
Floating point values for Channel 2
Floating point values for Channel 3
Floating point values for Channel 4

Figure 5.20 Pixel data in PE

However, since it is sometimes useful to be able to cluster more pixels, CAC has lately been experimenting with what we call "weighted clustering". This is based on the observation that within an area of LANDSAT data, pixel values tend to be repeated many times (5). Then, if each pixel is stored once, along with the number of occurrences (or weight) of that pixel and the clustering formulas are modified appropriately to take this weight into account, the same resultant statistics are obtained so that more pixels may be clustered. The input file for weighted clustering as read in by the Illiac IV has a two row header, followed by the weights (w_i) followed by the pixels (p_i); this is shown in Figure 5.21.

Each weight is stored as a 32-bit integer so that the weight falls into the same PE and the same part (inner or outer) of that PE (after some appropriate shifting on the Illiac IV) as does the pixel value to which it applies. Since for each pixel value, the weight will occupy an additional word, the total number of different pixel values to which weighted clustering may be applied is reduced to 33664. The program to generate weighted files is available as part of EDITOR on TENEX. The weighted cluster produces a valid statistics file, but does not produce an output file suitable for display. To get such an output file it is necessary to use the statistics file generated by the cluster to do a Euclidean minimum distance classification of the entire area. Such a classification is, of course, equivalent to Step 2 (category assignment) of a cluster analysis.

3.2. Classification

Classification is the process of assigning a category to each pixel in some (usually) large area based on a statistics file as obtained by one or more cluster analysis. Currently two classification algorithms are implemented on the Illiac IV: the statistical maximum likelihood classification as adapted from LARSYS (3,4), and the simple minimum distance Euclidean classifier (equivalent to Step 2 of cluster analysis).

In statistical classification, pixel X_k is classified into category i such that the discriminant function G_i is maximum where

$$G_i(X) = b_i - \frac{1}{2} [(X_k - M_i)^T \Sigma_i^{-1} (X_k - M_i)]$$

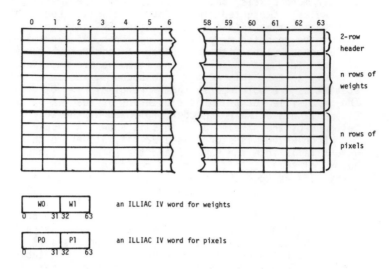

Figure 5.21 Input file for weighted clustering

and M_i is the mean value vector for category i

Σ_i is the 4 x 4 variance-covariance matrix for category i

$b_i = -\frac{1}{2} \ln |\Sigma_i|$ where

$|\Sigma_i|$ means the determinant of Σ_i.

The inversion of the matrix Σ_i and the computation of b_i for each category is done on TENEX in the statistics editor program of EDITOR before the statistics file is presented to the Illiac IV classification program.

In Euclidean classification, pixel X_k is classified into category i such that (the square of) the Euclidean distance, d^2_{ki}, is the minimal between the pixel and the mean value vector M_i where

$$d^2_{ki} = \sum_{j=1}^{4} (X_{kj} - M_{ij})^2$$

and

$$X_k = (x_{k1}, x_{k2}, x_{k3}, x_{k4})$$

$$M_i = (m_{i1}, m_{i2}, m_{i3}, m_{i4}).$$

It is readily seen that for both methods, the classification of any one pixel is entirely independent of that of any other pixel. Therefore, the procedure is parallel and may proceed very rapidly on the Illiac IV. Also, the classification procedure is not iterative so there is no reason for the data to be core-contained. It can handle as much data as will fit on the Illiac disk.

The input and output data have the same format as for clustering, except that for statistical classification a chi-square index indicating the probability of misclassification is put into the high order eight bits of the 16-bit field allotted to each pixel on output.

An enhancement of classification currently being worked on at CAC is "masked classification" in which different statistics files are used on different areas of the data. Which statistics file to use is determined by a mask file fitting the area to be classified. The mask file is generated by digitizing boundaries between different types of terrain. Such a procedure should be of use in areas where the terrain varies widely, as in certain areas of California where the transition from agricultural valleys to mountains is abrupt. The process of determining, for each PE, the mask field to which a pixel contained in the PE belongs is not particularly well-suited to Illiac IV processing. Some large mask file representation could be passed to the Illiac IV, but because of the problems incurred in handling the increased amount of data, it seems best to tolerate this relatively minor loss of parallelism.

3.3 Use of Multitemporal Data

It is sometimes useful to process multitemporal data, made up of data from two separate frames spliced together. Each pixel then has eight channels, four from each frame. Using frames from different seasons of the year over the same area makes it easier to distinguish certain ground covers, such as corn and trees, which may not be distinguishable on a single frame.

On the Illiac IV, programs are also available to cluster and classify eight-channel data. They are similar to the programs for four-channel data and so will not be described. The eight-channel classifier is a 32-bit mode program and since each eight-channel pixel takes up a full 64-bit word, a little extra data manipulation is necessary. The eight-channel cluster program is a 64-bit mode program. Both the eight-channel cluster and classify allow a maximum of 32 categories.

Another way to handle eight-channel data on the Illiac IV is to condense it back to four-channel data by taking two channels from each of the two pixels used to make an eight-channel pixel. We have found it useful to take channels 2 and 4 from each. The program to do this condensation (available as part of EDITOR) allows the user to select the channels desired. The procedure for taking channels 2 and 4 is shown in Figure 5.22. Once this is done, the four-channel cluster and classify programs may be used.

Finally, the construction of the eight-channel data is a process that lends itself in part to use of the Illiac IV. The process requires a correlation of many blocks of data paired between the two frames to generate a set of matched control points between the two images. Using a polynomial fitting these control points, pixels from one frame may be mapped to the other allowing pixels representing the same ground area to be spliced together. While there is already such a block correlation program available on the Illiac IV, it has been found to be unsatisfactory for overlay of pairs of frames from widely different seasons and so improved methods of image overlay are being studied.

3.4 Considerations for Illiac Use

It should be noted that in LANDSAT applications, one is dealing with large amounts of data which is presently stored on tapes. The handling of many tapes, reading them into TENEX disk and copying the output back to other tapes as needed to process large amounts of data on the Illiac IV presents some still unresolved problems. Thus we look forward to the implementation by IAC of more adequate tape to disk data handling facilities, which are now under development.

The classify programs - for a full frame of LANDSAT data covering approximately 8.5 million acres - typically take less than five minutes of actual time on the Illiac IV, including transfers between Illiac memory (PEM) and Illiac disk (I4DM). Timings are dependent on the number of pixels and on the number of categories. In addition, the time required for clustering can vary widely with different data sets since it is an iterative process. However, in the past, the time taken for transfers between the I4DM and TENEX disk far exceeded the time spent processing on the Illiac IV. In July of 1977, IAC made available a new system for handling these TENEX to Illiac disk transfers. Data in this particular application is now transferred quickly enough to cut the total processing and transfer time for a full LANDSAT frame from approximately 55 minutes to 12 minutes.

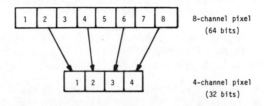

Figure 5.22 Condensing eight channel data

References

1. G. H. Ball and D. J. Hall, "ISODATA, A Novel Method of Data
    Analysis and Pattern Classification", Stanford Research
    Institute, Menlo Park, California, 1965.

2. P. H. Swain and K. W. Fu, "On the Application of Nonparametric
    Techniques to Crop Classification Problems", National Elec-
    tronics Conference Proceedings, 1968.

3. K. W. Fu, D. A. Landgrebe, and T. L. Phillips, "Information
    Processing of Remotely Sensed Agricultural Data", Proceedings,
    IEEE, Vol. 57, No. 4, April 1969.

4. P. H. Swain, "Pattern Recognition: A Basic for Remote Sensing
    Data Analysis", LARS Information Note 11572, Laboratory for
    Applications of Remote Sensing, Purdue University, West
    Lafayette, Indiana, 1972.

5. M. Goldberg and S. Schlien, "A Four-Dimensional Histogram
    Approach to the Clustering of Landsat Data", Fourth Purdue
    Symposium on Machine Processing of Remotely Sensed Data,
    Purdue University, West Lafayette, Indiana, June 1977.

6. M. Ozga, W. E. Donovan and C. Gleason, "An Interactive System
    for Agricultural Acreage Estimates Using Landsat Data",
    Symposium on Machine Processing of Remotely Sensed Data,
    Purdue University, West Lafayette, Indiana, June 1977.

3. Image Skeletonizing on the ILLIAC

The general problem of image pattern recognition is to assign each
of the patterns to be recognized to one of a prescribed number of
classes. The specific class to which a given pattern is assigned
is chosen on the basis of the values assumed by certain measurements applied to the pattern. These measurements are termed features. The effectiveness of a pattern recognition process depends
largely on significance of the features.
   One type of image pattern recognition has been implemented
on the Illiac IV for some time: multispectral classification.
Most commonly this processing has been applied to LANDSAT Multi-
spectral Scanner data. In this application the program assigns
each picture element to one of a prescribed number of land cover
classes such as bare soil, trees, wheat, water and snow. The
features used to perform this classification are the reflectances
of the particular ground point in each of four colors or spectral
regions. This set of four features is termed the spectral signa-
ture.
   Image pattern recognition is also concerned with other types
of patterns, for example, spatial temporal patterns, In the spatial domain patterns can be assigned to classes of the basis of
size, shape, location and orientation. If one seeks to recognize
patterns on the basis of size, then features are chosen that are
independent of shape, location and orientation. Such features
are then termed invariant with respect to these other characteristics.
   Generally invariant features cannot be obtained directly
from the original picture. Rather the picture is subjected to
some pre-processing which presents the information in a transformed way. This transformation process is termed feature extraction. One example of feature extraction is the two dimensional Fourier Transform, which is invariant with respect to the location of the pattern in the format of the original image.
   If, in binary images (just black and white, no grays), elongated objects of varying thickness are to be classified without
regard to thickness, then a transform which makes the features'
thickness invariant would be useful. Example applications would
include Chinese characters and chromosomes.
   A number of such transforms can be found described in the

203

image pattern recognition literature. They are referred to as thinning, skeletonizing or medial axial transforms. We will focus on one reported by Stefanelli and Rosenfeld (Journal of the Association for Computing Machinery, Vol. 18, No. 2, April 1971, page 255).

If we refer to a given picture element as P1, then we define P2, ..., P9, the neighbors of P1, by the diagram in Figure 5.23.

P9	P8	P7
P2	P1	P6
P3	P4	P5

Figure 5.23   Pixel neighbor diagram

Let $A(P1)$ be the number of 01 patterns in the ordered set P2, P3, ..., P9, P2. Let $B(P1)$ be the number of nonzero neighbors of P1. Then a nonzero point P1 is changed to zero in the image if all of the following 4 conditions prevail:

a) $2 \leq B(P1) \leq 6$

b) $A(P1) = 1$

c) $P2 * P4 * P8 = 0$ or $A(P2) \neq 1$

d) $P2 * P4 * P6 = 0$ or $A(P4) \neq 1$

This algorithm is applied iteratively until no further changes occur. This processing yields connected values given to that point and its eight neighbors at the (n-1)th iteration. Thus all the points of a figure can be processed simultaneously.

This algorithm has been implemented on the Illiac IV. A small test case has been executed with the results shown in Figures 5.24 through 5.27.

```
0 0 0 0 0 0 0 0 0 0 0 0 0 0 0 0 0
0 0 0 0 0 0 0 ★ ★ ★ 0 0 0 0 0 0 0
0 0 0 0 0 0 0 ★ ★ ★ ★ 0 0 0 0 0 0
0 0 0 0 0 0 ★ ★ ★ ★ ★ ★ 0 0 0 0 0
0 0 0 0 0 ★ ★ ★ ★ ★ ★ ★ 0 0 0 0 0
0 0 0 0 ★ ★ ★ ★ 0 0 ★ ★ 0 0 0 0 0
0 0 0 0 ★ ★ ★ ★ 0 0 ★ ★ 0 0 0 0 0
0 0 0 0 ★ ★ ★ 0 0 0 0 ★ ★ 0 0 0 0
0 0 0 ★ ★ ★ ★ ★ ★ 0 0 ★ ★ 0 0 0 0
0 0 ★ ★ ★ ★ ★ ★ ★ ★ ★ ★ ★ 0 0 0 0
0 0 ★ ★ ★ ★ ★ ★ ★ ★ ★ ★ ★ ★ 0 0 0
0 0 ★ ★ ★ 0 0 0 0 0 0 0 ★ ★ 0 0 0
0 0 ★ ★ ★ 0 0 0 0 0 0 0 ★ ★ 0 0 0
0 ★ ★ ★ 0 0 0 0 0 0 0 0 0 ★ ★ ★ 0
0 ★ ★ 0 0 0 0 0 0 0 0 0 0 0 ★ ★ 0
0 0 0 0 0 0 0 0 0 0 0 0 0 0 0 0 0
```

Figure 5.24   Input image

```
0 0 0 0 0 0 0 0 0 0 0 0 0 0 0 0 0
0 0 0 0 0 0 0 0 0 0 0 0 0 0 0 0 0
0 0 0 0 0 0 0 0 ★ ★ 0 0 0 0 0 0 0
0 0 0 0 0 0 0 ★ ★ ★ ★ 0 0 0 0 0 0
0 0 0 0 0 0 ★ ★ 0 0 ★ 0 0 0 0 0 0
0 0 0 0 0 ★ ★ 0 0 0 ★ 0 0 0 0 0 0
0 0 0 0 0 ★ ★ 0 0 0 0 ★ 0 0 0 0 0
0 0 0 0 0 ★ ★ 0 0 0 0 ★ 0 0 0 0 0
0 0 0 0 ★ ★ ★ 0 0 0 0 ★ 0 0 0 0 0
0 0 0 ★ ★ ★ ★ ★ ★ 0 0 ★ 0 0 0 0 0
0 0 0 ★ ★ 0 0 0 ★ ★ ★ ★ ★ 0 0 0 0
0 0 0 ★ 0 0 0 0 0 0 0 0 ★ 0 0 0 0
0 0 ★ ★ 0 0 0 0 0 0 0 0 ★ 0 0 0 0
0 0 ★ 0 0 0 0 0 0 0 0 0 0 ★ 0 0 0
0 0 0 0 0 0 0 0 0 0 0 0 0 0 0 0 0
0 0 0 0 0 0 0 0 0 0 0 0 0 0 0 0 0
```

Figure 5.25   Picture after 1 iteration

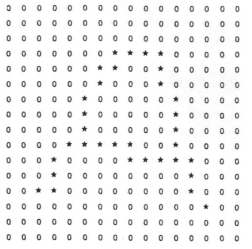

Figure 5.26 Picture after 2 iterations

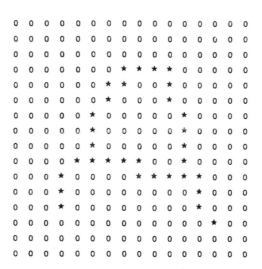

Figure 5.27 Picture after 3rd and final iteration

4. Two Dimensional Hadamard Transform on the ILLIAC IV

The Fourier Transform, the coefficients of a series expansion for a function in terms of sines and cosines, has quite properly found broad applicability throughout the scientific computation community. A wide range of IAC application efforts have employed the Illiac implemented FFT algorithm for quite some time. One prominent example is the generation of images from SEASAT Synthetic Aperture Radar data.

In the realm of general digital image processing, two dimensional Fourier Transforms are used for enhancement, compression, texture classification, smear removal, quality assessment, cross correlation, and a host of other operations. One simple example is contrast improvement. Here the Fourier Transform of an input image is obtained to ascertain the spatial frequency content of that image. If the zero frequency component or D.C. element of that transform is set to zero, the inverse of this "filtered" transform will be a new rendering of the image with the background haze removed. Hence, the contrast is improved and the image will be more interpretable.

Another transform, termed the Hadamard Transform, closely related to the Fourier Transform, for some applications has advantages over the Fourier Transform. Consider an n x n array of picture elements X_{ij} where i, $j = 1, 2, \ldots, n$. A transformation of this X_{ij} array into another n x n array $y_{k\ell}$ can be specified by

$$y_{k\ell} = \sum_{i=1}^{n} \sum_{j=1}^{n} a_{k\ell ij} X_{ij}, \qquad k, \ell = 1, 2, \ldots, k.$$

Similarly, the inverse transformation gives

$$X_{ij} = \sum_{k=1}^{n} \sum_{\ell=1}^{n} a_{ijk\ell} y_{k\ell}, \qquad i, j = 1, 2, \ldots, n.$$

207

The particular transform is defined by choosing the a's. For the Fourier transformation

$$a_{k\ell ij} = \frac{1}{n} \exp[-2\pi\sqrt{-1}\,(ki+\ell j)/n]$$

and the Hadamard transformation

$$a_{k\ell ij} = \frac{1}{n}\,(-1)^{\,b(k,\ell,i,j)}$$

where

$$b(k,\ell,i,j) = \sum_{h=e}^{\log_2 n-1} [b_h(k)b_h(\ell) + b_h(i)b_h(j)]$$

$b_h(\cdot)$ is the hth bit in the binary representation of $(\cdot)$, and n is a power of 2.

Stated differently, the Fourier Transform uses sines and cosines, while the Hadamard Transform uses Walsh functions. Figure 5.28 shows the first 16 of these Hadamard Transform waveforms.

One advantage of the Hadamard Transform over the Fourier Transform is computational simplicity. For an $n \times n$ image, the FFT requires $2_n^2 \log_2 n$ multiplications and a like number of additions, while the Hadamard requires just the additions.

For image data compression purposes large images are generally partitioned into a set of 26 x 16 sub-images(1). A computer program to generate the Hadamard Transform of a 26 x 16 sub-image has been experimentally implemented on the Illiac. Sample input and output arrays are shown in Figures 5.29 and 5.30. The program does not normalize the output. Fortuitously the inverse Hadamard Transform is produced by the same program to within a scale factor.

The Illiac IV as an array processor is particularly well suited for image processing applications. Consequently the Institute is experimentally implementing a number of general purpose image processing algorithms on the Illiac.

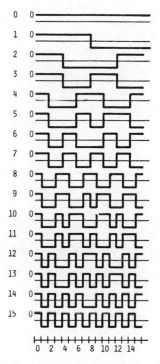

Figure 5.28   Hadamard transform of Figure 5.29

```
0  0  0  0  0  0  0  0  0  0  0  0  0  0  0  0
0  0  0  0  0  0  0  0  0  0  0  0  0  0  0  0
0  0  0  0  0  0  0  0  0  0  0  0  0  0  0  0
0  0  0  0  0  0  0  0  0  0  0  0  0  0  0  0
0  0  0  0  0  0  0  0  0  0  0  0  0  0  0  0
0  0  0  0  0  0  0  0  0  0  0  0  0  0  0  0
0  0  0  0  0  0  0  0  0  0  0  0  0  0  0  0
0  0  0  0  0  0  0  0  0  0  0  0  0  0  0  0
0  0  0  0  0  0  0  0  0  0  0  0  0  0  0  0
0  0  0  0  0  0  0  0  0  0  0  0  0  0  0  0
0  0  0  0  0  0  0  0  0  0  0  0  0  0  0  0
0  0  0  0  0  0  0  0  0  0  0  0  0  0  0  0
0  0  0  0  0  0  0  0  0  0  0  0  0  0  0  0
0  0  0  0  0  0  0  0  0  0  0  0  0  0  0  0
0  0  0  0  0  0  0  0  0  0  0  0  0  0  0  0
1  1  1  1  1  1  1  1  1  1  1  1  1  1  1  1
```

Figure 5.29
Input Array

```
 16  0  0  0  0  0  0  0  0  0  0  0  0  0  0  0
-16  0  0  0  0  0  0  0  0  0  0  0  0  0  0  0
 16  0  0  0  0  0  0  0  0  0  0  0  0  0  0  0
-16  0  0  0  0  0  0  0  0  0  0  0  0  0  0  0
 16  0  0  0  0  0  0  0  0  0  0  0  0  0  0  0
-16  0  0  0  0  0  0  0  0  0  0  0  0  0  0  0
 16  0  0  0  0  0  0  0  0  0  0  0  0  0  0  0
-16  0  0  0  0  0  0  0  0  0  0  0  0  0  0  0
 16  0  0  0  0  0  0  0  0  0  0  0  0  0  0  0
-16  0  0  0  0  0  0  0  0  0  0  0  0  0  0  0
 16  0  0  0  0  0  0  0  0  0  0  0  0  0  0  0
-16  0  0  0  0  0  0  0  0  0  0  0  0  0  0  0
 16  0  0  0  0  0  0  0  0  0  0  0  0  0  0  0
-16  0  0  0  0  0  0  0  0  0  0  0  0  0  0  0
 16  0  0  0  0  0  0  0  0  0  0  0  0  0  0  0
-16  0  0  0  0  0  0  0  0  0  0  0  0  0  0  0
```

Figure 5.30
Hadamard Transform of Figure 5.29

References

1. Paul Wintz, "Transform Picture Coding", Proc. IEEE, Vol. 60, No. 7, July 1972, p. 809.

2. A. E. Kahveci and E. L. Hall, "Sequency Domain Design of Frequency Filters", IEEE Trans. Comp., Sept. 1974, p. 976.

3. H. F. Harmuth, "A Generalized Concept of Frequency and Some Applications", IEEE Trans. Info. Theory, Vol. II-14, No. 3, May 1958, p. 375.

4. W. K. Pratt et al., "Hadamard Transform Image Coding", Proc. IEEE, June 1969, p. 58.

5. R. M. Haralick et al., "A Comparative Study of Data Compression Techniques for Digital Image Transmission", Cadre Corporation, Lawrence, Kansas, February 1972.

5. SAR Digital Processing Research

In 1972 NASA Special Programs Office of Applications began the
SEASAT program to gather information about the Earth's oceans in
the same manner as LANDSAT gathers data about the land's surface.
They conducted a survey of potential users of data on the condition of the seas; from this they determined a set of mission objectives and designed a vehicle to carry the sensors required to
meet these objectives. By testing the capabilities of this satellite under actual conditions, researchers will be able to
analyze all aspects of the program and design a system of satel-
lites to provide global coverage of the oceans.
It was obvious from the beginning that this program would
introduce new computational and data processing requirements.
In late 1975, the Institute for Advanced Computation began dis-
cussions with the SEASAT management regarding their computational
requirements. After reviewing the mission's requirements, it was
obvious that the most computationally intense process facing the
program was in the reduction of data from a microwave imaging
sensor, the synthetic aperature radar (SAR). The characteristics
for processing this data clearly matched the architecture of the
Illiac IV. This would also be the first attempt to use a SAR on
a satellite mission, and it would establish new requirements both
for the volume and for the transmission speed of remotely sensed
data. IAC proposed and was awarded research funding to investigate using the Illiac IV to develop, analyze, and evaluate algorithms for the reduction of SAR data. These algorithms will ultimately be implemented in hardware aboard future vehicles.
Simply put, a SAR is a microwave imaging radar whose beam is
focused by post-processing the return signal, rather than by having its beam focused by the size and shape of the emitting device.
The radar mounted on the satellite illuminated an area on the
earth about 15 km x 100 km. This area, called a "footprint", is
to the side of the satellite's orbital plane at an angle of 20°
degrees. (SAR's have been flown on aircraft for many years and
are called side-looking radars.) Because this beam is slanted,
the point nearest to the satellite is reflected sooner than the
point most distant from the satellite. This reflection is time
sampled at a frequency necessary to give a 25 meter ground resolution. Such orientation is on a line orthogonal to the orbital

plane and is called the range direction; the orientation along
the line parallel to the satellite's orbit is called the azimuth
direction. The positioning in the azimuth direction is determined by the direction in which the radar is pointed ("look angle")
and the doppler shift introduced by the relative motions of the
satellite and the target. Each point, called a resolution element, represents a 25 m x 25 m square of surface area. The images
to be produced from the SEASAT-A SAR are of 100 km square regions
with a resolution of 25 meters. This means that the final image
is composed of a grid of 40,000 x 40,000 resolution elements.
This processing is further complicated by having to compensate
computationally for the satellite's orientation and the earth's
rotation.

The role of the SAR is to gather data on ocean waves with
wavelengths of 50 meters and larger. This permits the computation of the wave energy spectra and direction. The resolution
of SAR permits the study of ice formations and movement.

As can be seen from the above description, SAR produces
large volumes of data at a very high rate. The only reasonable
approach to processing such volume is to do as much processing
as possible onboard the satellite so that it will transmit only
essential data to ground stations on earth. The processing of
this data will require new algorithms and techniques which are
being developed and analyzed on the Illiac IV.

The approach taken by IAC is to design a programmed environment which will manipulate the data from a SAR image. This environment is made up of a system of programs to read, convert, re-
order, and display the SAR data. It was designed so that various
subprograms to compute correlations and filter functions can be
included as modules to the system. The processing of an image is
done in two main steps; first along the range direction, then
along the azimuth direction. This requires transposing the image
(corner turning) between the range and azimuth processing. The
results of the processing are scaled and packed into a format
which will allow it to be reproduced on several commercial image
display devices.

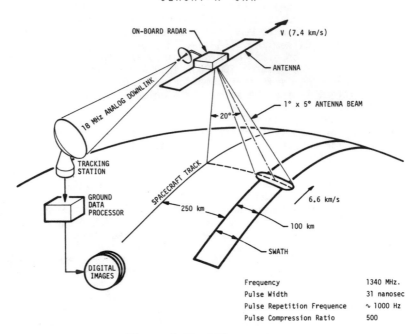

SEASAT-A SAR

ON-BOARD RADAR

V (7.4 km/s)

ANTENNA

18 MHz ANALOG DOWNLINK

1° x 5° ANTENNA BEAM

20°

TRACKING
STATION

GROUND
DATA
PROCESSOR

SPACECRAFT TRACK

6.6 km/s

250 km

100 km

SWATH

DIGITAL
IMAGES

Frequency	1340 MHz.
Pulse Width	31 nanosec
Pulse Repetition Frequence	~ 1000 Hz
Pulse Compression Ratio	500

Figure 5.31   SAR geometry

D. Mathematics

Numerical analysis activities on the Illiac IV are for the most
part research in nature and generally directed at seeking methods
for parallel processors in general rather than for the Illiac
specifically. For example, performing a two dimensional Fourier
transform on the Illiac involves the one dimensional transform of
the columns of the array down the PEs, a transpose of the array,
followed by the one dimensional transform of the rows of the array
again down the PEs. Research into efficient matrix transpose
methods is then applicable to other parallel processors.

1. Computing the Singular Value Decomposition on the ILLIAC IV

INTRODUCTION

In this report we study the computation of the singular value decomposition of a matrix on the Illiac IV computer. The singular value decomposition of a real m x n matrix A (e.g., see (10), can be defined as

$$A = U \Sigma V^t, \qquad (1)$$

where   U is an m x m orthogonal matrix,

                V is an n x n orthogonal matrix,

and Σ is an m x n matrix with a non-

              negative main diagonal and zeros

              everywhere else.

The columns U(V) are called the left (right) singular vectors of A, and the diagonal elements σ_i's of Σ are called the singular values. We assume that

$$\sigma_1 \geq \sigma_2 \geq \ldots \geq \sigma_\nu > 0$$

and

$$\sigma_{\nu+1} = \ldots = \sigma_k = 0,$$

where $\nu = \text{rank } (A)$ and $k = \min(m,n)$.

There are alternative representations of the singular value decomposition, for example,

$$A = U_\nu \Sigma_\nu V_\nu^t \qquad (2)$$

This Section is based on an article in the IAC Newsletter by Franklin T. Luk, June 1978.

with
$$U_\nu^t U_\nu = V_\nu^t V_\nu = I_\nu$$

and
$$\Sigma_\nu = \text{diag}(\sigma_1, \ldots, \sigma_\nu).$$

Over the past twenty years, various methods have been proposed for computing the singular value decomposition. The standard method, due to Golub (1965) (4), (6), uses the Householder transformations to bidiagonalize the given matrix, and then the QR method to compute the singular values of the resultant bidiagonal form. Hestenes (1958) (9) proposed a one-sided orthogonalization method, which is essentially a Jacobi algorithm and is not as efficient as Golub's method. Similar transformation algorithms were, however, subsequently studied by Chartres (1962) (1), who suggested the method for a computer with a magnetic backing store, and by Nash (1975) (12), who developed his version on a mini-computer. Since the algorithm can also be efficiently executed on a parallel computer, we (1977) have studied its implementation on the Illiac IV computer.

A ONE-SIDED ORTHOGONALIZATION METHOD

There are two reasons why the standard singular value decomposition method due to Golub may not be desirable on a parallel computer. First, although the Householder transformation is inherently parallel, the effective vector length decreases at each step, which may cause inefficiencies. Second, the parallel QR method (14) may be numerically unstable (see 7). In contrast, the one-sided orthogonalization method due to Hestenes et al., can be easily modified for efficient execution on a parallel machine.

Since neither Hestenes nor Chartres reported practical trials, Nash was apparently first to give implementation details. His algorithm is briefly described here. He uses plane rotations to orthogonalize the columns of the given m x n matrix A. The aim is to find an n x n matrix V as a product of plane rotations so that

$$AV = B,$$

with the columns of the m x n matrix B both orthogonal and non-increasing in norm (euclidean norm) from left to right. Those columns are then normalized so that

$$B = (U_\nu | 0) \left(\frac{\Sigma_\nu}{0} \right) ,$$

where U_ν and Σ_ν are the matrices defined in (2).
Consequently,

$$A = U_\nu \Sigma_\nu V_\nu^t,$$

where V_ν consists of the first ν columns of V.

A very similar algorithm based on row orthogonalization is proposed. m x m matrix U is sought as a product of plane rotations so that

$$U^t A = C$$

with the rows of the m x n matrix C orthogonal and non-increasing in length from top to bottom. Normalize those rows to obtain

$$C = (\Sigma_\nu | 0) \left(\frac{V_\nu^t}{0} \right).$$

Hence

$$A = U_\nu \Sigma_\nu V_\nu^t ,$$

where U_ν consists of the first ν columns of U.

Consider the effect of a plane rotation on a matrix. A rotation acts only on two rows of the matrix, say the i-th row a_i^t and the j-th row a_j^t, with $i < j$. We write

$$\begin{bmatrix} \cos\phi & -\sin\phi \\ \sin\phi & \cos\phi \end{bmatrix} \begin{bmatrix} a_{\sim i}^t \\ a_{\sim j}^t \end{bmatrix} = \begin{bmatrix} \hat{a}_{\sim i}^t \\ \hat{a}_{\sim j}^t \end{bmatrix}.$$

Choose ϕ such that

$$\hat{a}_{\sim i}^t \; \hat{a}_{\sim j} \; = \; 0,$$

and $\qquad \hat{a}_{\sim i}^t \; \hat{a}_{\sim i} \; \geq \; a_{\sim i}^t a_{\sim i} \; .$

The second condition ensures that the computation always proceeds towards an ordering of row norms. Nash suggests the choice so that

$$\cos\phi \; = \; \left[\frac{r+q}{2r}\right]^{\frac{1}{2}} ,$$

and $\qquad \sin\phi \; = \; \left[\frac{r-q}{2r}\right]^{\frac{1}{2}} ,$

where $\quad p \; = \; 2a_{\sim i}^t a_{\sim j}$,

$$q \; = \; a_{\sim i}^t a_{\sim i} \; - \; a_{\sim j}^t a_{\sim j} \; ,$$

and $\qquad r \; = \; (p^2 + q^2)^{\frac{1}{2}} \; .$

To minimize cancellation errors, Nash examines the sign of q and computes $\cos\phi$ ($\sin\phi$) using the above formula if q is positive (nonpositive). He then computes the other value using the following relation

$$\cos\phi \; \sin\phi \; = \; \frac{p}{2r} \; .$$

As in the traditional Jacobi algorithm, perform rotations in a set sequence called a sweep, each consisting of the $\frac{1}{2}m(m-1)$ rotations on the row pairs $(1,2),(1,3), \ldots , (1,m),(2,3), \ldots, (2,m), (3,4), \ldots, (3,m) \ldots, (m-1,m)$. The iteration is continued until all the rows are orthogonal. This guarantees convergence because the row norms become more ordered in each sweep. This one-sided method is in essence the Jacobi method implicitly applied to the matrix AA^t. Refer to the literature (8, 15, and 17) for the convergence properties of this method. It has a very desirable quadratic rate of convergence.

This row orthogonalization approach allows one to solve overdetermined linear equations efficiently. Suppose that

$$A\underset{\sim}{x} = \underset{\sim}{b}$$

is the current system of linear equations. Let R represent the next plane rotation. Then

$$(R\ A)\underset{\sim}{x} = (R\underset{\sim}{b}).$$

Since one can simultaneously apply the rotation on the right-hand vector as well as the matrix, one need not accumulate the rotations.

TEST FOR CONVERGENCE

Given the i-th row $\underset{\sim}{a}_i^t$ and the j-th row $\underset{\sim}{a}_j^t$ of the current matrix A (assume i < j), the two rows are orthogonal if the parameter

$$\tau = \frac{(\underset{\sim}{a}_i^t \underset{\sim}{a}_j)^2}{(\underset{\sim}{a}_i^t \underset{\sim}{a}_i)\ (\underset{\sim}{a}_j^t \underset{\sim}{a}_j)}$$

is less than a tolerance tol. If either

$$\underset{\sim}{a}_i^t \underset{\sim}{a}_i \quad \text{or} \quad \underset{\sim}{a}_j^t \underset{\sim}{a}_j$$

is less than another preselected value eps, one may also treat the two rows as orthogonal. One does not transform the orthogonal rows, but may permute them if necessary to order the row norms.

If all the row pairs satisfy the orthogonality criterion in a sweep, we terminate the iteration. Usually this takes the order of 6 to 10 sweeps, i.e., from $3m^2$ to $5m^2$ plane rotations (see 13).

APPLICABILITY

The singular value decomposition has many applications (see 5). Two are given here.

PSEUDOINVERSE (Subroutine SVD)

An n x m matrix X is called the pseudoinverse of an m x n matrix if X satisfies the following four properties:

$$(i) \quad AXA = A ,$$
$$(ii) \quad XAX = X ,$$
$$(iii) \quad (AX)^t = AX ,$$
$$(iv) \quad (XA)^t = XA .$$

The pseudoinverse is unique and is denoted by A^+. It can easily be verified that if $A = U \Sigma V^t$, then

$$A^+ = V \Sigma^+ U^t ,$$

where

$$\Sigma^+ = \begin{bmatrix} \frac{1}{\sigma_1} & & & 0 & \cdot & \\ & \cdot & & & \cdot & \\ & & \cdot & & \cdot & \\ & & & \cdot & \cdot & \\ 0 & & & \frac{1}{\sigma_\nu} & \cdot & \\ \cdot & \cdot & \cdot & \cdot & \cdot & \\ & & & & & 0 \end{bmatrix}_{n \times m} \quad \cdot$$

One may use the output from SVD to compute the pseudoinverse.

SOLUTIONS OF MINIMAL LENGTH (Subroutine MINFIT)

Let $\underline{b}$ be a given m-vector. Suppose one wishes to determine an n-vector $\underline{x}$ so that

$$\| \underline{b} - A\underline{x} \|_2 = min.$$

There is no unique solution if the matrix A is not of full rank. Usually the imposed condition is that the vector is of minimal length in the solution space. Such a solution, call it $\underline{\hat{x}}$, is unique and is given by

$$\underline{\hat{x}} = A^+ \underline{b}.$$

The subroutine MINFIT computes the minimal length solution to m linear equations in n unknowns, where m ≥ n.

FORMAL PARAMETER LIST

INPUT TO SUBROUTINE SVD

m	CU integer; number of rows of A, m ≥ 64.
n	CU integer; number of columns of A, n ≤ m.
withu	boolean; true if U is desired, false otherwise.
withv	boolean; true if V is desired, false otherwise.
A{0:m-1}	PE real vector; represents the matrix A to be decomposed. The rows of A lie across PE's.

OUTPUT OF SUBROUTINE SVD

D	PE real; a vector holding the singular values of A in non-increasing order.
U{0:m-1}	PE real vector; represents the orthogonal matrix U (if withu is true). The columns of U lie across PE's.
A{0:n-1}	PE real vector; represents the matrix V of orthonormalized columns. The columns of V lie across PE's.

INPUT TO SUBROUTINE MINFIT

m	CU integer; number of rows of A, m ≤ 64.
n	CU integer; number of columns of A, n ≤ m.
s	CU integer; number of columns of B, s ≤ 64.
cutoff	CU real, those singular values of A that are smaller than cutoff are set to zero.
A{0:m-1}	PE real vector; represents the regression matrix A. The rows of A lie across PE's.
B{0:m-1}	PE real vector; represents the data matrix B. The rows of B lie across PE's.

OUTPUT OF SUBROUTINE MINFIT

nrank	CU integer; number of singular values of A greater than cutoff.
X{0:s-1}	PE real vector; represents the solution matrix X. The columns of X lie across PE's.

GLYPNIR PROGRAMS

```
      BEGIN
$     SET DBUGA

      BOOLEAN WITHU, WITHV: CINT M,N,CMPLWD,ITER,INPROD,K,L; PREAL D;
      PREAL VECTOR A{63},U{63};

      ILLIACDISPLAY:
      AREA OUT;
```

```
%****************************************************************

SUBROUTINE SVD( CINT M, CINT N, PREAL OUT D,
                BOOLEAN WITHU, BOOLEAN WITHV );
    BEGIN
    %
    %
    %          ################################################
    %
    %          PROGRAMMER :      FRANKLIN LUK
    %                            VISITING APPOINTMENT PROGRAM
    %                            INSTITUTE FOR ADVANCED COMPUTATION
    %
    %          DATE :            AUGUST 1977
    %
    %          ################################################
    %
    %
    %          THIS SUBROUTINE COMPUTES THE SINGULAR VALUE
    %          DECOMPOSITION OF AN M-BY-N MATRIX A, VIZ.
    %
    %                    A  =  U D V' ,
    %
    %          WHERE   U IS AN M-BY-M ORTHOGONAL MATRIX,
    %                  D IS AN M-BY-N DIAGONAL MATRIX
    %                      WITH NONNEGATIVE ELEMENTS,
    %          AND     V IS AN N-BY-N ORTHOGONAL MATRIX.
    %
    %
    %          INPUT PARAMETERS :
    %
    %              M, N :      CU INTEGERS.  THE ROW AND COLUMN
    %                      DIMENSIONS OF THE INPUT MATRIX A; IT IS
    %                      ASSUMED THAT N .LE. M .LE. 64.
    %
    %              D :                     PE REAL.
    %
    %              WITHU :    BOOLEAN, TRUE IF U IS DESIRED,
    %                      FALSE OTHERWISE.
    %
    %              WITHV :    BOOLEAN.  TRUE IF V IS DESIRED,
    %                      FALSE OTHERWISE.
    %
    %              A :                     PE REAL VECTOR.  THE INPUT
    %                      MATRIX;  ITS ROWS LIE ACROSS THE PE'S.
    %
    %              U :        PE REAL VECTOR.
```

```
%      OUTPUT PARAMETERS :
%
%         D :                    PE REAL.  IT CONTAINS THE SINGULAR
%                 VALUES IN NONINCREASING ORDER ACROSS THE
%                 PE'S.
%
%         A :                    PE REAL VECTOR.  THE MATRIX V OF
%                 RIGHT SINGULAR VECTORS; ITS COLUMNS LIE
%                 ACROSS THE PE'S ( IF WITHV IS TRUE ).  NOTE
%                 THAT THE INPUT MATRIX HAS BEEN DESTROYED.
%
%         U :                    PE REAL VECTOR.  THE MATRIX U OF
%                 LEFT SINGULAR VECTORS; ITS COLUMNS LIE
%                 ACROSS THE PE'S ( IF WITHU IS TRUE ).
%
%
%      NOTE :
%         1.  GLYPNIR DOES NOT ACCEPT VECTOR PARAMETERS;
%         HENCE A AND U ARE GLOBAL TO THE SUBROUTINE.
%
%         2.  THE OUTPUT MATRIX V WILL BE A MATRIX OF
%         ORTHONORMALIZED COLUMNS BUT NOT AN ORTHOGONAL
%         MATRIX IF THE INPUT MATRIX A IS NOT OF FULL
%         RANK.
%

CINT IORTHG, COUNT, I, J;
CREAL P,Q,R,COSPHI,SINPHI,TOL,EPS,AIAI,AIAJ,AJAJ,LENGTH;
PREAL T;


%
%      INITIALIZE U TO THE IDENTITY MATRIX,
%      ASSUMING IT IS OF LENGTH 64.
%
IF (WITHU) THEN
    BEGIN
    FILL U WITH      (0.)4096;
    U{PEN} := 1.;
    END;


%
%         INITIALIZE THE CONTROL VARIABLES
%
IORTHG := (M*(M-1)) DIV 2;
TOL := 1.@-24;
EPS := 1.@-32;
COUNT := 0;
ITER := 0;
INPROD := 0;


%
%         ITERATE UNTIL THE ROWS OF A FORM AN ORTHOGONAL
%         SET
%
```

```
WHILE ( (ITER 50) AND (COUNT<IORTHG) ) DO
    BEGIN  % BEGIN WHILE LOOP
COUNT := 0;
ITER := ITER + 1;


%
%    ORTHOGONALIZE ROW I AGAINST ROW J, FOR I < J.
%
LOOP I : = 0, 1, M-2 DO
    BEGIN    % BEGIN LOOP I

    LOOP J : = I+1, 1, M-1 DO
        BEGIN     % BEGIN LOOP J

        AJAA := ROWSUM( A{J}*A{J}  );
        INPROD := INPROD + 1;

        IF ( AJAJ  < EPS  ) THEN
            BEGIN
            %
            %        SET ROW J TO ZERO IF ITS EUCLIDEAN
            %        LENGTH SQUARED IS LESS THAN EPS
            %
            A{J} := 0.;
            COUNT := COUNT + 1;
            END
        ELSE
            BEGIN           % BEGIN ELSE BLOCK

            AIAI := ROWSUM( A {I}*A{I} );
            INPROD := INPROD + 1;

            IF ( AIAI < EPS ) THEN
                BEGIN
                %
                %   SET ROW I TO ZERO IF ITS EUCLIDEAN
                %   LENGTH SQUARED IS LESS THAN EPS;
                %   INTERCHANGE ROWS I AND J.
                %
                A{I} := A{J};
                A{J} := 0.;

                IF (WITHU) THEN
                    BEGIN
                    T      := U{I};
                    U{I} := U{J};
                    U{J} := T;
                    END;
                END
            ELSE
                BEGIN

                    %
```

```
%     BOTH ROWS I AND J ARE NONTRIVIAL
%     VECTORS
%
AIAJ := ROWSUM( A{I}*A{J}  );
INPROD := INPROD + 1;

IF ( (AIAJ*AIAJ)/(AIAI*AJAJ) < TOL )
THEN
%
%        ROWS I AND J ARE ALREADY
%        ORTHOGONAL
%
BEGIN
COUNT := COUNT + 1;

IF ( AIAI < AJAJ  ) THEN
        BEGIN
        T    := A{I};
        A I  := A{J};
        A J  := T;

        IF (WITHU) THEN
            BEGIN
            T    := U{I};
            U{I} := U{J};
            U{J} := T;
            END;

        END;

    END
ELSE
    BEGIN

    %
    %        ORTHOGONALIZE ROW I
    %        AGAINST ROW J
    %
    P := AIAJ + AIAJ;
    Q := AIAI - AJAJ;
    R := SQRT( P*P +Q*Q );

    %
    %        CHOOSE THE APPROPRIATE
    %        FORMULA FOR COMPUTING
    %        COSPHI AND SINPHI TO PRE-
    %        SERVE NUMBERICAL STABILITY
    %
    IF ( Q>0.) THEN
        BEGIN
        COSPHI := SQRT( (R+Q)/(R+R) );
        SINPHI := P/(2.*R*COSPHI);
        END
    ELSE
```

```
                    BEGIN
                    SINPHI := SQRT( (R-Q)/(R+R) );
                    COSPHI := P/(2.*R*SINPHI);
                    END;


            %
            %        ORTHOGONALIZE THE I-TH AND
            %        J-TH ROWS OF A WITH RESPECT
            %        TO EACH OTHER, AND ORDER
            %        THEM SO THAT THE I-TH ROW
            %        HAS A GREATER EUCLIDEAN
            %        LENGTH.
            %


            T    := A{I}*COSPHI + A{J}*SINPHI;
            A{J}:=-A I *SINPHI + A{J}*COSPHI;
            A{J}:= T;


            %
            %              MODIFY THE COLUMNS OF U
            %              ACCORDINGLY
            %
            IF (WITHU) THEN
                BEGIN
                T    := U{I}*COSPHI + U{J}*SINPHI;
                U J  := -U{I}*SINPHI + U{J}*COSPHI;
                U{I} :=  T;
                END;

                END;

            END;

        END;   % END ELSE BLOCK

      END;   % END LOOP J

    END;   % END LOOP I

  END;   % END WHILE LOOP

%
%      COMPUTE THE EUCLIDEAN LENGTHS OF THE ROWS OF A;
%      THEY GIVE THE SINGULAR VALUES OF A.  THE NORMAL-
%      IZED ROWS BECOME THE ROWS OF V'.
%
LOOP I := 0, 1, N-1 DO
    BEGIN
    LENGTH := SQRT( ROWSUM( A{I}*A{I}  ) );
    WORD(I,D) := LENGTH;

    IF ( WITHV AND ( LENGTH > 0. )  ) THEN
        A{I}:= A {I} /LENGTH;
    END;
```

```
    END;    % END SUBROUTINE SVD

%***************************************************************


    %
    %          SET UP MATRIX A
    %
    M := 64;
    N := 64;
    WITHU := TRUE;
    WITHV := TRUE;

    FILL A WITH      (0.)4096;

    A{PEN}  := 1.;

    LOOP K :=0, 1, M-2 DO
        LOOP L := K=1, 1, M-1 DO
            WORD( L, A{K} ) := -1.;

    %
    %          IT IS NECESSARY TO OPEN DISPLAY
    %          BEFORE SETTING CLOCK
    %
    OPNDISP OUT;

    %
    %          SET CLOCK
    %
    CODE
    USE CMPLWD;
    BEGIN
    SET CLOCK O,CMPLWD;
    PAUSE CMPLWD;
    HALT;
    END CODE;

    %
    %          CALL SUBROUTINE SVD
    %
    SVD( M, N, D, WITHU, WITHV );

    %
    %          READ CLOCK
    %
    CODE
    USE CMPLWD;
    BEGIN
    READCLOCK CMPLWD;
    PAUSE CMPLWD;
    HALT;
    END CODE;
```

```
%
%         PRINT RESULTS
%
CODE
USE CMPLWD,ITER,INPROD,D,U,A;
BEGIN
DISPLO "TIME",16,CMPLWD, CMPLWD;
DISPLO "ITER",16,ITER,ITER;
DISPLO "INPROD",16,INPROD,INPROD;
DISPLE "UT",16,U,U+4095;
DISPLF "VT",16,A,A+4095;
CLSDISP OUT;
END CODE;
END.

BEGIN
SET DBUGA

CINT M,N,S,NRANK,CMPLWD,K,L;
CREAL CUTOFF;
PREAL VECTOR A{63}, B{63}; X{63};

ILLIACDISPLAY;
AREA OUT;


%************************************************************

SUBROUTINE MINFIT( CINT M, CINT N, CINT S, CINT OUT NRANK,
                   CREAL CUTOFF );
BEGIN
%
%
%         ##################################################
%
%         PROGRAMMER :    FRANKLIN LUK
%                         VISITING APPOINTMENT PROGRAM
%                         INSTITUTE FOR ADVANCED COMPUTATION
%
%         DATE :          AUGUST 1977
%
%         ################################################## ,
%
%
%         THIS SUBROUTINE USES THE SINGULAR VALUE DECOMPOSI-
%         TION TO COMPUTE THE LEAST SQUARES SOLUTION TO THE
%         FOLLOWING S SYSTEMS OF M LINEAR EQUATIONS IN
%         N UNKNOWNS :
%
%              A X = B ,
%
%         WHERE A IS AN M-BY-N DESIGN MATRIX,
%               X IS AN N-BY-S SOLUTION MATRIX,
```

```
%           AND   B IS AN M-BY-S DATA MATRIX.
%
%
%           INPUT PARAMETERS :
%
%               M, N :      CU INTEGERS. THE ROW AND COLUMN
%                   DIMENSIONS OF THE DESIGN MATRIX A; IT IS
%                   ASSUMED THAT N  <= M <= 64 .
%
%               S :             CU INTEGER. THE NUMBER OF DATA
%                   VECTORS; IT IS ASSUMED THAT S <= 64 .
%
%               NRANK :    CU INTEGER.
%
%               CUTOFF :   CU REAL. A SINGULAR VALUE IS SET
%                   TO ZERO IF ITS COMPUTED VALUE IS LESS
%                   THAN CUTOFF; HENCE CUTOFF SHOULD BE GIVEN
%                   A VERY SMALL VALUE, E.G.  1.@-8 .
%               A :             PE REAL VECTOR.  THE DESIGN
%                   MATRIX WHOSE ROWS LIE ACROSS THE PE'S.
%
%               B :        PE REAL VECTOR. A MATRIX CONSISTING
%                   OF THE DATA VECTORS; THE I-TH DATA VECTOR
%                   LIES IN THE (I-1)-TH PE, FOR 1 <= I <= S.
%
%
%           OUTPUT PARAMETERS :
%
%               NRANK :     CU INTEGER. THE NUMBER OF SINGULAR
%                   VALUES OF A THAT ARE GREATER THAN CUTOFF.
%
%               X :             PE REAL VECTOR.  A MATRIX CONSISTING
%                   OF THE SOLUTION VECTORS; THE VECTORS LIE
%                   ACROSS THE PE'S SO THAT X{I-1} IS THE I-TH
%                   SOLUTION VECTOR, FOR  1 <= I <= P .
%
%
%       NOTE :
%           1. GLYPNIR DOES NOT ACCEPT VECTOR PARAMETERS;
%           HENCE A, B AND X ARE GLOBAL TO THE SUBROUTINE.
%
%           2. THE PE VECTORS B AND X ARE LAID OUT IN
%           SUCH A WAY THAT HIGH EXECUTION EFFICIENCY CAN
%           BE ACHIEVED.
%
%           3. BOTH INPUT DESIGN AND DATA MATRICES ARE
%           DESTROYED.
%

CINT IORTHG, COUNT, I, J;
CREAL P,Q,R,COSPHI,SINPHI,TOL,EPS,AIAI,AIAJ,AJAJ,LENGTH,S1,S2;
PREAL Y, T;

%
```

```
%          INITIALIZE CONTROL VARIABLES
%
IORTHG := (M*(M-1)) DIV 2;
TOL := 1.@-24;
EPS := 1.@-32;
COUNT := 0;


%
%          ITERATE UNTIL THE ROWS OF A FORM AN ORTHOGONAL
%          SET
%
WHILE ( COUNT < IORTHG ) DO
    BEGIN  % BEGIN WHILE LOOP

    COUNT := 0;

    %
    %   ORTHOGONALIZE ROW I AGAINST ROW J, FOR I < J.
    %
    LOOP I := 0, 1, M-2 DO
        BEGIN    % BEGIN LOOP I
    LOOP J : = I+1, 1, M-1 DO
        BEGIN    % BEGIN LOOP J

        AJAJ := ROWSUM( A{J}*A{J} );

        IF ( AJAJ  < EPS  ) THEN
            BEGIN
            %
            %          SET ROW J TO ZERO IF ITS EUCLIDEAN
            %          LENGTH SQUARED IS LESS THAN EPS
            %
            A{J} := 0.;
            COUNT := COUNT + 1;
            END
        ELSE
            BEGIN         % BEGIN ELSE BLOCK

            AIAI := ROWSUM( A{I}*A{I}  );

            IF ( AIAI < EPS  ) THEN
                BEGIN
                %
                %   SET ROW I TO ZERO IF ITS EUCLIDEAN
                %   LENGTH SQUARED IS LESS THAN EPS;
                %   INTERCHANGE ROWS I AND J.
                %
                A{I} := A{J};
                A{J} := 0.;
                B{I} := B{J};
                B{J} ;= 0.;

                END
```

```
ELSE
    BEGIN

    %
    %   BOTH ROWS I AND J ARE NONTRIVIAL
    %   VECTORS
    %
    AIAJ := ROWSUM( A{I}*A{J});

    IF ( (AIAJ*AIAJ)/(AIAI*AJAJ) < TOL )
    THEN
        %
        %       ROWS I AND J ARE ALREADY
        %       ORTHOGONAL
        %
        BEGIN
        COUNT := COUNT +1;

        IF ( AIAI < AJAJ ) THEN
            %
            %   PUT THE LONGER VECTOR
            %   IN ROW I OF A
            %
            BEGIN
            Y    := A{I};
            A{I} ;= A{J};
            Y    := B{I};
            B{I} := B{J};
            B{J}.:= Y;
            END;

        END
    ELSE
        BEGIN

        %
        %       ORTHOGONALIZE ROW I
        %       AGAINST ROW J
        %
        P := AIAJ + AIAJ;
        Q := AIAI - AJAJ;
        R := SQRT( P*P + Q*Q );

        %
        %       CHOOSE THE APPROPRIATE
        %       FORMULA FOR COMPUTING
        %       COSPHI AND SINPHI TO PRE-
        %       SERVE NUMERICAL STABILITY
        %
        IF  (Q>0.) THEN
            BEGIN
            COSPHI := SQRT( (R+Q)/(R+R) );
            SINPHI := P/(2.*R*COSPHI);
            END
```

```
                        ELSE
                            BEGIN
                            SINPHI := SQRT( (R-Q)/(R+R) );
                            COSPHI := P/(2.*R*SINPHI);
                            END;


                %
                %
                %            ORTHOGONALIZE THE I-TH AND
                %            J-TH ROWS OF A WITH RESPECT
                %            TO EACH OTHER, AND ORDER
                %            THEM SO THAT THE I-TH ROW
                %            HAS A GREATER EUCLIDEAN
                %            LENGTH.
                %
                Y    := A{I}*COSPHI + A{J}*SINPHI;
                A{J} :=-A|I}*SINPHI + A|J}*COSPHI;
                A{I} := Y;


                %
                %            MODIFY THE DATA VECTORS
                %            ACCORDINGLY
                %
                Y    := B{I}*COSPHI + B{J}*SINPHI;
                B{J} :=-B{I}*SINPHI + B{J}*COSPHI;
                B{I} := Y;

                END;

            END;

        END;    % END ELSE BLOCK

        END;    % END LOOP J

    END:    % END LOOP I

  END:    % END WHILE LOOP
%
%     1.  COMPUTE THE EUCLIDEAN LENGTHS OF THE ROWS OF
%     OF A; THEY GIVE THE SINGULAR VALUES OF A.  THE
%     NORMALIZED ROWS BECOME THE ROWS OF V'.
%
%     2.  SOLVE D Y = B IN THE LEAST SQUARES SENSE,
%     WHERE D IS THE DIAGONAL MATRIX CONSISTING OF THE
%     SINGULAR VALUES OF A, AND Y IS STORED IN B.
%
NRANK := 0;
LENGTH := SQRT( ROWSUM({A}O *{O} ) );

WHILE ( ( LENGTH < CUTOFF ) AND ( NRANK < N ) ) DO
    BEGIN
    A{NRANK} := A{NRANK}/LENGTH;
    B{NRANK} := B{NRANK}/LENGTH;
    NRANK := NRANK + 1;
```

```
            IF ( NRANK < N ) THEN
                LENGTH := SQRT( ROWSUM( A{NRANK}*A{NRANK} ) );

            END;


    %
    %         COMPUTE X = V Y
    %
    LOOP I := 0, 1, S-1 DO
        BEGIN
        X{I}:= 0.;

        %
        %   X{I} IS A LINEAR COMBINATION OF THE ROWS OF V' .
        %
        LOOP J := 0, 1, NRANK-1 DO
            X{I}:= X{I} + WORD(I,B {J}*A{J};

        END;

    END;    % END SUBROUTINE MINFIT

%**************************************************************


    %
    %    SET UP MATRIX A
    %
    M := 64;
    N := 64;
    S := 64;
    CUTOFF := 1.@-8;

    FILL A WITH      (0.)4096;
    A{PEN} := 1.;

    LOOP K := 0, 1, M-2 DO
        LOOP L := K+1, 1, M-1 DO
            WORD( L, A{K} ) := -1.;

    %
    %         SET UP DATA VECTORS B
    %
    FILL B WITH      (0.)4096;

    B PEN := 1.;

    %
    %         IT IS NECESSARY TO OPEN DISPLAY
    %         BEFORE SETTING CLOCK
    %
    OPNDISP OUT;
    %
```

```
%        SET CLOCK
%
CODE
USE CMPLWD;
BEGIN
SETCLOCK 0, CMPLWD;
PAUSE CMPLWD;
HALT;
END CODE;

%
%        CALL SUBROUTINE MINFIT
%
MINFIT( M, N, S, NRANK, CUTOFF );

%
%        READ CLOCK
%
CODE
USE CMPLWD;
BEGIN
READCLOCK CMPLWD;
PAUSE CMPLWD;
HALT;
END CODE;

%
%        PRINT RESULTS
%
CODE
USE CMPLWD,NRANK,X;
BEGIN
DISPLO "TIME",16,CMPLWD,CMPLWD;
DISPLO "RANK",16,NRANK,NRANK;
DISPLF "X",16,X,X+4095;
CLSDISP OUT;
END CODE;
END.
```

ORGANIZATIONAL AND NOTATIONAL DETAILS

SUBROUTINE SVD

(1) This algorithm accesses and modifies the matrix A by rows and
     the matrix U by columns. Hence lay out A such that its rows
     lie across PEs, and U such that its columns lie across PEs.
     Note that skewed storage is not required.

(2) The assumption that n ≤ m is no restriction. One can always
     compute the singular value decomposition of the transpose.
     A change in the code will drop the constraint: replace n by
     min(m,n) in the block where it computes the matrices Σ and V.

(3) One can handle a matrix with less than 64 columns by disabling
     the last (64-n) PEs whenever a row inner product is computed.
     One can view the given matrix as an m x 64 array whose last
     (64-n) columns are zeros. Take the second approach in this
     program.

(4) One can handle a matrix with more than 64 columns in the follow-
     ing way. Divide the rows of the given matrix into segments
     each of width 64. One can thereby represent the given matrix
     A by

     k PE real vectors A1,A2,...,Ak, each of length m, where

$$k = \{\frac{n}{64}\} \ ,$$

     i.e., k equals the smallest integer greater than $\frac{n}{64}$.

     There is a need to modify the code accordingly. Observe that it
     works with the rows of A to compute (a) their lengths, (b) their
     inner products, and (c) the new rows after a rotation. To
     compute the norm squared of a row of A, say the (i+1)-th row,
     in the new representation, call

          ROWSUM(A1[i]*A1[i] + A2[i]*A2[i]

          + ...+ Ak[i]*Ak[i])

     The extension if similar in computing the inner product of two
     rows. One may handle (c) by computing the segments of the new
     rows one at a time, for example, instead of

          A[j] := -A[i]*sinphi + A[j]*cosphi,

write the following k lines of code:

```
Al[j] := -Al[i]*sinphi + Al[j]*cosphi
A2[j] := -A2[i]*sinphi + A2[j]*cosphi
  .
  .
  .
Ak[j] := -Ak[i]*sinphi + Ak[j]*cosphi
```

Similarly, divide the columns of U into segments and represent U using k PE real vectors. The modification to codes involving U is also in the same way.

(5)   The subroutine presets the values of the parameters tol and eps at 10^{-24} and 10^{-32} , respectively. Experiments indicate that the computed solution is then accurate to 12 decimal digits (see Section 6), about the most that one can ask for from a 14-decimal digit machine. The user can increase those preset values to trade accuracy for speed.

SUBROUTINE MINFIT

Since MINFIT is derived from SVD, the appropriate comments in Section 5.1 apply here as well.

One may choose to lay out the data and solution matrices in the "natural" way, which is also the way for efficient computation. Lay out the data matrix B so that its rows lie across PEs, just as the rows of the regression matrix A do; and lay out the solution matrix X so that its columns lie across PEs, to facilitate output.

DISCUSSION OF NUMERICAL PROPERTIES

Wilkinson (1965) (18) gave an error analysis of the action of plane rotations on a matrix. His error bound was improved by Gentleman in 1975 (3). We apply their results to examine the effects of the rotations in one sweep of our algorithm.

Let $M = 1/2\, m(m-1)$ and let R_j , $1 \leq j \leq M$, represent the j-th rotation. We can show that the computed matrix $\bar{A}_M$ after a sweep satisfies the inequality

$$\| \bar{A}_M - R_M R_{M-1} \cdots R_1 A \|_F \leq 2^{-48}(m+n-2)$$

$$(1+2^{-48})^{m+n-2} \| A \|_F ,$$

where

$$\| \cdot \|_F \quad \text{is the Frobenius matrix norm,}$$

i.e.,

$$\| B \|_F^2 = \sum_{ij} b_{ij}^2 \quad \text{for } B = (b_{ij}).$$

The right-hand side of the inequality is an extreme upper bound. The statistical distribution of the rounding errors reduce the error to well below the level of the bound; for this reason alone, a factor of the order of $(m + n -2)^{\frac{1}{2}}$ in place of $m + n -2)$ might be more realistic. This shows that the algorithm is extremely stable.

Since the matrix U is formed as a product of plane rotations, one is also interested in the deviation from orthogonality of such a product. Let $\overline{P}_M$ represent the computed product of the rotations in a sweep. One has the inequality

$$\| \overline{P}_M - R_M R_{M-1} \cdots R_1 \|_F \leq 2^{-48} m^{\frac{1}{2}}$$

$$(m+n-2) \ (1+2^{-48})^{m+n-2}$$

Again statistical consideration indicates that a factor of the order of $m^{\frac{1}{4}}$ $(m+n-2)^{\frac{1}{2}}$ instead of $m^{\frac{1}{2}}$ (m_n-2) is probably more realistic.

The value of the parameter tol controls the accuracy of the solution. After the Jacobi process has converged,

$$\| V_\nu^t V_\nu - I_\nu \|_F \leq (\nu \cdot tol)^{\frac{1}{2}}.$$

The previous paragraph showed that U will deviate very slightly from orthogonality. Indeed experiments show that the accuracy of the singular values and vectors is of the order of $(tol)^{\frac{1}{2}}$.

TEST RESULTS

Tests were carried out on the Illiac IV computer and on an IBM 370/168 computer at the Standord Linear Accelerator Center. In the following, tol = 10^{-24}, eps = 10^{-32} and cutoff = 10^{-8}.

First Example:

$$
A = \begin{bmatrix}
22 & 10 & 2 & 3 & 7 \\
14 & 7 & 10 & 0 & 8 \\
-1 & 13 & -1 & -11 & 3 \\
-3 & -2 & 13 & -2 & 4 \\
9 & 8 & 1 & -2 & 4 \\
9 & 1 & -7 & 5 & -1 \\
2 & -6 & 6 & 5 & 1 \\
4 & 5 & 0 & -2 & 2
\end{bmatrix}, B = \begin{bmatrix}
-1 & 1 & 0 \\
2 & -1 & 1 \\
1 & 10 & 11 \\
4 & 0 & 4 \\
0 & -6 & -6 \\
-3 & 6 & 3 \\
1 & 11 & 12 \\
0 & -5 & -5
\end{bmatrix}.
$$

The singular values of A are $\sqrt{1248}$, 20, $\sqrt{384}$, 0, 0. The subroutine SVD computed those values to machine precision. The
minimal length solution to the overdetermined system is

$$
X = \begin{bmatrix}
-\dfrac{1}{12} & 0 & -\dfrac{1}{12} \\[2mm]
0 & 0 & 0 \\[2mm]
\dfrac{1}{4} & 0 & \dfrac{1}{4} \\[2mm]
-\dfrac{1}{12} & 0 & -\dfrac{1}{12} \\[2mm]
\dfrac{1}{12} & 0 & \dfrac{1}{12}
\end{bmatrix}
$$

The computed solution from the subroutine MINFIT is accurate to
all 14 significant digits.

Second Example:

$$A = \begin{bmatrix} 1 & -1 & -1 & -1 & -1 & \cdots \\ & 1 & -1 & -1 & -1 & \cdots \\ & & 1 & -1 & -1 & \cdots \\ & 0 & & 1 & -1 & \cdots \\ & & & & 1 & \cdots \\ & & & & & \cdots \end{bmatrix}_{n \times n}$$

The matrix is ill-conditioned with respect to inversion because it has a very small singular value, as can be seen by applying the matrix to the column vector

$$(1, 2^{-1}, 2^{-2}, \ldots, 2^{-n+2}, 2^{-n+2})^t.$$

The matrix becomes singular if one adds -2^{-n+2} to its $(n,1)$ position.

The subroutine SVD was applied to this matrix for different values of n. For comparison purpose, the subroutine SVA in the EISPACK eigenvalue package from the Argonne National Laboratory was chosen (2). The EISPACK subroutine implements Golub's method and has been coded for high execution efficiency. Similar tests with the Argonne routine on an IBM 370/168 computer at the Stanford Linear Accelerator Center were run using the FORTRAN H (opt=2) compiler.

The following table gives the execution time in seconds on the two machines.

n	ILLIAC IV		IBM 370/168	ILLIAC Time/
	iter	time	time	IBM Time
16	7	0.26	0.101	2.57
32	8	1.25	0.57	2.19
48	8	2.89	1.76	1.64
64	9	5.57	4.03	1.38
96	10	15.94	12.81	1.24
128	9	26.81	29.68	0.90

Note that the Illiac routine becomes more efficient compared with the Argonne routine as more of the Illiac parallel computing ability can be exploited. The latter is an $O(n^3)$ process, while the machine time of the former is proportional to (iter $x\{\frac{n}{64}\}$ x n^2); this shows therefore, the potential of parallel computers with a large number of processing elements. Unfortunately, the GLYPNIR compiler does not produce very efficient code. Another program in CFD implementing this method ran on the same matrix with n=64. The execution time was 3.31 seconds, about 59% of the execution time of the GLYPNIR code.

MINFIT was applied to the following linear equation

$$AX = I$$

with n=64. The execution time was 5.29 seconds. This example serves to indicate how MINFIT can be an effective linear equations solver. The exact solution to

$$A x_{\sim n} = e_{\sim n} \, ,$$

where $\quad e_{\sim n} = (0,0,\ldots,0,1)^t \, ,$

is $\quad x_{\sim n} = (2^{n-2}, 2^{n-3}, \ldots, 2, 1, 1)^t \, .$

A Gaussian elimination method with row pivoting will give the above solution since the matrix is already upper triangular. But such solution is likely to be unacceptable because $2^{n-2} > 10^{18}$ for n=64. The computed result from MINFIT is approximately

$$(-2^{-n-2}, -2^{-n-1}, \ldots, -2^{-3}, 2^{-2})^t \, .$$

It may be argued that the residual is not close to zero. But if y is the vector obtainable from x_n by rounding the latter to 14 decimal digits, then the residual produced by $\tilde{y}$ will be of the order of 10^4.

ACKNOWLEDGEMENTS

The author acknowledges the generous support of the Institute for Advanced Computation. He is grateful to D. Stevenson and H. Brown for their invaluable help in programming the ILLIAC IV.

References

1. B. A. Chartres, Adaptation of the Jacobi method for a computer with magnetic-tape backing store. Computer J. 5 (1962), 51-60.

2. B. S. Garbow, J. M. Boyle, J. J. Dongarra, and C. B. Moler, Matrix Eigensystem Routines - EISPACK Guide Extension. Springer-Verlag, Berlin (1977).

3. W. M. Gentleman, Error analysis of QR decompositions by Givens transformations. Lin. Alg. Applics. 10 (1975), 189-197.

4. G. Golub and W. Kahan, Calculating the singular values and pseudoinverse of a matrix. J. SIAM Numer. Anal., Ser. B 2 (1965), 205-224.

5. G. Golub and F. Luk, Singular value decomposition: applications and computations. ARO Report 77-1, Transactions of the 22-nd Conference of Army Mathematicians (1977), 577-605.

6. G. Golub and C. Reinsch, Singular value decomposition and least squares solutions. Numer. Math. 14 (1970), 403-420.

7. D. Heller, A survey of parallel algorithms in numerical linear algebra. Technical Report, Dept. of Computer Science, Carnegie-Mellon University (February 1976).

8. P. Henrici, On the speed of convergence of cyclic and quasicyclic Jacobi methods for computing eigenvalues of Hermitian matrices, J. Soc. Indust. Appl. Math. 6 (1958), 144-162.

9. M. R. Hestenes, Inversion of matrices by biorthogonalization and related results. J. Soc. Indus. Apl. Math. 6 (1958), 51-90.

10. C. Lanczos, Linear Differential Operators, Van Nostrand, London (1961).

11. D. H. Lawrie, T. Layman, D. Baer, and J. M. Randal, GLYPNIR - a programming language for ILLIAC IV. Comm ACM 18 (1975), 157-164.

12. J. C. Nash, A one-sided transformation method for the singular value decomposition and algebraic eigenproblem. Computer J. 18 (1975), 74-76

13. H. Rutishauser, The Jacobi method for real symmetric matrices. Numer. Math. 9 (1966), 1-10.

14. A. H. Sameh and D. J. Kuck, A parallel QR algorithm for tridiagonal symmetric matrices. Technical Report, Dept. of Computer Science, University of Illinois, Urbana (July 1974).

15. A. Schoenhage, Zur Konvergenz des Jacobi-Verfahrens. Numer. Math. 3 (1961), 374-380.

16. K. G. Stevens, Jr., CFD - a FORTRAN-like language for the ILLIAC IV. ACM Sigplan Notices 10 (1975), 72-76.

17. J. H. Wilkinson, Note on the quadratic convergence of the cyclic Jacobi process. Numer. Math. 4 (1962), 296-300.

18. J. H. Wilkinson, The Algebraic Eigenvalue Problem. Clarendon, Oxford (1965).

19. J. H. Wilkinson and C. Reinsch, Linear Algebra. Springer Verlag, New York (1971).

2. Exploitation of Parallelism in Number Theoretic and Combinatorial Computation

The concept of doing tasks in parallel in order to multiply one's output has always been an intriguing idea. As applied to computing, this notion has been less than completely successful. I hope to indicate how some comparatively straightforward serial problems in Number Theory and Combinatorics can take advantage of parallelism in a computer.

The history of parallelism in computing is a rather spotty one. The earliest reference, that I know, to many computers working on the same job goes back to the French Revolution. A large group of computers working together under the direction of Legendre produced the Tables du Cadastre, high precision tables of the elementary functions. These were never published. In the mid-19th century a proposal was made in England to put vast numbers of school children to work subtabulating highly accurate logarithm tables to produce in a few weeks a large easily usable table to seven or eight decimals. The proposal was never carried out. The W.P.A. Tables Project of the great depression certainly accomplished wonderful parallel work.

As regards to parallelism in machines, one can say that Babbages Difference Engine had the rudiments of what is now called "pipelining". From their very beginning desk calculators have used a parallel adding mechanism. Hollerith's original punched card machines employed much parallelism.

The mechanical sieves that I built from 1927-1936 were highly parallel devices. As we shall discuss this problem later, it is perhaps not out of place here to indicate at this time the difference between such a device and the old hand serial method of sifting. The problem is to find the least positive integer not belonging to a given set of arithmetical progressions. In the serial procedure one began by purchasing a good supply of paper ruled in small squares. Each square by virtue of its row, column and page numbers represents a unique positive integer. Next, one has to guess a reasonable upper bound for the answer and thereby select the appropriate number of pages to use. In step three one makes a number of strips of paper of different lengths and marks their edges in accordance with the given arithmetic progressions. Each strip in turn is now moved carefully down the columns of each page. Crossing out square cells as

This section is based on an article in the IAC Newsletter by D.H. Lehmer, April, 1978.

indicated by the markings on the strip, one finally reduces the number of surviving cells to a sufficiently small set that can be examined individually for a minimum answer.

In contrast, with the mechanical sieve all the "strips" are applied simultaneously. We soon find the least survivor without having to guess in advance how large it is, and we don't waste time ruling out all the larger numbers. Small wonder hand sifting, or "criblage" as the French used to call it, is a lost art.

The first electronic computer, the ENIAC was a parallel machine in many ways. It had 20 arithmetic units with a paternal overall supervisor. Its organization resided in the network of interconnections, with interlocks, demanded by the problem to be solved. In contrast, its predecessor the Harvard Mark I was tape driven and therefore serial in operation. The ENIAC was designed for systems of five ordinary differential equations. The Harvard Mark I or "Bessel Engine" could (and did) make tables of $J_n(x)$.

It was soon suggested by von Neumann that since electronic computing was so very fast, as compared with relay computing, it was silly to try for parallel operations. "What's the hurry?" Following this suggestion the ENIAC was crippled to save set-up time. Only one arithmetic unit was used as such. The others were made into one-word registers. From the same idea emerged the Edvac type machine which was even more serial. Even the adder was serial, the digits of the sum being produced one after the other, somewhat like a zipper.

Even before the Edvac became operative, parallelism began to creep back into the hardware in the form of parallel adders, parallel data transmission and parallel memory access as in the SWAC. There was a hurry, after all.

This next period (1960-67) in the history of machine development saw big increases in speed due to solid state circuitry. These increases tended to delay the advance of parallelism. Any criticism of the architecture of a machine was answered by increasing the speed by a factor of 10. Still they were all "one bottleneck" machines.

During this era three principles were discovered by the designers that we shall refer to.

Principle 1   Time can be saved by using more space. Space can be saved by using more time.

Principle 2   Circuits should not be allowed to stand idle.

Principle 3   Versatility can be achieved at almost no cost by modifying the flow of information.

During this period the development of software systems and languages began to control the computing styles of the users. This held back parallelism also. More emphasis was put on recursive procedures, as in Algol. Those of us who are in Number Theory and Combinatorics will not have failed to notice how the quest for speed has damaged the integrity of the arithmetic unit by the introduction of floating point arithmetic. For some years

now it has been difficult, if not impossible, to obtain the exact
product or the remainder on division, on some machines.

One can almost hear the design engineer asking the rhetori-
cal question: "Who needs it?" The answer is, of course, "We
do!" By parallelism in computing we can mean any instance of
two or more numerical activities taking place at the same time.
For example in the ENIAC the square rooter was supplied with an
interlock circuit so that once a square root was called for, the
rest of the program could go ahead to the point where the square
root was actually needed. If the square root was ready, it meant
that the square rooter had been waiting for the rest of the program. If not, the rest of the machine sat down to wait for its
square root.

The modern version of this kind of parallelism is called
"pipelining" and it often serves to increase the speed of certain operations by a factor of 3-5. This is achieved by segmentation of the operation. Each serial segment performs a certain
suboperation on the incoming data. Without pipelining, only one
segment would be active during a given nanosecond. With optimal
timing of input, every segment will be active each with a different input. This is an instance of Principle 2.

Thus for floating point addition there might be four segments

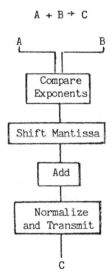

$$A + B \rightarrow C$$

If we had a large number of additions to make, as in vector addition, we could pipeline the job by sending in two streams of components via A and B. At any nanosecond all four boxes would be active each doing "its thing" with a different addition problem. We would get at C one result every minor cycle even though one addition itself takes 4 cycles. If addition took 6 cycles the saving would be still greater. It is fair to say that this is parallelism since several additions are going on simultaneously.

In the CDC STAR 100 for example, with its 40 nanosecond minor cycle, 25 million 32 bit floating point sums can be formed in one second. By using 128 bit words of 4 vectors each, the star claims 100 million additions per second. What can we say about this breath-taking performance?

Three things:

1. If we had fixed point addition only one of these boxes would be needed so the parallelism disappears.

2. The stress on the programmer to keep such a stream of instructions going would appear to be great. Of course this problem is as old as the ENIAC. It is solved by the special STAR vector software.

3. Who needs it?

A more recent machine the CRAY-1 also uses pipelining and vector features are supplied as hardware. In this case 6 additions occur simultaneously. Oh yes, the speed has gone up. A minor cycle for the CRAY is only 12.5 nanoseconds. Both machines give exact results in their address arithmatic registers only and so are not always suitable for our purposes. The one machine that takes parallelism seriously is the Illiac IV(=I4) designed at the University of Illinois, Urbana and operated by NASA, Moffett Field, California (node 15 on the ARPA network). It is an ensemble of 64 identical computers supervised by a central control unit that issues the instructions. Originally it was planned to have 256 processing elements, not 64. Accounts of the I4 always say that all 64 processing elements (= PE's) are executing the same instruction at any particular nanosecond. Fortunately for the usefulness of the I4 this is false. What is true is that some of the PE's are carrying out the same operation while the others are standing idle. This is an instance of Principle 3 despite Principle 2. We shall see the utility of this versatility. I plan to discuss the exploitation of the powerful parallelism of the I4 in the programming of four different problems. Enough information on the architecture of the I4 will be given to render intelligible what I have to say.

Even what little I have said already makes it evident that the I4 can be operated like 64 Harvard Bessel Engines calculating 64 values of a function $J_n(x)$ for 64 values of x provided

the same algorithm is applicable to all 64 cases. We consider
such a use of the I4 as laudable but verging on the trivial.
This consideration applies in particular to all vector operations with 64 or fewer components.

    We turn, instead, to a familiar but relatively simple prob-
lem made famous by the Illiac IV, namely the discovery of
Mersennes Primes, 2^P-1. Most of you will recall the test that
one uses here. For a given Mersenne number 2^P-1 one forms the
sequence $\{S_n\}$ defined recursively by

$$S_{n+1} \equiv S_n^2 - 2 \quad (\text{mod } 2^P-1)$$

with $S_1 = 4$, $S_2 = 14$, $S_3 = 194,\ldots$.

Then 2^P-1 is a prime $\leftrightarrow S_{p-1} = 0$.

    For p > 20000, where we must start since Tuckerman's last
search with the IBM 360, the great cost of such a program is the
scarcity of such primes. Only 24 are known. How, you ask, can
we parallel the calculation of S_n? The answer is simple. We
can test 64 candidates at once. This is how it's done. One
chooses a set of 64 primes

$$20000 < P_0 < P_1 < \cdots < P_{63}$$

that are good candidates in the sense that $2^{P_i}-1$ is not already
divisible by a known small prime of the form $q = P_j\, x + 1$.

    We set

$$\Delta_i = P_{i+1} - P_i \quad (i=0(1)62).$$

Loading this redundant input data we begin by assigning the test
of $2^{P_i}-1$ to the i-th processing element, PE(i), (i = 0(1)63).
We then compute S_n in parallel for n = 1(1)P_0-1. At this point,
we "disable" PE(0). We now proceed with Δ_0 more steps of the
S sequence and then disable PE(1) etc., until $S_{p_{63}-1}$ is found
mod $2^{p63}-1$. We now "reenable" all PE's and ask of all PE's, in

one instruction, whether its S is zero. If any PE answers "yes"
it does so by raising a flag bit of 1 in an otherwise 0 bit
register. In the next instruction the control unit gathers the
64 votes into a single word and asks itself if this word is zero.
If so, we have just found 64 cases of composite Mersenne numbers.
If not, there is a mad scramble to find the position of the 1
bit (or bits) which will identify the p_i for which $2^{p_i}-1$ is the
largest known prime. Needless to say, this part of the program
need not be very elegant since it is almost never used. Since
Δ_i is small compared with p_i the first part of the program, i.e.,
getting up to S_p0 is the major effort. Hence it is fair to say
that this is an application of parallelism. A much more elaborate
procedure could attempt to keep all 64 PEs alive throughout the
calculation in accordance with principle number 2 rather than
number 3. This would save less than 2% of the effort however.
In any case, the I4 would handle tests of Mersenne numbers at
the rate of about 1 per minute. This program has not been
written. There has been coded a somewhat similar program that
searches for primes p for which

$$2^p \equiv 2 \pmod{p^2} \quad (p > 2.10^9).$$

The same technique of handling 64 values of p at once
through their differences is used. Of course, in this case the
cycle length is not $O(p^3)$ but rather $O(\log p)$ so there is no
time to prepare an input list of primes. Each new p is obtained
by

$$p + 240 \rightarrow p$$

since $\phi(240)=64.$, a procedure which is simple if not optimal.
Needless to say, many composite p's are processed uselessly.
Speaking of primes in arithmetic progressions brings me to
a fairly elaborate program for searching for small factors
$(< 2^{48})$ of a large multiprecise integer N. Every computer center
has its own version of this useful program (perhaps without the
multiprecise feature). The one run on the I4 examines N for 64

different trial divisors at once. The program has another feature. It often happens that we know in advance that for some a and b all the prime factors of N are of the form ax + b (x=0,1,111). In a prelude to the main routine the I4 sets up an optimum set of 64 arithmetic progressions, one for each of the 64 PEs to use as a source of possible divisors of N. This prelude is also done in parallel as explained later.

In a typical problem of triple precision (n had $\leq$ 48 decimal digits) 1178048 trial divisors are performed and remainders examined every second. A still more elaborate use of parallelism, more combinational than number theoretic, has to do with solving the general diophantine equation in two integer variables $f(x,y) = 0$ by Gauss' method of exclusion. Here f is a polynomial with integer coefficients and we seek solutions (x,y) in integers ≥ 0. If we can find the x then the y can be easily found. For $f(x,y)$ to vanish it is necessary that

$$f(x,y) \equiv 0 \quad (\text{mod } E)$$

where E is any integer > 1. We ask: For which of the E values of x(mod E) is it true that there exists a y such that the above congruence holds? This question is easily answered in less than E^2 steps simply by evaluation $f(u,v)$ for $u,v = 0(1)E - 1$. Let the answers be

$$x \quad x_1, x_2, \ldots, x_{n(E)} \quad (\text{mod } E).$$

If this set σ is empty we are through because the original equation $f(x,y) = 0$ is then impossible. We can represent σ by a characteristic binary word whose k-th bit is 0 or 1 according as k belongs to σ or not. We think of this word as infinite, its bits being periodic of period E.

Since E is arbitrary we can take a large number of them, say 64, and get the I4 to construct 64 different periodic patterns of 0's and 1's corresponding to 64 different sets σ. If indeed $f(x,y)=0$ has a solution (x_0,y_0), when we come to examine the x_0-th binary bit in each of 64 infinite words it will be a 0.

Conversely if the k-th binary digit is 0 in all 64 cases, k is a likely candidate for x in f(x,y) = 0.

It is now clear what must be done. We must OR together these 64 infinite words and search the result for 0 bits. The I4 has a marvelous instruction

LDC(N) $A

which causes the contents of all 64 A registers of the PEs to be ORed into the n-th register of the control unit. This register can now ask whether its contents consist of all 1's (which is usually the case) and according transfer control to an appropriate part of the program. Thus 64^2 = 4096 bits are examined in two instructions. This is parallelism in two dimensions.

Besides these two instructions the rest of the program is in three parts.

1) Choice of the Es

2) Generation of the bit patterns

3) Shifting and maintenance of pattern words.

As to 1, we need to OR a full word of bits so we must take E ≥ 64. One standard choice is the set of the first 64 primes or their powers or small multiples. It starts with 64, 81, 100, 98, 121, 65, 68, 76, 69, 87,..., 293, 307, 311.

We have already indicated how to program part 2. I leave it to your ingenuity as a "bit pusher" to design part 3 using address arithmetic and a special long shift of 128 bits depending on E_i (mod 64). Of course, "it is best that it be done quickly," as this is the main loop. With speeds of up to 15 million values of x per second this program competes strongly with my best sieve which is capable of 20,000,000/sec.

The use of as many as 64 moduli E_i is for most equations f(x,y) = 0 a considerable overkill. Forty moduli is usually enough. However, no time is saved by the use of fewer than 64. There are polynomial's f where 64 are needed.

One place where parallelism plays an important role is in so called modular arithmetic system for dealing easily with large integers. In this system the integer N is represented by the vector of small integers

$$N \sim \{n_0, n_1, \ldots, n_{63}\} = \{n_i\} \begin{smallmatrix} 63 \\ 0 \end{smallmatrix}$$

where

$$N \equiv n_i \quad (\text{mod } m_i)$$

(small letters stand for one word integers $< 2^{48}$. This representation of N is unique for

$$|N| < \frac{1}{2} \text{ LCM } (m_0, m_1, \ldots, m_{63}).$$

In this system, addition, subtraction and multiplication can each be executed in a single step

$$A \oplus B \sim [a_i \oplus b_i]_0^{63}$$

where $\oplus$ stands for $+$, $-$ or $.$ and the quantities inside $\{\}$ are understood to be reduced mod m_i. The operations are of course done in parallel. Comparing this system with the ordinary multiprecision package one sees that, whereas in the latter case costs increase as log N and (log N)2 respectively for addition and multiplication, in the former case there is no increase at all. Passing from one system to the other makes only slight use of the multiprecision package when the m's are chosen relatively prime in pairs. The use of as many as 64 different moduli is again overkill.

In the above discussion we have really been comparing modular arithmetic as done on the I4 with multiprecision arithmetic as done on a standard machine. The I4 can do multiprecise arithmetic in parallel as we saw in discussing the Mersenne Test problem. We conclude with a couple of remarks or precepts for parallel programmers. Of course very few people have access to the I4 but I predict that soon conglomerations of mini-arithmetic units will be assembled for special problems that will involve this type of programming.

Principle 3 is familiar when the information flowing is data. But we must be prepared to encounter flow modification

when the flow is an instruction stream. We meet our simplest problem in
the conditional transfer situation. A familiar instance is exemplified
by the flow chart (Figure 5.32). If this chart is being followed by
64 processing elements in parallel we can expect (if ? is reasonable)
that some of them will answer ? by "yes", and the rest by "no". The
instructions for OP2 would need to be supplied to the former PE's and
those for OP3 to the latter. This is obviously unsatisfactory with
only one control unit.

An alternative procedure is pictured in Figure 5.33. Here   D
means disable all PE's where answer is "yes" and E means enable all
PE's that were previously disabled. (The whole diagram could be operating under a subset of the PE's previously enabled.) OP5 would be
the result of "undoing" OP2 and following this by OP3, assuming that
OP2 has a single valued inverse. With this procedure there is no real
branching in the time sense as there is in Figure 5.32.

Another technique exploiting Principle 1 rather than 3 may be used
in the following situation. A program may consist of pieces that can
be programmed in parallel mode, interspersed with parts that seem to
require serial mode operation.

For example in dealing with matrices with 64 columns one may wish
to perform row manipulations, with row vectors, in parallel but from time
to time the problem requires the calculation of a new vector each component of which is obtained by a different formula. Assigning each
column to its own PE and following the preceding idea we could method-
ically disable all but one of the PE's and execute the instruction
appropriate to that column. Finally arriving at our new vector, all
PE's would be enabled before entering the next parallel stretch of the
program. Instead, we can use 4096 words of temporary storage and
avoid any disabling of the PE's by the following device. At starting
time we introduce the vector

$$V = \{ 0,1,2,\ldots;63 \} \quad .$$

When we come to the calculation of the separate components of our
new vector we begin by computing its first component not just in PE(0)
but, in parallel, in all PE's. The identical results A_0 are deposited
in the first row of temporary storage.

$$R: A_0,\ldots,A_0$$

next we compute

$$R + 1: A_1,a_1\ldots,A_1$$

and finally

$$R + 63: A_{63},A_{63},\ldots,A_{63} \quad .$$

By using V to set index registers in the PE's, the command
"Fetch R" will fill the A registers with the main diagnonal of the R
matrix with, in fact, the desired vector. The time saved by not disabling and enabling is 17.65 = 1105 clock pulses.

This concludes what I had planned to say about the exploitation
of parallelism. I hope that these ideas, principles, and examples
will serve to interest some of you in parallel computing. Perhaps the
next few years will see more hardware development along these lines
and, recalling this 1976 discussion, some of you will be able to con-
sult about machine development of the 1980's. The recent past has
shown that no such consultation took place when the machines in current
use were designed. Meanwhile from time to time I hope to report on
what parallel computations are being done on the Illiac IV. I wish,
in closing, to acknowledge the assistance given me by the Institute
for Advanced Computation, Sunnyvale, California in carrying out experiments in parallel programming.

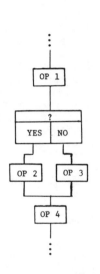

Figure 5.32 Algorithm
with branching

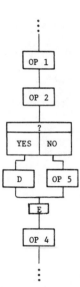

Figure 5.33 Algorithm
with branching removed

E.   Seismic

Seismic models have been addressed on the Illiac for some time.
Often they are characterized by regular data structures and
computationally intensive algorithms. In these cases the Illiac
is attractive not only for speed but for the large main memory
that allows grid sizes of more realistic size to be addressed.

1. A Three-Dimensional Finite Difference Code for Seismic Analysis on the ILLIAC IV Parallel Processor

EMPIRICAL EVIDENCE

Since empirical evidence for the complex earthquake fault behavior, deep within the earth, is normally gathered from motions at surface stations, there has been increasing interest in the computerized prediction of the ground motions which would result from postulated earthquake fault models. In addition, two dimensional models cannot adequately represent the complex three dimensional effects surrounding a fault. Therefore, a number of researchers have developed three dimensional seismic codes. One such code, TRES, was developed by Systems, Science and Software for their UNIVAC 1108 computer (1). Unfortunately, this code, like most three dimensional codes, required excessive amounts of computational time to run. For even a moderately sized problem (51x51x101 finite difference mesh, 253 time steps), 15 minutes of computer time were required for each time step on the full grid. To reduce run times to reasonable levels, a decision was made to implement the TRES code on one of the world's most powerful computers, the Illiac IV.

This paper describes the implementation and some of the results obtained. To facilitate understanding of the details of the implementation, descriptions of the architecture of the ILLIAC IV computer and of the numerical algorithms used by TRES will first be presented.

THE TRES COMPUTER PROGRAM

The problem predicting ground motions resulting from earthquake sources may be divided into three smaller problems. The first step is to simulate the earthquake source and collect motion data on a sphere surrounding the fault. The second step is to use this

data to define an "Equivalent Elastic Source". The Equivalent
Elastic Source is a collection of coefficients of a spherical expansion (in terms of Bessel functions, trigonometric functions
and associated Legendre functions), where each coefficient is a
function of frequency. The third step is to use these Equivalent
Elastic Source coefficients to analytically predict the motion at
selected sites. The TRES code is only concerned with the first
of these steps. Thus, TRES simulates the earthquake faulting process, calculates the resulting wave motion in the earth surrounding the fault, and collects divergence and curl histories on a
spherical surface surrounding the fault. The problem geometry is
illustrated in Figure 5.34.

THE FAULT MODEL - Currently, the only fault model is a bilateral
strike-slip fault using a stick-slip rupture mechanism (2). For
this type of fault, the fault plane is vertical and the motion involves symmetric horizontal slip of the sides of the fault relative to one another. The rupture is initiated at the center of
the fault, the focus, and spreads radially at a specified rupture
velocity until the limit of the fault plane is reached. The grid
is split on the fault plane, that is two nodes are used at each
grid point on the fault plane. Until rupture occurs, the two
nodes must move identically. After rupture, they are free to
slide relative to one another in the plane of the fault. While
they are sliding, the force between them is just the kinetic fric-
tion. When the relative velocity drops to zero, the rupture is
said to heal and no further relative motion between the two nodes
is permitted. The maximum size of the fault plane was 4x6 in the
UNIVAC 1108 version of the code.

THE PLASTIC ZONE - The fault plane is surrounded by a zone in
which inelastic behavior is permitted. The size of this zone was
9x11x9 in the UNIVAC 1108 code. The material in this region is
modeled as ideally elasto-plastic. The material behaves as if it
were perfectly elastic until the yield strength of the material
is exceeded. The Huber-Von Mises-Hencky yield criterion is used
to determine incipient yield. When this shear-distortion energy
limit is violated, the material behaves in a perfectly plastic
fashion. The usual stress-strain relationships are replaced by
the Prandtl-Reuss equations. That is, the rate of plastic strain
is proportional to the state of stress and the elastic strains
are considered to not exceed the yield surface. Since the stress
is no longer proportional to strain, six stress components are
carried with each node in the plastic zone. In addition, the
work done by the plastic deformation is calculated. So a seventh
plastic variable is carried with each node (the current integrated total of the plastic work).

THE ELASTIC ZONE - The remainder of the grid (surrounding the
plastic zone) is treated as ideally elastic. In the UNIVAC 1108
version of the code, the total grid is limited to a maximum of
51x51x101 nodes. Six variables are carried at every node in the
grid. These are the three displacements at each node and the

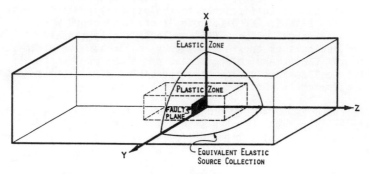

Figure 5.34   I4TRES geometry

three velocities. Thus, a grand total of 13 variables are carried at each node in the plastic zone, and 19 variables for the split nodes in the fault plane.

THE BOUNDARY CONDITIONS - The initial conditions in TRES consist of zero displacement and velocity. However, a uniform state of horizontal shear stress is permitted. On the six surfaces of the grid, either the force or the displacement must be constrained to be zero. Since the three coordinate directions on each surface may be independently prescribed, symmetry conditions may be imposed. In fact, it is customary to apply symmetry conditions on both planes normal to the fault, thus treating only a quarter of the fault. The current fault algorithm does not permit a symmetry condition across the plane of the fault (even though such a condition could be formulated for this class of fault). This is the reason for the final dimension being double the first two.

THE COMPUTATIONAL ALGORITHM - The basic computational cycle in TRES consists of integration for one time step. The cycle starts by numerically approximating the derivative of the displacement field to obtain the strain field. A central difference of displacement values at adjacent nodes approximates the partial derivative at the midpoint. By combining these partial derivatives and averaging, an estimate is obtained for the strains at the center of the block of material determined by eight nodes. The constitutive relationships (Hooke's Law in the elastic region) are then used to obtain the stress at the center of the block. Then the equilibrium relationships (Newton's Law) are used to determine the acceleration. The partial derivatives of the stress required in the equilibrium relationships are obtained in a fashion similar to the strains. In this case, the stresses at the centers of the eight blocks surrounding the node are used to estimate the acceleration at that central node. The velocity, V, and the displacement, U, of a node are obtained as

$$V(T+.5xDT)=V(T-.5DT)+DTxA(T), \text{ and } U(T+DT)=U(T)+DTxV(T+.5xDT)$$

where A is the acceleration, T is the current time, and DT is the time step. This calculation is analogous to the centered difference technique used for the strain and acceleration calculations. Although this description covers the more important aspects of the calculation, it must be noted that there are other features in the code to treat damping, plasticity and to control a form of instability observed to occur in such centered difference techniques of a rectilinear grid (3).

IMPLEMENTATION ON THE ILLIAC IV

The Illiac IV (I4TRES) code is designed to handle a substantially larger grid than the UNIVAC 1108 TRES. The maximum size of the fault plane is increased from 4x6 to 32x32. Similarly, the maximum dimensions of the plastic zone have been increased from 9x11x9 to 32x32x64. Finally, the maximum dimensions for the full grid have been increased from 51x51x101 to 80x80x160. The goal of this project was to implement on the Illiac IV a code which was computationally equivalent to TRES but executed an order of magnitude faster on a grid four times as large. Consequently, the algorithms were redesigned to maximize the number of PE's in use at any time, to minimize routing costs, and to minimize ILLIAC IV Disc Memory latency time.

USER INPUT AND OUTPUT - Since reading card input is a highly serial process and because more flexibility in input was desired, no direct input is done in the Illiac IV program. Rather an interactive preprocessor was written to aid the user in preparing the program's input data. This preprocessor, the I4TRES File Editor, executes under the TENEX timesharing system on the Institute for Advanced Computation's DEC PDP-10 computer. The I4TRES File Editor prepares a file in Illiac IV binary word representation which is moved to Illiac IV Disc Memory at the start of a run and is the sole source of input information for the Illiac IV code. Similarly, since the creation of formatted output in a program is highly serial and since extensive post-processing was to be done, no formatted output is prepared by the Illiac IV program. Rather binary output files in the user's machine word format are prepared and transferred to the user. Thus, the Illiac IV time is not spent on these highly serial tasks, but is reserved for the highly parallel computational tasks.

COMPUTATIONAL METHODOLOGY - Referring again to Figure 5.34, the basic computational strategy is to calculate results in the X direction in parallel. Using J, K, and L as the indices in the X, Y and Z directions of the grid, respectively, results for 60 J indices are all calculated simultaneously. A second calculation is then used for the remaining 20 indices. With this technique, the two outermost PE's are not used. The two PE's adjacent to the main data block (PE 1 and 62) are used to make it appear as if there were actually 62 variables. Values from the beginning of the block of 20 or the end of the block of 60 are moved into these PE's so the correct differences can be obtained. Boundary conditions are created by turning off the boundary PE during displacement calculation to enforce a constant zero displacement or by loading values which produce zero difference, strain, and consequently stress, to enforce a load free boundary condition.

DATA BASE DESIGN - A key element in the design is the data layout within an Illiac IV disc memory page. Each page in the main data base contains the three displacements and three velocities for the nodes at all 80 J indices, for 2 K indices and for 1 L index,

and is referred to as an elastic page. Recalling that a page is
16 rows in PE memory, the first four rows contain displacements
for all J's and the first K; the next four contain the corresponding velocities. The remaining eight rows contain the displacements and velocities for all J's and the second K in the same format. Within each group of four rows, the first row carries 60
values of the X component of displacement or velocity surrounded
by two zeros on each side (i.e., in PE's 0, 1, 62 and 63 when
moved to PE memory). Similarly, the second and third rows each
contain 60 values of the Y and Z components, respectively. The
fourth row contains the values for the remaining 20 J indices for
all three components.

The stress data for the plastic zone is contained in another
block of pages. Each of these plastic pages contains the six
stresses and the plastic work for all 32 J's, 4 K's and 1 L. The
first four rows contain values associated with the first K index,
the next four for the second K index, etc. The six stress components and plastic work are packed into four rows with half in PE's
0-31 and the remainder in PE's 32-63.

DATA MANAGEMENT SCHEME - In TRES, J's were scanned most rapidly,
K's next and L's last. The net result was that every point had
to be read three times per cycle. To minimize the number of I4DM
accesses in I4TRES, a different order was used. In I4TRES, of
course, all J's were processed simultaneously; this was the paral-
lelization. However, only a quadrant of the K's was scanned at a
time. Thus, 20 K's were scanned most rapidly, L's were next, and
quadrants were scanned least rapidly. The net result of this
strategy was most variables only had to be read once. Only the
K's at the quadrant interfaces (e.g., K=19, 20, 21, 22) were read
twice.

In both codes data was moved to and from mass storage into
and out of buffers in core. The buffers were configured to permit the minimum number of data transfers for the selected scanning order. In the UNIVAC 1108 version of TRES, the working data
buffer contained all 51 J's, 5 K's, and 3 L's. This buffer was
used in a circular fashion with 3 K's for computation, 1 K for
input, and 1 K for output. A somewhat different system was used
in I4TRES. In I4TRES, the input data buffer contains all 80 J's,
24 K's, and 3 L's (36 elastic pages). Results are calculated and
placed in the output data buffer which contains all 80 J's, 20 K's,
and 1 L (10 elastic pages). (The variables at all 24 K indices
cannot be updated for two reasons: first, to update a node all
26 of the surrounding nodes must be present to allow differencing.
And second, only full pages of data are updated.) A plastic input data buffer is used similarly. It contains all 32 J's, 24 K's,
and 2 L's (12 plastic pages) and a plastic output data buffer contains all 32 J's, 20 K's, and 1 L (5 plastic pages).

The integration method is explicit. (Calculations are based
only on values at the previous time step.) So new values cannot
replace the old ones until all calculations requiring that value
are complete. In the UNIVAC 1108 TRES, two separate files were
maintained. During a cycle, data (values at T) was read from one

file and results (values at T+DT) were output to the other. Their
roles were then switched for the next time step. For the Illiac
IV version, I4TRES, the two file scheme was replaced with a dynamic disc allocation scheme which requires only about half as much
space. The key to this technique is keeping two copies of the
interfacing nodes only. For instance, if K=1 to 20 have just
been updated, a copy of the old K=19 and 20 page must be kept to
permit differencing at K=21. The way this is implemented on
Illiac IV disc memory is illustrated in Figure 5.34 and may be
described as follows. Imagine for each L that an empty page is
in position zero and the data follows in positions 1 to 40. After
updating, the results for K=1 to 20 (10 elastic pages) are written
in positions 0 to 9. Thus, position 9 contains the new values for
K=19 and 20 and position 10 still contains the values from the
previous time step. After updating the complete grid, every value
is one position in front of where it was in the previous step.
The complete data base is treated as circular so that when a page
goes off the front of the data base, it is wrapped around and
added to the vacancy left at the back.

RESULTS OBTAINED WITH THE I4TRES PROGRAM

The I4TRES code was compared to the UNIVAC 1108 TRES code in three
test cases. The first test case was plane wave propagation and
consisted of nine subcases, one for each coordinate direction of
propagation and each coordinate direction of motion. The second
test case involves a smoothly varying load on a small, approximately circular area on the surface. This test case permits comparison with two dimensional (axially symmetric) simulations.
The third test case is an actual earthquake simulation. In each
case, the numerical results obtained with I4TRES on the Illiac IV
were identical to those obtained with TRES on the UNIVAC 1108 in
all of the five digits printed. The solution times on the Illiac
IV are about one and one half minutes per time step, whereas on
the UNIVAC 1108 they were 15 minutes. Moreover, the number of
nodes has been increased from approximately a quarter million to
over one million nodes (an overall speed up to approximately 60).
These solution times are for an Illiac IV code before optimization. Optimizing Illiac IV disc memory organization to minimize
latency and overlapping computation and input/output operations
would be expected to make further substantial reductions in run
time.
Activities are currently focused in several areas. Several modifications to I4TRES are being considered. These include taking
advantage of symmetry across the fault plane, allowing material
inhomogeneities, modifying the treatment of the observed instability, as well as code optimization. In addition, plans are currently being made for development of a code based on finite element
(instead of finite difference) technology.

ACKNOWLEDGEMENT

The design which has been reported here is the result of the collaborative efforts of a number of members of the Institute for Advanced Computation. The author wishes to acknowledge their contributions to the project.

References

1. T. C. Bache, et al, "A Deterministic Methodology for Discriminating Between Earthquakes and Underground Nuclear Explosions." Final Report to Advanced Research Projects Agency under Contract No. F44620-74-C-0063, July 1976.

2. J. T. Cherry, et al, "A Deterministic Approach to the Prediction of Free Field Ground Motion and Response Spectra from Stick-Slip Earthquakes." Earthquake Engineering and Structural Dynamics, Vol. 4, pp. 315-332, 1976.

3. G. Maenchen and S. Sack, "The Tensor Code." Methods in Computational Physics, Vol. 3. Academic Press, 1964.

2. Seismic Data Processing

INTRODUCTION

The purpose of this study was to determine the suitability of the Illiac computer for processing seismic data. We have done this by looking at the computing requirements of each of several algorithms; and then, by comparing these requirements with the characteristics of the Illiac, we have investigated the feasibility of programming each of the algorithms on the Illiac. Finally, the procedure FKCOMB was actually coded for the Illiac and the program has been tested and run. FKCOMB is a long-period seismic signal analysis procedure, which is important in calculating discriminants between earthquakes and nuclear explosions; it may become an integral part of data processing on the seismic network. FKCOMB was chosen for this experiment because the large amount of processor time required prohibits its use in-house. Also, known results are available with which to compare the Illiac version.

This Section is based on "A Study of the Illiac IV Computer for Seismic Data Processing", by A. Kerr, G. Wagenbreth, E. Smart, and Z. Der, SDAC-TR-74-16, Teledyne-Geotech Report to DARPA, October 1974.

The first step in designing a seismic algorithm to run on Illiac is to examine similar or repeated data structures and determine how they could be organized in the processor memory and to analyze similar or repeated operations and determine how they could be divided among the processors.

Long and short period seismic data are recorded at seismic arrays consisting of a group of sensors sampled at a constant time interval. The data so recorded consists of a series of data scans. Each data scan is a time sample from each sensor. There are two structures repeated throughout the data. First, there are several channels, each identical in structure to the rest. Second, there are many identically structured time samples. In order to utilize either of these structures, time must be spent transposing the data. It would be convenient if it were possible to process the data without transposing in any way - but the input consists of data records which are formatted differently for each array.

Since the data must be restructured, it is reasonable to build a new structure which makes processing as fast and straight forward as possible. The choice between the two data structures is dependent upon the requirements of the algorithm. General discussion of the several seismic algorithms and their data requirements is contained in Section 3. A detailed discussion of the design of FKCOMB is found in Section 4.

SEISMIC APPLICATIONS ON THE ILLIAC IV COMPUTER

General

In the following paragraphs we shall discuss the suitability of the Illiac computer for processing seismic data using several tested algorithms.

Our investigation has revealed that the Illiac computer is generally suited for processing of seismic data which involves frequently repeated or simultaneous identical operations using different sets of data, and can be programmed in such a way that the processing is performed simultaneously in the 64 processing elements of this computer. Thus, if desirable, it will be feasible to use Illiac to process routinely all long-period data for the planned seismic network. In addition, it can also be used for off-line processing of selected data.

In this discussion we shall concentrate on the possibilities of this computer for the detection and discrimination of seismic events using seismic array data. The computer can also be used in other seismic applications too numerous to treat here. Seismic arrays record the earth motion in two separate frequency bands, short-period and long-period, which for some purposes require different treatments because of the different nature of seismic waves recorded in the two bands. Some of the processes discussed are used for data in both bands while others are commonly used only for long or short period data.

The most common signals for investigation in the short-period band are the short-period body waves, particularly the short-period P first arrival. P waves can arrive at a seismic station with a wide range of apparent velocities and from all possible azimuths. Since the bandwidth of the signal is limited, frequency filtering tends to enhance the signal/noise ratio. The detection threshold in the short-period band is low relative to that of the long-period band, and events are usually detected in this band. The arrival azimuth and apparent velocity of the short-period P waves at an array yield a preliminary epicenter location which can be used to narrow the search for waves in the long-period band. In the long-period band, long-period body waves are the signals of interest. When used in conjunction with short-period data, they are all proven or potential discriminants between explosions and earthquakes. The most important of these is the long-period Rayleigh wave, which is used in the M_s-m_b discriminant. The Rayleigh wave has several characteristics which can be utilized by detection algorithms:

1. Waveform (path-dependent);

2. Particle motion; and

3. Azimuth and apparent velocity.

Since in most cases detection has already occured on the short-period data, it is only necessary to prove or disprove the presence of Rayleigh or other long-period waves arriving from

roughly the direction of the preliminary epicenters, and to measure the wave amplitude if present.
The following seismic processing algorithms will be discussed in this report:

1. Frequency (convolution/recursive) filtering

2. Beamforming

3. Matched filtering

4. PHILTRE

5. Maximum likelihood f-k spectra

6. FKCOMB

The last four of these have only limited or no application
for the short period band. One processor (FKCOMB) is discussed
in more detail since it was selected to be demonstrated on the
Illiac.

Convolution and Recursive Filtering

Simple filtering is the convolution of a seismic trace with some
arbitrary function which limits the bandwidth of the output. Recursive filtering accomplishes the same result, but makes use of
a feedback loop to reduce the number of arithmetic operations required.
This operation can be represented mathematically in the form:

$$y_n = \sum_{1=n}^{m} a_1 x_{n-1} + \sum_{i=1}^{k} b_i y_{n-1}$$

where all indices are integers, x_i are values of the original dig-
itized trace and y_i are values of the filtered output, and a_1,
b_i, n, m, and k are constants the choice of which is dependent on
the filter function to be performed.

The Illiac is well suited to perform convolution of recursive
filtering simultaneously on all processing units. These algorithms
can be used for filtering all elements of an array using the same
filters to enhance a band limited signal in wideband noise, or
utilized for filtering the same trace with a set of filters to
perform a fast Fourier analysis or to compute spectral ratios for
discrimination. The parallel algorithm can also be used to simultaneously deconvolve sixty-four seismic traces, remove instrument
response, simulate seismograms produced by different instruments,
or to reduce the seismogram traces simultaneously to accelerations,
velocities, and displacements as functions of time.

Figure 5.35 is a schematic representation of possible arrangements of data in the Illiac memory for frequency filtering. In Figure 5.35a, a different channel of data is input to each PE, with the same filter applied to all PE's. In Figure 5.35b, a given channel of data is input to all PE's, with a different filter applied to each PE. Figure 5.35c represents a combination of the previous examples in which the PE's are partitioned into several sets, all of the PE's in a given set receiving the same data channel but operating with different filters.

Beamforming

Beamforming is the process of time-shifting several channels of array data and summing them to form a single channel. The time shifts chosen are the natural delays in time of arrival of a hypothetical signal crossing the array. The delays are defined with respect to some arbitrary point in space. For plane waves of constant velocity, the delays are

$$\tau_i = \vec{r}_i \cdot \vec{S}$$

where i is the index of the ith sensor, $\vec{r}$ is the location of the sensor and the slowness of the signal is:

$$\vec{S} = \vec{V}/(\vec{V} \cdot \vec{V})$$

where $\vec{V}$ is the velocity of the signal across the array. If one has computed delays from the true $\vec{S}$ of a given signal, that is, from its true speed and arrival azimuth, and has assumed that the signal waveform does not vary during transit, the effect of time shifting is to make all the channels appear to have been recorded at the arbitrary reference point. The effect of summing, therefore, will be to add the signal to itself N-1 times, where N is the number of channels. The signal is thus reinforced. If the noise is random and uncorrelated between array elements, it is reduced to $N^{-1/2}$ of its original amplitude by the summation. Thus beamforming has the function of increasing the effective signal-to-noise ratio.

One can estimate the speed and direction of propagation of signals by finding the maximum of the time average of the squared beam values (denoted $\overline{B^2}$) on the $\overline{S}$-plane:

$$\overline{B^2} = \sum_{j=0}^{J-1} [\frac{1}{N} \sum_{i=1}^{N} x_i (j\Delta t - \tau_i)]^2 = \sum_{j=0}^{J-1} B_j^2$$

where B_j is the expression in brackets, the beam of the array; x_i are the ith channel data samples; Δt is the sampling interval, j is the time index; J is the number of time points over which average is taken.

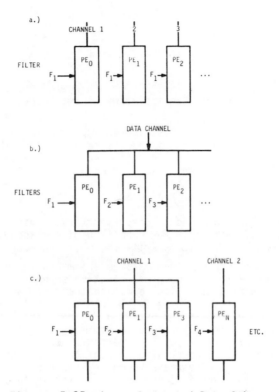

Figures 5.35a, b, c   Suggested Data Schemes
for Convolution-Recursive Filtering

The probability of the presence of the signal can be estimated by the statistic

$$F = \frac{N-1}{N} \frac{\overline{B^2}}{\sum\limits_{i=1}^{N} (x_i - B)^2}$$

where the denominator is the time average of the sum of the square (or power) of the individual input traces x_i after the beam is subtracted.

This statistic is distributed approximately as a non-central F variable with degrees of freedom determined by the number of channels, bandwidth, and the time length of averaging (assuming that only uncorrelated noise is present).

The standard F tables can be used to determine the significance of detection, or the detection can be automated (Blandford, 1971).

The beams can also be displayed for the visual detection of the waves of interest. For detection of surface waves and the measurement of M_s this is still the best procedure. Experienced analysts can recognize and measure seismic wave arrivals in many cases where automatic machine detection schemes fail. Routine computation of long-period beams and their storage in the mass store event files would be a valuable routine function for the NEP and would require a substantial computational power easily met by the Illiac. Therefore beamforming might well be the single most useful algorithm for implementation on the Illiac computer.

Several basic computational configurations can be used in beam processing. These are shown in Figure 5.36 in the first configuration (a) each PE contains one sensor trace and the beam values are accumulated by forming row sums on the several PE's. This configuration is suitable to process several arrays simultaneously, and computing the desired beams from a single data set sequentially may use long time windows such as those needed for the recognition of dispersed surface wave trains. Another advantage of this configuration is that preprocessing of traces such as filtering processing can also be performed simultaneously prior to beaming without the need to remove the data from memory. The output of such a scheme can be directly used in network event processing. This configuration, uniquely possible on the Illiac' IV, is the most efficient if the maximum number of PE's can be utilized. This can be achieved if the total number of sensors in the arrays are close to sixty-four, or alternatively the remaining PE's are used to compute different beams on the same arrays. To obtain continuous seismograms of long duration this seems to be the most efficient approach, since various preprocessing schemes, such as convolution filtering, coordinate rotation to obtain Rayleigh Love, SH and SV components can be performed on them without the need for excessive numbers of overlaps in the successive time windows which would be required if, as we discuss

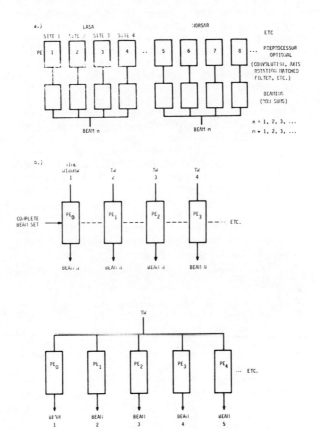

Figure 5.36   Suggested data schemes for beamforming

below, each PE were to contain all the channels of data required
for a particular beam. Incidentally, PHILTRE can be used as a
postprocessor for 64 array beams previously obtained (for 64
events) which can be run in parallel.

There are two other alternate but generally less effective
computational configurations which are indicated in Figure 5.36.
One loads all sensor traces from one array into one PE and each
PE contains a different time window. The desired beams for a
given time window may then be computed sequentially (Figure 5.36b).
The other scheme (Figure 5.36c) loads the same time window, all
traces, into as many PE's as there are desired beams and the beams
are computed simultaneously. The disadvantage of the last mentioned methods is that since each PE contains all traces the corresponding time windows must be shorter due to PE memory limitations.
This processing, including beaming, will require more complicated
buffering schemes between core and disk. Therefore it seems that
the first computational scheme has the most practical value,
although the others may be used advantageously, for instance, for
enhancing short body wave arrivals. The maximum utilization of
the computer requires the consideration of the type of processing
required, number of traces or arrays and the length of time windows to be processed.

Matched Filtering

This technique utilizes the waveform of the signal to be detected
(Alexander and Rabenstine, 1967a,b). The expected waveform of
the signal is used on the seismic trace as a convolution filter.
Ideally the expected waveform is identical to the actual one and
in the resulting output trace the signal is transformed into a
pulse which is shaped like the autocorrelation of the signal
waveform. In practice it is not possible to predict the actual
waveform precisely, so the matched filtering results in the con-
traction of the actual signal, which for surface waves can be a
long wave train, into a much shorter waveform. By compressing
the same amount of energy into a shorter time interval, the sig-
nal/noise is increased. It also de-emphasizes signals which do
not match the waveform used for filtering. The technique has
been successful in detecting surface waves, and preliminary results indicate that it is a very effective preprocessor for f-k
spectra analysis (FKCOMB or maximum likelihood f-k spectra) if it
is applied to all elements of an array. Application of matched
filtering requires that the signal waveform be known, which in
turn presupposes knowledge of the approximate epicenter, which
may be acquired by short-period detection. If the epicenter is
known, the recordings of a nearby large event can be used as the
expected waveforms. Alternatively, if the dispersion characteristics of the path are known sufficiently well, the signal waveforms can be synthesized and the resulting waveform used as a
matched filter.

An alternative application of matched filtering can be relative location of events. If recordings of a reference event
(preferably of an explosion) are available at a set of seismic

stations, the times of maxima resulting from the matched filtering of seismic traces of nearby events with waveforms of the reference event, can be considered as relative arrival times for the
purpose of event relocation in the general region surrounding the
reference event. The technique also has a potential as a discriminant since azimuthal variations in the initial phases of earthquakes will cause inconsistencies in the times of occurrences of
matched filter output maxima when compared to explosions.

Matched filtering is essentially convolution, and the computational advantages of convolution or recursive filters on the
Illiac stated above apply in this case.

Possible applications of the Illiac (Figure 5.37) include
matched filtering of many sites simultaneously (each with a different matched filter), filtering several sets of array elements
simultaneously with matched filters corresponding to each array,
or filtering independent sites (such as LRSM sites) with their
own respective matched filters. One can also use matched filters
corresponding to several areas of interest routinely on the data.

PHILTRE

This process is designed for a single three-component set of long-
period data. It uses a nonlinear weighting scheme of Fourier
spectral components in overlapping time windows to enhance Love
or Rayleigh particle motion associated with a given arrival direction (Simons 1968). First the three components of long period
recordings are rotated to obtain radial transversal and vertical
motion. The rotated traces are broken up into overlapping time
windows and Fourier transformed, yielding the Fourier coefficients

$$a_c(nf) = \frac{2}{T} \int_0^T c(\tau) \cdot \cos 2\pi nf\tau \cdot d\tau;$$

$$b_c(nf) = \frac{2}{T} \int_0^T c(\tau) \cdot \sin 2\pi nf\tau \cdot d\tau;$$

where $c(\tau)$ is the radial, transverse or vertical component to be

analyzed, T is time, $n = 0,1,2,3,...,N-1$, Nf - folding frequency,

and $f = \frac{1}{T}$ = fundamental harmonic of Fourier series.

Using the absolute value of a Fourier component

$$A_c(nf) = \sqrt{a^2_c(nf) + b^2_c(nf)}$$

one computes three quantities used in the weighting scheme

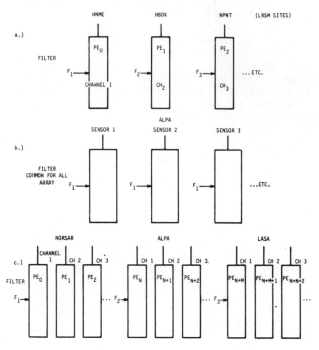

Figure 5.37   Suggested data schemes for matched filtering

a.) The apparent horizontal azimuth (the angle from the radial direction)

$$\beta(nf) = arctan \frac{A_t(nf)}{A_r(nf)}$$

b.) A measure of the accentricity of the particle motion ellipse

$$\Psi(nf) = arctan \frac{A_r^2(nf) + A_t^2(nf)}{A_z(nf)}$$

c.) The phase difference between the vertical and radial components

$$\alpha(nf) = \Theta_r(nf) - \Theta_z(nf).$$

The Fourier amplitude coefficients of each direction components are then weighted in the following manner

$$A_z'(nf) = A_z(nf) \cdot cos^M[\beta(nf)] \cdot cos^K[\Psi(nf)-.21\pi] \cdot sin^N[\alpha(nf)]$$

$$A_r'(nf) = A_r(nf) \cdot cos^M[\beta(nf)] \cdot cos^K[\Psi(nf) - .21\pi] \cdot sin^N[\alpha(nf)]$$

$$A_t'(nf) = A_t(nf) \cdot sin^M[\beta(nf)] \cdot sin^K[\Psi(nf)] \cdot 1$$

where $sin^N[\alpha(nf)] \equiv 0$ if $\pi \leq \alpha(nf) \leq 2\pi$.

The $A_c'(nf)$ are the "weighted amplitude coefficients". No weights or adjustments are applied to the phase angles. The exponents M, K, and N are parameters that are read into the program. Values of M, K, and N which have worked reasonably well in practice range from 4 to 8. Note that on the vertical radial components all weighting factors vary from 1 to 0 as powers of sines and cosines depending upon the degree to which the particle motion resembles pure Love or Rayleigh waves.

The effects of the first weighting factors (functions of β) are to attenuate transverse energy on the vertical and radial components and radial energy to the transversed component.

The second set of weighting factors depends upon the angle Ψ - a measure of the accentricity of the Rayleigh orbit providing transversal trace does not contain too much non-Rayleigh type motion.

On the vertical and radial traces, the angle desired (0.21π) is the one corresponding to a representative value of the horizontal/vertical displacement ratio (~0.8) for fundamental long-period Rayleigh waves.

The resulting Fourier coefficients are subsequently transformed back into the time domain to yield transverse traces containing only Love motion and radial and vertical traces with only Rayleigh motion and greatly reduced noise since the weighting scheme de-emphasizes noise which, even if coherent, is liable to come from a direction different from that of the epicenter.

The data dependent nature of this algorithm does not lend itself well to utilize the parallel computing feature of Illiac. However if large sets of data need to be processed each PE can process three components of data from a given location (Figure 5.38). This may make PHILTRE a practical preprocessor for arrays. Recent work by von Seggern and Sobel (1974) indicates that it is effective in revealing Rayleigh waves hidden in noise. Although further tests are needed to establish its effectiveness as a preprocessor for an f-k detector, it utilizes a neglected aspect of surface wave detection.

Maximum Likelihood f-k Spectra

A maximum likelihood f-k spectrum is the mapping of the power passed by a set of maximum likelihood filters in the plane. A maximum likelihood filter is an optimum filter which is constrained to pass a plane wave in the direction to be looked at while rejecting all the rest of the energy present, in a least mean square sense. It has the mathematical form for a given frequency

$$P(\vec{K}) = \frac{1}{\vec{u}\Phi^{-1}\vec{u}t}$$

where Φ is the power sepctral matrix of the sensors, K is the wavenumber and u is a vector

$$\vec{u} = (e^{i\vec{K}\vec{r}_1}, e^{i\vec{K}\vec{r}_c} \ldots e^{i\vec{k}\vec{r}_n}).$$

The position vector of the i'th sensor of the array is $\vec{r}_i$.

The maximum likelihood f-k spectrum is one of a wide family of high-resolution spectral estimators. It is characterized by reduced side lobes and higher resolution as manifested in the reduction of the width of the main lobe when compared to the simple frequency domain beam used in FKCOMB. The processor requires the estimation of the inverse of the input spectral matrix; there are fast practical ways to make this estimate, after which the multiplications with the various $\vec{u}$ vectors can be done rapidly by using all 64 parallel processors. The parallel feature can also be used to Fourier transform the individual seismic trace segments simultaneously. Algorithms are available to estimate the inverse of the array spectral matrix without actually inverting a matrix

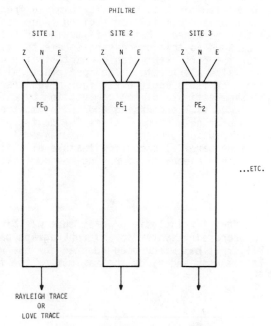

Figure 5.38   Suggested data schemes for PHILTRE

(J. W. Woods, personal communication, 1972).

If the detection of surface waves from a known epicenter is desired, the range of search in the $\vec{k}$ plane is reduced. Moreover, the absolute value of k is fixed for a given frequency, since the surface wave phase velocity for a given frequency at a given array site can be determined. Matched filtering or PHILTRE can be used as preprocessors to this processing scheme to utilize the dispersion and/or the particle motion characteristics of the signal and reduce the false alarm rate. The most practical way to use the Illiac computer is to apply sixty-four $\vec{u}$ vectors simultaneously using the same estimate of the computation by a factor of 64 relative to sequential processing and is the most efficient for the computation of finely spaced values in the f-k plane needed by this high-resolution process. A flow diagram in Figure 5.39 shows how the unique parallel computing feature of Illiac can be used to increase the efficiency of computing maximum likelihood f-k spectra.

FKCOMB

FKCOMB is a fast f-k analysis program that was first used in an automatic processing system for microbaragraph data (Smart and Flinn 1971). It has since been adopted for use with LP seismic data. It computes and finds the maximum of the function

$$P(\omega,k) = \left| \sum_{n=1}^{N} \{A_n(\omega) \exp[i\alpha_n(\omega)]\} \cdot \exp(ik \cdot r_n) \right|^2$$

which is essentially the power in the frequency domain beam. Here ω is the angular frequency, $\{A(\omega) \exp i_n(\omega)\}$ is the Fourier transform of the n'th seismic trace, N is the number of traces, and $\exp(ikr_n)$ are the components of the vector $\overline{u}$ in the previous section. The maximum of the function can be associated with the presence of a signal. The F test is used to determine whether a signal is present.

The methods take advantage of the fact that the signal-to-noise ratio varies with frequency, so beamforming is done frequency by frequency. Also, by staying in the frequency domain a great many beams can be examined rapidly, the number being limited only by the resolution cell of the array response. The low resolution of the process is actually an advantage when one desires to search f-k space rapidly, since the wide main lobe of the process enables one to use a wide grid spacing in the search.

The azimuth and velocity of a signal need not be assumed: one merely accepts the beam with maximum power. This fact is

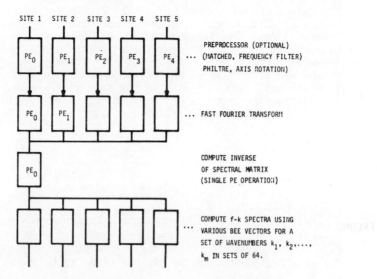

Figure 5.39   Computation of maximum likelihood f-k spectra

important for signals such as long-period seismic surface waves, which not only are dispersive (i.e., their phase velocities vary with frequency) but whose arrival azimuth may also vary with frequency because of lateral inhomogeneities in their paths.

Since the main advantage of the FKCOMB method is the possibility of fast search in the wavenumber vector space at a given frequency, changing frequencies as the search requires, we programmed the processor to operator on sixty-four successive time windows. This uses the Illiac most effectively for signal detection. The other type of application, searching sixty-four frequency levels simultaneously on the same time window, is not so efficient, since not all of the frequency bands may be needed for the search in a given iteration.

FKCOMB ALGORITHM DESIGN

General

The FKCOMB algorithm can be divided into the following steps:

1. Input raw long period data. Separate it by array. Extract the long period data samples and the timing words associated with those samples.

2. Divide the input into time windows. As originally input the data is ordered in the following manner:

$T(1,1),T(2,1),...T(N,1), T(1,2),T(2,2),...T(N,2),$

$T(1.S),T(2,S),...T(N,S)$

where $T(i,j)$ represents the data sample from channel i at time j, N is the number of channels and S is the number of time periods. After division into time windows the data is ordered as follows:

$T(1,1),T(1,2),...T(1,TW, T(2,1),T(2,2),...T(2,TW),...$

$T(N,1),T(N,2),...T(N,TW),T(1,TW+1),T(1,TW+2),...T(1,2TW),...$

where TW is the time window length and $T(i,j)$ and N are as above.

3. The data is converted from the raw data format to the internal representation of the machine used. Glitches or spikes are removed and dead or noisy channels are detected and removed. (Portions of this step may be performed before step 2.)

4. A Fourier transform is applied to each time window.
After FFT the data is arranged as follows:

F(1,1,1),F(1,1,2),...F(1,1,TW),F(1,2,1),F(1,2,2),...
F(1,2,TW),...
F(1,N,1),F(1,N,1),...F(1,N,TW),F(2,1,1),F(2,1,1),...
F(2,1,TW),

F(2,2,1),F(2,2,2),...F(2,2,TW),...

where F(i,j,k), the Fourier transform output, represents frequency k, channel j, time window i.

5. Re-order the data so that it is arranged by frequency.
It is then arranged as follows:

F(1,1,1),F(1,2,1),...F(1,N,1),F(1,1,2),F(1,2,2),...
F(1,N,2),...

F(1,1,TW),F(1,2,TW),...F,N,TW),F(2,1,1),...

where F(i,j,k), TW, and N are defined as above.

6. Search frequency - wavenumber space for power maxima.

Data Editing Module One (DEM1)

Since step one is a process common to all seismological algorithms
and because large input/output buffers are required it was coded
as a stand alone module. The input to this module (DEM1) is the
raw data as read from a low rate tape. The format of input records is shown in Figure 5.40. The output consists of several
files, one per array, containing only the data samples applicable
to long period processing. The data movement required to isolate
and properly structure this data is nonparallel. There are no
general structures repeated often enough to allow efficient use
of the ROUTE instruction. The CU is used to move one word at a
time between input buffers and output buffers. (Actually the
BIN instruction is used to move blocks of eight words to the CU.)
A description of each array format is given in the block data subroutine initialization of the vector CNTRL.
The reordering of data in steps 2 and 5 is not required if
all data is available on a random access device, since it reflects
the order in which the data will be accessed. It is necessary on
Illiac since the size of core and long disk access time prohibit
random access.
Assuming approximately 20 channels for each of three arrays,
each sampling at the rate of once per second, one twenty-four hour
tape contains:

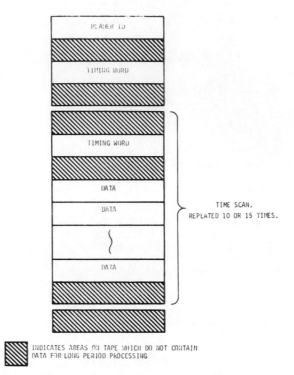

Figure 5.40   Memory allocation

3 arrays/sample * 20 channels/array * 1 sample/second *

60 seconds/minute * 60 minutes/hour * 24 hours/day =

5,184,000 channels.

Moving each sample involves two memory accesses (one load and one store). Given that a memory access from the CU takes approximately .5 microseconds, the total time spent in memory accesses by DEM1 to process twenty-four hours of data is on the order of 5 seconds. This is small enough that more complicated algorithms which may have permitted use of the ROUTE instruction were not considered.

Twenty-four hours of data is approximately ten to the eight bits. In order to read these into core without losing a great deal of time waiting for disk access a buffer of 128 rows (512,000 bits) of core is used. 200 disk accesses are required for input. This takes up to eight seconds. Since there are several output files, the output buffers are somewhat smaller. The total size of the output is smaller, since at least half of the input is not used in long period processing. The I/O time spent in output is therefore approximately equal to that spent in input even though the output buffers are smaller.

The actual movement of data by DEM1 is done within three nested loops. The outermost loop is gone through once for each input record.

The next inner loop is gone through once for each time scan in each record. The innermost loop is gone through once for each channel per time scan. All buffering is handled by an input routine and an output routine called once for each channel to transfer. In order to reduce overhead spent in subroutine calls it may be necessary to recode calls on these routines as in line code.

DEM1 transposes data in a serial fashion. It is coded so as to minimize time lost in disk and memory accesses. It puts array data in a standard format to reduce the size of the data and allow the straight forward execution of subsequent modules.

Data Editing Module Two (DEM2)

Steps 2 through 5 are performed by DEM2. The primary reason that this module was coded separately from step 6 was to shorten coding and debugging time. The relatively small amount of core memory available in each PE would necessitate the overlaying of various vectors used by step 6 and those included in DEM2 if all were included in one module. The I/O times spent writing the output from DEM2 and reading it in before step 6 would be saved, but this time is estimated to be less than 5 seconds.

Steps 2 through 5 are performed one time window at a time. A complete multi-channel time window is taken through steps 2 through 5 and the resulting output placed in an output buffer before the next time window is processed.

One multi-channel time window consists of approximately 20 channels of up to 512 samples each or approximately 10,000 data items. During step 2 it is impossible to include a complete

multi-channel time window within one processing element memory.
It is possible to include a single channel time window within one
processing element memory, but due to the variable number of channels used for each time window, keeping track of which channels
and time windows have been processed is complicated, though feasible.

An alternate approach is to use 64 PE's to process each time
window. An FFT routine is available (written at the University
of Illinois) which utilizes all 64 PE's to perform one FFT which
runs very close to 64 times faster than one PE would do. Conversion to floating point involves no interaction between processing
elements. Deglitching involves the comparison of each sample with
the previous and next sample. With this data arrangement these
samples are in adjacent PE's and the ROUTE instruction can be
effectively utilized. The original structuring of the data into
time windows (step 2) and the final transposition (step 3) are
each performed serially by the CU, so are not affected by the
data arrangement chosen. Spreading time windows across PE's was
the approach chosen for steps 2 through 5.

Step 2 thus consists of extracting timing information from
the input and, using this information, from time windows. Each
time window is spread across the PE's, occupying between one and
eight rows per channel, depending upon the time window size in
use. Overlapping of time windows is performed by retaining whatever part of the most recent time window is still of interest and
using the ROUTE instruction to back it up properly. For this
reason, the buffer in which time windows are built is alternated
between two halves of an array so that the last time window built
is not overwritten.

Conversion to internal floating point format is the first
step performed once the time windows have been formed. Each PE
converts all samples within its memory and no inter PE communication is required. Deglitching is performed by routing the values
from adjacent PE's and adjusting them if a glitch is encountered.
(See program documentation for exact procedure.) The rowsum procedure described in section 2 is used in the variance calculation,
since a summation across PE's is required. The FFT is then performed and the frequencies prepared for output. Due to the fact
that not all frequencies output by FFT are of seismological interest, the output from step 4 is much smaller than the input to
step 4. This data reduction is significant in that after FFT a
multi-channel time window consists of approximately 20 channels
and 20-30 frequencies and will fit within one processing element
memory. Placing each separate time window wholly within one PEM
is very convenient since the search of frequency wavenumber space
for one time window is completely self contained and independent
of other processing (see Figure 5.41). In step 5, the FFT output
is written into one PEM of an output core buffer. This is done
serially by the CU. When the buffer is full it is written to
disk.

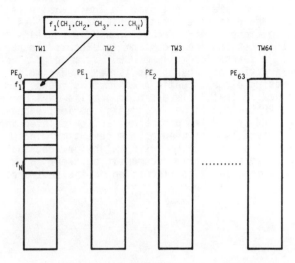

Figure 5.41   Input format for FKCOMB

FKCOMB Algorithm

Since each PE completely contains one time window after step 5,
the algorithm used in the search of frequency wavenumber space is
essentially the same as that used in the serial version. The program reads the data file created by DEM2, which has been arranged
as shown in Figure 5.41. Each time window contains the frequencies of interest and the algorithm is executed in parallel on
the data. A search for maximum power is made on a coarse grid
and then a series of finer grids is searched simultaneously in
all processing elements until a maximum is found. In a given
PE the mode for that PE is disabled until a maximum is found in
all other PE's. The Fisher statistic, period, signal azimuth and
velocity, and associated parameters are calculated and stored,
and the process is continued on the next time window of data.
The design of the algorithm was straightforward, and the reader
is referred to the program documentation (Kerr and Wagenbreth,
1974) for a more detailed discussion of the software.

PROJECT NOTES

The operational aspects of using Illiac differ significantly
from those of other machines. In addition to the parallel architecture, there are two other characteristics which are important
considerations for the user of the Illiac system. First, all of
the support software such as editors and compilers run on processors other than Illiac. There is currently support software available on DEC, IBM, and Burroughs machines. The choice of which
machines and software to use is an integral part of system development, for Illiac is accessible only via the ARPA Network and is
routinely used remotely. The bandwidth, availability, and reliability of the network directly affect the performance of the
Illiac system as seen by a user.

Program Entry and Storage

A basic requirement for any long-term coding effort is a
reliable file system permitting easy access and modification of
source codes. Two basic options were available in using the
Illiac system. One, used by several Illiac coding efforts, is
to maintain files on a host computer and transfer the files to
the Illiac system via the ARPA Network whenever necessary. The
second is to utilize the Tenex file system and editors included
in the Illiac system. The first approach required frequent
ARPA Network transfers and a reliable and economical host machine.
Since such a host was not available to SDAC, the Tenex file system was used and was found reliable and convenient. No work was
lost due to disk or file system failures during the duration of
this project. The editor DED fulfilled all requirements regarding both modification and examination of source files.

Languages

Three languages are available for preparation of Illiac code.
There are two high-level languages, GLYPNIR and CFD, and an assembly language, ASK. The large amount of coding necessary made the
use of assembly language impractical except for specific portions
where bit manipulation or efficiency made it a necessity. The
majority of coding was done in high-level language. A comparison
of the syntax and semantics of GLYPNIR and CFD revealed the
following significant differences:

1. Ease of understanding - CFD looks much like FORTRAN and
is easily interpreted or learned by a scientific programmer.
GYLPNIR resembles ALGOL and is somewhat more confusing and difficult to learn.

2. Ease of coding - Once learned, GLYPNIR permits faster and
clearer coding than CFD. GLYPNIR's macro facilities are a convenience not provided by CFD. GLYPNIR has some higher level con-
structs which require several CFD statements to implement.

3. Efficiency - CFD produces more efficient code than GLYPNIR in many instances.

The two languages are very similar in their treatment of unique Illiac characteristics and both provide all facilities necessary for the implementation of seismic analysis programs. Certain types of code are better suited to one language than the other, but consideration of the syntax and semantics alone indicated no clear preference.

The choice of language ultimately depended upon the support and availability of GLYPNIR and CFD. GLYPNIR is supported by the Institute for Advanced Computation as part of the Illiac system. It is implemented on a Burroughs 6700 located at the Illiac computer center and must be accessed via the Illiac batch queue (as discussed below). CFD is implemented on the IBM 360/67 located at NASA Ames Research Center. It is accessible routinely via the ARPA Network. The source for CFD is transportable, and a version of CFD is available on the UCLA IBM 360/91. Also supported on the Ames IBM 360/67 is a translator, CFDX, which translates CFD to FORTRAN. With some modification due to I/O differences and inserted assembly language code, CFD programs may be translated to IBM FORTRAN. The translator is designed to generate code equivalent to that generated by CFD for Illiac. CFDX is not designed to replace Illiac in production mode since the FORTRAN generated by writing a CFD program and translating it will not be nearly as efficient as coding in FORTRAN directly.

Due to the superior availability of CFD and the existence of the CFDX translator, the decision was made to implement the FKCOMB algorithm in CFD.

As actually experienced, the availability of CFD was not as good as had been hoped, for several reasons. First, availability of the Ames IBM 360 is very poor. Between the hours of 8:00 am and 12:00 midnight (PST) use of the machine by non-priority accounts is restricted. During the eight remaining hours, the requirement that both the Illiac Tenex system and the Ames IBM 360 be operational for file transfers caused much lost programmer and computer time. The hours were also inconvenient. The UCLA version of CFD, due to lack of overlays, requires 400K core and runs in a slow queue (6-8 hours turnaround). Efforts to implement CFD on the SDAC IBM 360/44 were frustrated due to incompatibility of the operating systems of the IBM 360/44 and the IBM 360/67. The large core requirement also posed a serious problem. It was found that the effort required to implement CFD at SDAC would not be worth the convenience of an in-house compiler. The availability of Illiac was sufficient (see below) to make the use of the CFDX translator uneconomical due to the alterations necessary to accommodate I/O differences and inserted assembly language statements.

Run Procedures

Coding of the FKCOMB algorithm in CFD began in April 1974. What follows is the set of procedures developed for the day to day process of running and debugging an Illiac program, along with experience gained and observations made during the use of these procedures.

The primary site at which compiles were done was the Ames IBM 360/67. A CFD restriction is that all subroutines must be separately compiled. Our code was divided into three programs, each consisting of a main driver and four to six subroutines. Initially all subroutines had to be compiled, but thereafter only those with code modifications required compilation. Compiling a module consists of four steps. First, after having logged in on the Ames 360/67, the source file is transferred over the ARPA network from the I4-Tenex File System, where the source files are maintained, to the Ames 360. This process is done interactively and typically takes one to ten minutes of real time, depending upon the length of the source and the load average on each machine. Approximately one out of three transfers terminated abnormally and had to be reinitiated. The failure rate increased greatly when the load on either machine was heavy. The next step is to initiate the CFD compiler. The time between the submission of a compile and its completion varied from five minutes to several hours, again dependent upon the machine load. After termination of the compile the listing generated by the CFD compiler is examined with the TSS editor, REDIT, to check for syntax errors or other abnormal termination. If errors are detected, they are corrected (being careful to make the same corrections to the original source at I4-Tenex) and the compile reinitiated. After a successful compile, the ASK assembly language source module is copied back to I4-Tenex via network transfer. This file is usually several times larger than the original source and the time taken to transfer the file is several times longer than that for the source. If several subroutines are to be recompiled, this process can consume several hours. When only small changes are necessary, this time can be saved by changing the assembly language code directly with the text editor at I4-Tenex, again being careful to make the same changes to the original source.

Once the necessary assembly language modules have been created, a batch job is submitted at I4-Tenex to perform the following tasks:

1. Assemble the ASK modules

2. Linkedit the resultant relocatable modules

3. Create a disk map file describing the actual layout of any Illiac disk areas to be used by this run

4. Allocate the map file created in the last step

5. Move any input files required to the appropriate Illiac disk area

6. Run the Illiac code

7. Move any output from the appropriate Illiac disk area to the I4-Tenex file system

8. Release the Illiac disk areas used.

CONCLUSIONS

Seismic Processing on Illiac

The Illiac computer programmed to perform seismic processing on large data bases can be a valuable tool in the development of seismic event detection and discrimination procedures. It is feasible to implement some existing algorithms on the Illiac which are not currently used to process large data bases, or some algorithms which are proposed but not tested due to a lack of computing power. Our experience with one algorithm (FKCOMB) which is representative of seismic analysis programs shows that a major benefit of the Illiac to seismic processing is its ability to operate in parallel on sixty-four different data streams, thereby reducing the time required to process large data bases. Efficiently arranging these data streams for the processing element memories is an important consideration for designing any seismic algorithms for the Illiac.

It is feasible to program Illiac to perform the algorithms reviewed in this study: convolution-recursive filtering, PHILTRE, matched filtering, beamforming, and maximum likelihood f-k estimation. Since a major factor in programming any of these algorithms is the data arrangement in core, a more detailed study of the data configurations for these algorithms would be needed to optimize the use of the computing power of Illiac. One algorithm (FKCOMB) was studied in detail and implemented on Illiac IV. Data editing schemes were devised for FKCOMB which can be used with appropriate modifications for all the seismological algorithms we received.

Two independent uses for Illiac are suggested. First, FKCOMB and other algorithms now used selectively could be run routinely on larger data bases to better provide the services they already give on conventional machines. Second, experimental methods impractical to test via conventional machines could be tested on Illiac. The experience of implementing FKCOMB illustrates that the design and coding of new algorithms for Illiac is not significantly more difficult than for serial machines. The only phase not experimentally explored by this effort is the operational problems of manipulating the large amounts of data involved in routine processing of long and short period data on Illiac.

References

1. S. S. Alexander and D. B. Rabenstine, 1967a, Detection
    of surface waves from small events at teleseismic distance:
    SDL Report No. 175, Teledyne Geotech, Alexandria, Virginia.

2. S. S. Alexander and D. B. Rabenstine, 1967a, Rayleigh
    wave signal-to-noise enhancement for a small teleseismic
    using LASA, LRSM and observatory stations: SDL Report No.
    194, Teledyne Geotech, Alexandria, Virginia.

3. R. R. Blandford, 1971, An automated event detector at TFO:
    SDL Report No. 263, Teledyne Geotech, Alexandria, Virginia.

4. J. Capon, 1969, High-resolution frequency-wavenumber
    spectrum analysis, Proc. IEEE 57, 1408-1418.

5. CFD, A Fortran based language for ILLIAC IV, 1973, Compu-
    tational Fluid Dynamics Branch, Ames Research Center,
    National Aeronautics and Space Administration.

6. ILLIAC IV Systems Characteristics and Programming Manual,
    1971, Burroughs Corporation, Defense, Space and Special
    Systems Group.

7. A. U. Kerr and G. Wagenbreth, A long-period processing
    package for ILLIAC IV, 1974 (in preparation).

8. H. Mack, 1972, Evaluation of the LASA, ALPHA, NORSAR long
    period network: Seismic Array Analysis Center Report No.
    6, Teledyne Geotech, Alexandria, Virginia.

9. R. S. Simons, 1968, PHILTRE, A surface wave particle
    motion discrimination process. Bull. Seism. Soc. Amer.,
    58, p. 629-637.

10. E. Smart, 1971, Erroneous phase velocities from frequency
    wavenumber spectral sections: Geophys. J. Roy. Astr. Soc.,
    26, p. 247-254.

11. E. Smart and E. A. Flinn, 1971, Fast frequency-wavenumber
    analysis and Fisher signal detection in real time infrason-
    ic array data processing: Geophys. J. Roy. Astr. Soc.,
    26, p. 279-284.

12. J. E. Stevens, 1971, A fast Fourier transform subroutine
    for ILLIAC IV: C.A.C. Document No. 17, Center for Advanced
    Computation, University of Illinois at Urbana-Champaign,
    Urbana, Illinois 61801.

13. System Guide for the ILLIAC IV User, 1974, Institute for
    Advanced Computation, Ames Research Center, Moffet Field,
    California 94035.

14.   D. H. von Seggern and P. Sobel, 1974, Performance of the PHILTRE processor at low signal to noise ratios (in preparation).

15.   J. W. Woods and P. R. Lintz, 1972, Plane waves at small arrays: Geophysics, 38, p. 1023-1041.

F.   Astronomy

Introduction

Very little astronomical research has been undertaken using the
Illiac. The following galaxy simulation is an exception. It can
be expected, however, that stellar collapse with inhomogeneous
mixing and rotation will be modelled on a machine of the Illiac
class in the not too distant future.

1.   Three Dimensional Galaxy Simulations

THE ASTRONOMICAL PROBLEM

The dynamic properties of galaxies are not adequately understood. This is especially true of the galaxy in which we live.
Because stars represent most of the mass of galaxies and because
a star moving in a galaxy is well represented as a mass point, a
dynamic model of a galaxy consists of a large number of point
masses that move in the force field generated by the Newtonian
gravitational attraction of the stars themselves. This is a form
of the gravitational n-body problem. In computer simulations of
galaxies, n is usually in the range of 10,000 to 250,000 -- far
fewer than the 10^{11} stars in a typical galaxy. But a difficulty
arises: models intended to represent the galaxy collapse within
the period of one galactic rotation. The difficulty is physical
in origin and does not result from the relatively small number of
particles in the model nor from other computational features.

As part of a study directed toward understanding the origin
of this difficulty and toward discovering the physical principles
that must be included in order to build stable models that agree
with our observations, we have used a fully three-dimensional
galaxy simulation on the Illiac IV. The fully three-dimensional
form is important. Several earlier computer simulations have
been designed with restricted geometries, and it is important
to understand the consequences of these restrictions. For example, a restricted geometry which admits only axisymmetric forms
misses essential features of galactic dynamics because the domi-
nant instabilities of galactic models are non-axisymmetric and
because angular momentum transfers among particles are not properly handled. Most galaxies are non-axisymmetric: The beauti-
ful spiral galaxies often shown in photographs are dominated by
twofold symmetries in the plane.

This Section is based on an article in the IAC Newsletter by
R. H. Miller, May/June, 1977.

The stability problem first became apparent from two-dimensional disk galaxy simulations with point masses constrained to move on a plane. The masses interact with $1/r^2$ forces. The models developed from such simulations showed spiral density waves, but the velocity dispersions were much too large. Systems with smaller velocity dispersions quickly formed bar-like structures and later developed large velocity dispersions. Since real galaxies do not have these properties, something must be present to stabilize the galaxy--possibly some mass that is stable and produces a gravitational potential within which the observed stars move; otherwise the velocity dispersion in the galaxy would be too small for stability. This has ramifications far beyond the immediate question: if typical galaxies have much more mass than has been thought, the universe may be fairly close to the critical density for closure. Other possible physical stabilizing mechanisms include a dissipative drag on stars as they move through the interstellar medium.

While stability questions provided the principal motivation for undertaking the development of the three-dimensional program on the Illiac IV, many other problems can be studied with this tool. Several have been investigated so far.

1) Early Stages of Galactic Evolution

Any particle in the simulation can be made to represent either a star or a gas cloud, but the dynamics are different. Gas clouds, unlike stars, undergo inelastic collisions, which may result in the formation of a star. A galaxy is thought to form from the collapse of an initially extended, turbulent, gravitationally unstable gas cloud. Experimentally, the system does not behave as expected. The gas quickly settles into a thin sheet in the equatorial plane, and continues to form stars long after star formation should have stopped. The stars formed in the early stages of the collapse have velocities that do not agree with observation. More detailed studies of these collapse and formation processes may be carried out with two-dimensional disk galaxy simulations because the most important processes happen after the gas settles into a thin sheet.

2) Stability of Bar-Like Systems

Particle systems settle into a prolate bar that rotates end-over-end in space. This bar is a long-lived form, but the reasons for its peculiar stability are not known. We have studied the dynamics of the bar by graphic methods: computer-generated motion pictures of particle motions, as viewed from a rotating coordinate system in which the bar is at rest, show a net streaming motion around the bar in the direction of rotation. Individual particle orbits are similar to trajectories in an anisotropic harmonic oscillator within a rotating coordinate system. There is empirical evidence for extra isolating integrals of the motion. This study is well started, but not yet complete.

3)   Are Elliptical Galaxies Prolate?

The peculiar stability of prolate systems raises the question
whether elliptical galaxies that have a flattened outline on the
sky are oblate objects seen in projection, as is commonly supposed. They are more likely to be prolate. Systems that appear
circular on the sky may well be spherical in three-dimensions.
This opens the question of how flat an oblate object can exist
stably. A series of experiments is underway to study this
question. First, a spherical equilibrium system had to be constructed and shown to be stable in the computer. Next, the spherical system was made to rotate, which caused it to flatten. Pre-
sumably, it should assume an oblate form. At a certain degree
of flattening, the oblate form becomes unstable and shifts over
to a prolate form. We are now searching for that stability
limit.

4)   Colliding Galaxies

An interesting set of planned experiments refers to colliding
galaxies. This problem is inherently three-dimensional. The
initial galaxies must be self-consistent and stable, like those
used for (3) above. Self-gravitation in the bridges and tails
formed during the collision can be taken into account in an
Illiac simulation. This has not been possible with previous
simulations. The galaxies may merge into one large galaxy. The
dynamics of merging is not well understood -- a lot of energy
gets transferred from the center-of-mass motion of the colliding
galaxies into internal degrees of freedom of the resulting system. The Illiac simulation will provide information on this
exchange.

5)   Ring Galaxies

Another form of galaxy that is occasionally observed is a ring
structure. The usual picture for the formation of rings requires a collision. But a ring galaxy was formed in the collapse of a rotating stellar configuration in one simulation, which
demonstrates that rings can be formed by means other than galaxy
collisions. Rings are very short-lived forms. The ring in the
Illiac IV simulation was formed under circumstances favorable
for a long lifetime, but it became oval-shaped and collapsed into
a bar in less time than that required for a star in the ring to
complete one circuit around the center.

6)   Reliability of Disk Galaxy Simulations

The three-dimensional Illiac IV simulation of collapsing stellar
configurations has shown why disk galaxy simulations are so reliable for stability studies. The reliability results from an
essential separability of the motion into directions along an
axis of rotation and directions perpendicular to the axis of
rotation. Since components of the motion along the axis of ro-

tation do not affect the stability significantly, simulations that take account of motions perpendicular to the axis of rotation provide a good representation of the stability problem. The basic stability problem that motivated the development of the three-dimensional simulation is still open, but it can be studied by means of disk galaxy simulations.

PROGRAM DESIGN

The three-dimensional n-body program constructed for the Illiac IV is designed to be quite general so that it can be used for a variety of astronomical problems. It can handle as many as 10^6 particles within a cubic volume, with forces computed in a manner that allows details down to 1/64 of the linear dimension of the configuration space. Long-range effects are correctly handled by the force calculation. Each particle is represented by one Illiac word. In addition to the configuration coordinates and the velocities, 10 bits are allowed for other attributes. These attributes may be defined to suit the particular problem.

Computationally, the program designs are pleasing in the way they fit the Illiac IV architecture and utilize the parallel features of the Illiac. Like most large n-body programs designed for the Illiac IV it consists of two principal parts: the potential solver or subroutine in which the forces are calculated, and the particle-pusher or subroutine in which the particle velocities and positions are advanced according to these calculated forces. The potential solver makes use of the densities (or the projection of the particle phase space density onto the configuration space), which are tabulated by the particle-pusher as the new velocities and positions are computed. Summaries and tabulations are handled by other subroutines, as is the establishment of starting conditions.

Although two-dimensional calculations can be core-contained, this is no longer possible for reasonably sized three-dimensional calculations. However, it is not necessary that all of the particle data be available at once, since data for one particle can be completely processed independently of the rest. Particle interactions occur through the force field. One way to handle such a three-dimensional calculation is to sort the particles so that only a portion of the force field and of the density count need be in the core at any one time. All of the particles whose configuration coordinates are within a limited region are processed to completion before starting another region. In the design of our Illiac IV program, matching portions of the particle data, of the force field, and of the density count are in the memory at the same time, during the particle-pushing part of the calculation.

The cubic volume occupied by the system of particles is partitioned into 64 subdivisions along each edge; the force of calculation returns values at the center of each subdivision. Force values at points other than at the centers are found by linear interpolation. Densities are determined by counting the particles in each subdivision. The Cartesian coordinates are designated as follows: the 64 subdivisions along the x-coordinate

are each assigned respectively to one of the 64 PEs of the
Illiac IV. All 64 subdivisions of the y-coordinate and 8 of the
64 subdivisions of the z-coordinates are in the PE memory simultaneously. Eight such loadings are required to process the entire accessible configuration space. Each band of 8 subdivisions
of the z-coordinate is called a "z-sheet" (see Figure 5.42).

The cube represents the entire accessible configuration
space. The x-coordinate increases to the right, the z-coordinate
increases upward, and the y-coordinate increases into the page.
The eight z-sheets are shown. The volume of configuration space
for which particle data can be in one PE is the long thin rectangular parallelopiped that extends from one face of the cube to
the other in the y-direction, extends the depth of a z-sheet
(8 subdivisions = 8 L) in the z-direction, and for just one subdivision in the x-direction. All particles present in the volume shown are processed by one PE (PE number 25 in z-sheet number
2, starting from 0); the entire set of 64 PE's handle the full
volume of the z-sheet in parallel.

Allowable velocities are limited to +8 subdivisions per
time-step. After the particle pushing part of the integration,
those particles initially in one PE and in a certain z-sheet have
x- and z-values such that they may now belong in a different PE
(within 8 of the present PE number). Because diffusion is a dynamic process, those particles initially contained in one PE will
have diffused to other parts of the configuration space while
other particles will have diffused into this volume during the
same integration step. The particles now belong somewhere within the larger, dashed volume in Figure 5.42, but the data which
represent the particles are still in the original PEs.

The programming problem is to arrange for the particle's
data to be reassigned to the correct PE and brought back in the
proper z-sheet on the next integration step. This feature, along
with the need for frequent access to backup storage on the
Illiac disk, is the principal complication in the design of particle-pushing programs. With this partitioning of the configuration space, only those potential values which correspond to the
current z-sheet and those density counters which correspond to
the current z-sheet plus its immediate neighbors need be in the
core during the integration. The part of the program which
handles the actual integration is divided into several subprograms for readability and to simplify debugging.

Values for the potential at the center of each subdivision
are calculated from the new density data. Potentials go to zero
at infinite distance, the boundary condition that is appropriate
for the gravitational problem. The calculation proceeds through
Fourier transformations of the density; then the convolution theorem is used to obtain the transformed potentials, which are finally retransformed to yield values of the potentials at the grid
points. Forces are obtained in the particle pusher by quadratic
interpolation of the potential values.

These potential values need be in the core only for the
eight z-values in the current z-sheet; an additional z-value
above and below the current z-sheet is also in the core to facilitate interpolation. Potentials are packed two per Illiac word,

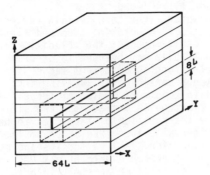

Figure 5.42   Memory allocation

with logical packing that permits full use of all 64 bits.
Density counters need be in the core only for the present z-sheet
and for the two neighboring z-sheets. Density counters are
packed four per Illiac word.

All data which refer to a certain particle are packed into
a single 64-bit Illiac word in seven sections: the position requires three 10-bit numbers; the velocity, three 8-bit numbers.
The remaining 10 bits may be used to describe other attributes
of the particle, such as different masses. At present, one bit
is used to flag a particle for plotting into an output file
which is used to construct motion pictures. Another bit has
been used to distinguish between gas and stars. The 10-bit des-
criptors allow the position of particles to be defined within
1/16 of the interval between PEs or up to 1/1024 of the edge of
the full configuration. All velocities and coordinates are packed as positive integers. A word of all 0's (not a valid particle
descriptor) is used to flag an empty location.

A major design consideration for a program such as this is
the selection of an output form which will make the state of the
program comprehensible. As we are able to manipulate increasingly massive data bases and more complex programs, the results
may be overwhelming. The author strongly believes that graphic
forms are the best means of comprehending large systems and their
components. The principal output from these simulations is taken
in the form of motion pictures that show the development of particle configurations, though other run summaries are occasionally
generated for special purposes (see Figure 5.43). These are generated on other computers from plot files produced in the Illiac
IV at run time. Approximately 2000 particles are flagged for
plotting. At each integration step, both the position and the
velocity of each flagged particle are copied onto the plot file.
Flagging assures that the same set of particles appears in the
plot file at each step. This provides continuity in the motion
pictures and also permits individual particle orbits to be followed. The plot file is generated by a special subroutine that
is called at each integration step, after the particle-pushing
and before looping back to the potential solver subroutine.

Figure 5.43 shows three orthogonal views of the configuration at
fixed times near the end of the run sequence. The body rotation axis
is along z. The three views in a row, left to right, are (x,y)
(x horizontal, y vertical), (y,z), and (x,z). The corner marks
show the limits of the available configuration space. The first
set of three views shows the configuration at step 108, while
there remains a part of a transient S-shape, with tails trailing
off the vertical bar. The second set of three views shows the
bar reached at the end of this run. This bar rotates end-over-
end in space, and has been followed for 1 1/2 complete rotations
past the end of this run. It is a long-lived form, and may represent the prolate shape of an elongated elliptical galaxy.

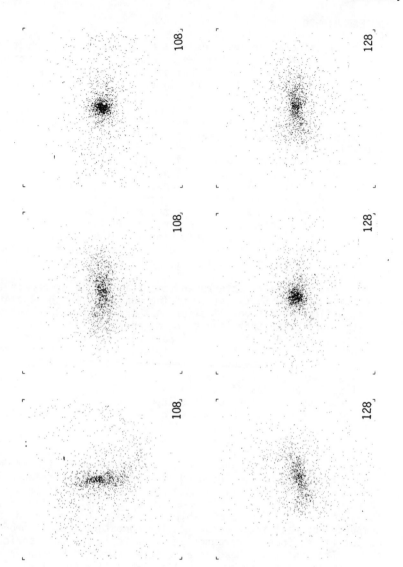

Figure 5.43   Development of particle configurations

OPERATING EXPERIENCE

The galaxy simulation routines were first used in a production
run in July 1976. Since then we have made about 50 production
runs and 40 debugging runs. Most of the debugging runs were
used to design and check out new initial conditions, but some
involved modifications to incorporate different intermediate
file formats, gas dynamics, and so on. While concurrently con-
ducting other research, the author designed, wrote, and checked
the programs in about one year, though some help with day-to-day
operations was available.

Galaxy simulations are initial value calculations. Other
experiments can use the same routine and the same boundary conditions with different initial loads. Most simulations have been
run with about 116,000 particles. Normal experimental sequences
span 128 integration steps, which represent about eight times as
long as the characteristic "dynamic" period for the system. Calculations of this kind are useful for studying phenomena which
occur on a "dynamic time scale"; eight of these units are normally adequate to probe the stability which is the object of these
investigations.

A run is usually interrupted after a certain number of integration steps with the state of the run saved in checkpoint
files. This permits verification that the program is running
satisfactorily and that it has not degenerated into some unin-
teresting condition, such as all particles having escaped, or all
having collapsed to a very small region. Runs are interrupted
after 16 integration steps and tape copies of the checkpoint
files are saved after each 32 steps. Checkpoints require space
for 1158 Illiac pages of storage (4632 TENEX pages); safe operation requires space for both the input and output files on the
TENEX disk as well as the dump file (34 Illiac pages of output).
A tape copy of the checkpoint file fills one reel.

The efficiency of 16-step runs is due mainly to the handling
of output files. Longer runs or more particles in the plot files
would entail correspondingly larger output files, which are more
troublesome to handle. The need to inspect results frequently,
the mean time to failure, and the priority ranking of jobs in the
batch queue also make shorter runs more desirable. Other features make longer runs preferable; because slow turnaround is
compunded by restricted access to the computers used to process
output files, four turnarounds per week represent good performance. The system overhead is also more costly with shorter runs
because most of it appears in Illiac-TENEX file transfers.

Recently a program revision has been tested which reduces
the size of the checkpoint files at a considerable loss of parallelism in the program's execution. It represents about a 50%
increase in Illiac run time for the particle-pusher subroutines
but works with 268 Illiac pages of checkpoint files. Yet because of system overhead, the total Illiac IV sequence time is
reduced so that the revision achieves an overall savings. A substantial increase in throughput is achieved because several run
sequences can proceed concurrently within the same file space on
TENEX.

CONCLUSION

In addition to the investigation of the stability problem in
current disk galaxy models, other studies planned or in progress
with the three-dimensional Illiac galaxy simulation programs are:
(1) The effects of gas dynamics and star formation on the early
collapse history of a galactic model; (2) An investigation of
how flat a stellar system can remain oblate; (3) The generality
of the phenomenon of strongly anisotropic velocity distributions
among collapse models; (4) Particle motions in the final state
bar in a free collapse of a rotating sphere of stars; (5) A variety of solar-system problems, in which particles may collide
inelastically. Readers are invited to send questions to the
author in care of the IAC Newsletter.

VI.   Commentary

The Illiac IV is a controversial machine. It cost too much, it took too long to get to work, it was offered to users before it was ready, and so on. Still it was a quantum jump forward in computer technology and it has produced some handsome accomplishments.

It is inappropriate to judge the reality of the Illiac in terms of the original goals for the Illiac. Rather, the Illiac should be assessed in terms of the progress it has achieved in computer technology and the utility it exhibits for today's requirements.

There have been many failed application projects on the Illiac. For the most part these have been software failures, at least since the Illiac was declared operational on November 1, 1975. Users of the Illiac were just not prepared for how different coding for a parallel computer is from coding for a conventional computer.

To some degree these issues have been addressed earlier in this book. This chapter looks more closely at these and tries to provide a sense of perspective for the reader.

A. Comments on Some Case Studies

The following are some selected observations on several programs which have been written for the Illiac. The intention is that they may shed some light on the nature of scientific computing that may be amenable to parallel computation. These case studies are important both for the problem formulation strategies, program design decisions and coding techniques.

1. Sparse matrix multiply

The following three paragraphs are a somewhat edited quotation from a report on three-dimensional stress wave simulation for the Illiac, authored by Gerald Frazier and Christian Peterson (DNA 331F report by Systems, Science and Software), pages 48 and 49.

> The time stepping process for this problem consists of the calculation U=V+A*W for each time step. The first term V is a vector and its calculation involves vector operations which require no interaction among the Illiac PE's. As a result, it is easily computed in parallel. Similar operations are involved in the calculation of the vector W. The significant calculation is the multiplication of the vector W by the large sparse matrix A. This multiplication accounts for almost all of the computation time that is required to complete one numerical time step. A sophisticated but simple mechansim has been developed to perform the sparse matrix multiply in parallel. The non-zero terms of A lie in 3x3 sub-matrices of A, no more than 27 such submatrices in any row of A. These are arranged on disk so that when read into memory each arrives in the PE which contains the three elements of W which enter into the computation of the product of the submatrix of A and W. Furthermore, as successive terms of A are read from disk the matrix row numbers increase monotonically (but not

Based on "Programming the Illiac", by David Stevenson, Sept. 1975 Appendix.

necessarily sequentially). This is done so that the
sparse matrix multiply can be completed in the order
of ascending row number.

The first submatrix to arrive in each PE from
the disk is multiplied by the appropriate three components of the vector W and the results are accumulated
in a buffer along with the row number identifier. This
operation allows some PE's to work ahead on other row
numbers. Since several rows may be processed simultaneously, a look-ahead buffer is maintained in each
PE which contains both the elements and their row numbers. Since rows will continuously be completed as new
ones are started, the buffer need only be large enough
to contain the maximum number to be worked on at one
time in any given PE. On the average, all of the multiplies for about 2.4 rows of the sparse matrix multiply are completed at a time.

During the matrix multiply, a test is made to see
if all contributions from the sparse matrix multiply
are ready to be summed for the node numbered n. If all
of the row numbers from the submatrix multiply are greater than n, then all contributions for n are calculated
(all PE's are now working on contributions to higher node
numbers). The contributions for n are then summed and
added to the other terms to obtain the advanced nodal
displacement U(n). This displacement vector is stored
in PEk, where k=n mod 64. If the contributions from row
n+1 are completed, then node n+1 is also advanced in
time, otherwise the next submatrix multiply in line for
each PE is performed. The parallel submatrix multiplies,
row sums, and disk reads continue until all of the A
matrix has been processed and all nodes have been advanced in time. The entire operation is repeated for
each time step.

This ends the quotation from the text. Some points are worth
mentioning here. First of all is the surprise that the matrix-vector
product is not programmed as vector operations but rather as separate
processes (the Illiac is being used not as a vector processor, but as
multiple processors, each working largely in its own "context"). The
difference in this case is essentially 99 vector component-wise multiplies (of vectors of length 3N, where N is the number of mesh nodes)
plus aligning and summing the 99 result vectors, versus 27N matrix-
vector products (involving 3x3 matrices) plus aligning and summing the
27N vectors (of length 3). The vector formulation costs about 18%
more storage -- the added padding of zeros is necessary for alignment
purposes -- plus the concomitant increase in arithmetics -- the multiplications by the padding zeros; the use of zero here is exactly analogous to its use for positional notation in number systems. On the
other hand, the vector formulation eliminates the control structure
which tests to see when all information for updating each node has
been assembled and can be combined. It also eliminates the buffer
management for these intermediate results. The real subtlety of the
problem lies in the aligning and summing involved in the two approaches,

plus the possible necessity (based on small core memory) to partition
long vectors,but we will leave the matter here.

The non-vector approach does lend itself to matrices which arise
from arbitrarily connected grids. But the automatic grid generation
used by this project generates grids which are unions of regions homeo-
morphic to a cubical lattice, hence the structure of the matrix A will
have large blocks along its diagonal where the above vector approach
will hold, and its off-diagonal blocks, most of which are identically
zero, will have an analogous vectorizable structure.

2. A Model for Disaster

The Tensor code (Final Report of the Tensor/Illiac IV Project,
ARPA Order 1839 (UCRL-51467) by Tad Kishi, 1973) is based on a grid
which moves with the material; the solution at a grid point involves
information from nine neighboring points nearest to it. Here whatever
regularity exists in the grid at the beginning of the simulation is
rapidly destroyed over the iterations, so a vector formulation of the
sparse matrix is clearly inappropriate. The next question is, can an
Illiac-type architecture, viewed as each processor working in its
separate context but doing roughly the same thing, provide a suitable
environment for such calculations? Or is this a formulation best
suited for some other type of computer?

Unfortunately, the project gives no answer, since it was a complete failure. In fact, the charitable thing would be to forget this
fiasco entirely, but since a computer is what it appears to its users
to be, it is important to consider this project, if only as a study in
cognitive psychology.

> The project was essentially doomed by its charter.
> "Bound by the primary requirement to reconfigure an
> existing production code, the development of effec-
> tive parallel processing methods for the Illiac com-
> puter system has been an exceedingly difficult one.
> It could not have been accomplished by a simple trans-
> lation of the existing FORTRAN code to a comparable
> language for the Illiac. The FORTRAN listing of the
> Tensor code is a poor substitute for documentation.
> It is next to impossible to understand the Tensor
> code or to derive effective algorithms for parallel
> processing from a code that was programmed in assembly
> language for a conventional computer and then brute
> force converted to FORTRAN. The task has only been
> accomplished by reformulating and reexamining the basic
> finite difference equations. Unfortunately, neither a
> consistent nor complete set of equations of the exist-
> ing code was available and had to be redeprived (sic)
> by members on the ARPA Tensor project." (One can only
> wonder what the sequential code has actually been com-
> puting all this time). (p. 3)

To seal the project's fate, it was decided to code in an assembler language. The reasons given were that the higher level languages

were undergoing development and hence (a) did not generate reasonable
object code (which is irrelevant; bad code can be selectively tuned)
and (b) their programming support was minimal at best. The result of
this decision was predictable, "Once a course of action was decided
upon, it was literally embedded in "cement'. Programming in assembly
language left little or no flexibility in our code development"
(pp. 3-4). Thus the conclusions drawn by this project were largely due
to the propagation of poor early design decisions. A stunning example
of this occurred when the program was restructured, proving "that skewing of data, which we originally believed to be essential for efficient
boundary calculations, was immaterial. To reconsider the skewing of
data at this point in our code development was next to impossible.
This is the price one pays when a code of this complexity is programmed
in assembly language." (p. 14) There was an even greater price:
the code never ran. "Two simulation runs have been attempted in this
configuration. The code has crashed in loop 1 in the k=0 boundary
routine. The results have been evaluated, but there are no plans to
continue debugging." (p. 15)

        What were the perceived problems of programming this formulation
on the Illiac? There were essentially three. First, "The inherent
geometric structure of the 64-PE Illiac computer system imposes an
artificial boundary (modulo 64) on the grid system and must be contend-
ed with throughout the program for an array not commensurate with this
base". (p. 6) Second, "considerations of the boundary calculations...
required skewing as a fundamental requirement of the problem logistics
for efficient PE usage. However, a given storage assignment for one
phase of the calculation may not be suited for another part of the
calculation." (p. 7) And finally, third, "the calculational procedures of the slip lines for the Illiac array processors require extensive movement of data across the PE's in order to meet the nearest
neighbor requirements for the nine-point difference scheme. This is
the result of the change in the nearest neighbor relationship with
time. Thus the values necessary for interpolation may be in some arbitrary assignment across the processing elements." (p. 63)

        The first perceived problem is illusory; it is solved by logic-
ally programming in a system of N processing elements and then simula-
ting N processors using 64 or fewer processors (this is what a higher
level language should be able to do). As seen above, the second problem actually turned out to be a red herring, and probably a costly one
at that. The third problem, which is the heart of the matter of whether this formulation can be effectively used on an Illiac-type computer,
arises from assuming a fixed data structure; but if the grid moves with
the physics of the process, it seems reasonable to entertain the notion
that its representation moves with the computation of the algorithm;
this probably won't solve the problem, but it might mitigate its pre-
sumed seriousness. Another possible approach would be to use a grid
structure fine enough so that slip lines and any other physically interesting phenomenon could be derived from calculations performed on
the fixed grid--this would be an example of using raw computational
power in place of the potentially staggering overhead of bookkeeping
and routing of information needed for a more sophisticated formulation. This solution may not be aesthetically pleasing, but it might
be the best cost-effective method (or even the only technologically

feasible method for very large models). Since the purpose of computing is insight, the only question is whether this insight should be
derived directly from the mechanics of the algorithm or be inferred
from the results of the calculation.

Notice that all three problems have a common thread: the vagar-
ies of the programming language, in revealing all of the machine characteristics, have given the greedy programmer more than enough rope to
hang himself in trying to pull the last bit of speed out of the machine.
This is a very serious problem, since it distracts from the real issues.
"Skewing and the pseudo 64-PE boundary are new experiences and add to
the difficulties in visualizing parallel processes in the Illiac."
(p. 7)

3. Monte Carlo Methods on the Illiac

The real problem with the slip-line is the interaction among dynamically varying groups of nodes, and the attendant bookkeeping necessary to locate specific nodes or assemble the necessary information.
Monte Carlo methods which are formulated so that interactions among
constituent elements are implicit can effectively minimize this overhead problem, but at the expense of substituting an apparent "random-
ness" in the control-flow. That this substitution can be successful
on the Illiac must certainly be one of the ironies of contemporary
computing, since "conventional wisdom" had held that the single-instruc-
tion stream was the constraining factor to the efficient utilization
of the Illiac, which does not obviously lend itself to branch-driven
programs. (Conventional wisdom also ignored completely the impact of
the memory structure on effective data utilization, which probably will
be the constraining factor once more experience with the Illiac is
reported).

A successful Monte Carlo code for the Illiac is reported in
SAM-IV: a three dimensional Monte Carlo radiation penetration code
for the Illiac IV by E. S. Troubetzkoy, M. H. Kalos and H. Steinberg
of Mathematical Applications Group, Inc., DNA 3303F, 1973. Of particular interest are the mechanics used to implement a disorderly control
flow (one which takes many different branches when executed successively of different data by a sequential computer).

> "The major difficulty with attempting to implement
> a Monte Carlo code ... on the Illiac lies in the
> intrinsic disorderly nature of Monte Carlo logic.
> ... The order and the nature of the physical events
> have little, if any, correlation from (particle to
> particle). The naive approach of following 64 his-
> tories simultaneously is therefore not feasible as
> the parallelism breaks down almost immediately.
> Our approach is to initiate many histories in each
> PE, and hold all of them in abeyance until any cal-
> culation is required" -- that is, until enough PE's
> have particles upon which the same calculation can
> be performed. (p. 10)

The basic idea here is reminiscent of the control mechanism in a production system, or Markov algorithm, where, at least conceptually, processes are activated in an associative manner whenever certain specified conditions in the data base arise. In the Monte Carlo program, certain computations are performed whenever a certain amount of parallelism is possible.

4. Conclusions

A general statement of the philosophy underlying the successful programming strategy would be: divide the problem formulation into as many independent steps as possible -- steps which would have to be executed repeatedly on varying data by a sequential computer -- and then at each point of the parallel computation, choose to execute that step which will utilize the greatest amount of parallelism. The ultimate success of any code seems to lie in the ability to minimize the overhead of bookkeeping, either implicitly (as for example, when the computation required for a particular node is known to be completed when all PE's are working on computations involving higher numbered nodes) or explicitly (as where the formulation is in theory without any dynamically varying interrelationships among distinct components; that is, the aggregate effects of interest can be viewed as data reduction which can be done without regard to order and in a cumulative fashion, and hence lends itself well to homogeneous parallel processing).

One of the unifying characteristics of these three projects is their unwillingness to view the Illiac as a vector computer. This may be because of the small random access memory or because of the short natural vector length. Or it could be a (perhaps deserved) infatuation with a sequential program. However, if one generalizes the notion of a vector operation from component-wise scalar operations to more complex operations on structured components, then these programs may be interpreted as attempts to simulate generalized vector computations.

B. Assessing the ILLIAC for Wind Tunnel Simulations

The ever-increasing complexity and broadening performance envelopes of modern aircraft have fostered a dramatic increase in the quantity and quality of flow simulation data required in the aerodynamic design process. As this trend continues, the cost in both time and money to obtain these data by experimental means becomes increasingly burdensome. If this rise continues, the test time for each new aircraft will, by 1980, exceed 10 years (equivalent, for example, to two wind tunnels working day and night for 5 years) at a corresponding cost of approximately $100 million. The situation is further complicated by the fact that, in many cases, it is impractical or even impossible to obtain needed data by ground-based experimental facilities. Consequently, there is a strong motivation to seek more efficient methods for providing reliable flow-field simulations.

An alternate approach receiving growing attention is to use large, high-speed computers. The differential equations governing fluid motion are solved for a large number of grid points appropriately spaced throughout the flow field. Such simulations, which form the basis of computational aerodynamics, can be intricate and very time-consuming if the geometries are realistic and the flow has regions of turbulence. Thus, the completeness and accuracy of computed flow simulations depend heavily on the computer power available.

*Based on "Computational Aerodynamics-Illiac IV and Beyond", by F. R. Bailey, Digest Compcon, Spring 1977, pp 8-11.

311

STATUS OF COMPUTATIONAL AERODYNAMICS

The set of nonlinear, partial differential equations (Navier-Stokes equations) governing fluid flows has been known for over a century. However, solution of these equations for realistic aerodynamic flow fields defies analytical treatment, and a purely computational approach requires a resolution many orders of magnitude beyond present computer capability. As in analytical techniques, progress to obtain numerical solutions is made by investigating suitable approximations to the full fluid-dynamic equations. These approximations can be conveniently classified into four stages (1) outlined in Table 6.1. For each stage, the table lists the nature of the approximation, its principal limitations, its developmental status, and the computer class needed for its application to three-dimensional aerodynamic design simulations. Briefly, the four stages are summarized as follows:

Stage I - Linearized Inviscid Approximation

This highly simplified approximation, whose roots go back to the 1930's, is based on the superposition of basic known solutions and requires spatial divisions only along the configuration surface. With the development during the 1960's of computers of the IBM 360/65 and CDC 6600 class, it became practical to compute linearized, inviscid flows over quite realistic aircraft configurations. This approximation is limited, however, to purely subsonic and supersonic flows and does not treat viscous effects.

Stage II - Nonlinear Inviscid Approximation

The addition of nonlinearity requires numerous evaluations of the flow variables at grid points in the fluid volume surrounding the configuration as well as on its surface. The computation of nonlinear, inviscid flows about three-dimensional configurations is practical today with CDC 7600 class computers. Although limited to attached boundary-layer flows where viscous effects are not large, this stage makes possible the simulation of important transonic and hypersonic flows.

Stage III - Viscous, Averaged Navier-Stokes Equations

This approximation describes the mean fluid motion of turbulent flows by averaging the Navier-Stokes equations. No terms in these equations are neglected, but the averages of certain terms involving the turbulent mass, momentum, and energy transfer must be modeled, which is the main limitation to the accuracy. This approximation is a significant step toward the simulation of turbulent flow regions critical to the prediction of aerodynamic forces. While it is now possible to obtain two-dimensional simulations on the CDS 7600 and Illiac IF class computers, three-dimensional simulations for aircraft design are estimated to need a computing power at least 100 times larger.

State of approximation	Approximation to governing flow equations	Principal limitations	Status	Computer class for practical three-dimensional engineering calculations
I Inviscid linearized	Viscous and nonlinear inviscid terms neglected	Slender configurations; small angle of attack; perfect gas; no transonic flow; no hypersonic flow; no flow separation	Two-dimensional flows, 1930's; three-dimensional flows, 1960's; used in current aircraft design	IBM 360/65 CDC 6600
II Inviscid nonlinear	Viscous terms neglected	No flow separation	Two-dimensional flows, 1971; three-dimensional flows, 1975; early stages of application to aircraft design	CDC 7600 ILLIAC IV STAR 100
III Viscous, averaged Navier-Stokes	No terms neglected, turbulent transport terms modeled	Accuracy of turbulence model	Two-dimensional flow development; early stages of three-dimensional development	10^2 x CDC 7600
IV Large eddy simulation	Subgrid-scale motion modeled	Accuracy of Navier-Stokes equations and modeling	Development for very simple flows	10^2 x CDC 7600

Table 6.1   Stages of approximation in computational aerodynamics

Stage IV - Large Eddy Simulation

For practical aerodynamics purposes, this could well be the final
stage of approximation in which the significant large-scale turbulent eddies would be computed from the Navier-Stokes equations
for a sufficiently long time to yield a satisfactory solution of
both attached and separated turbulent flows. The relatively large
eddies responsible for most mass, momentum, and energy transport
would be computed directly, while transport due to subgrid motion
would be modeled to permit use of the largest practical grid spacing. Even so, the number of grid points required for good resolution may be very large, and present estimates indicate a computer power on the order of 10^4 larger than the CDC 7600 would
be needed.

Clearly, the realization of the full potential of computational aerodynamics depends heavily on advances in computer technology as well as modeling accuracy and algorithm efficiency.
That is not to say, however, that activity is stalled, for a great
deal of research and development is currently under way in all
four stages using present computers. For example, Figure 6.1
shows the dramatic improvements that have been achieved in numerical methods for stages II and III. (2)

Another area of activity, centered at Ames Research Center,
is the application of the Illiac IV computer to aerodynamic problems, which consumes about 20% of the machine availability. The
goal of this effort is to use the parallel computing ability of
Illiac IV to take advantage of the parallel nature of most fluid
dynamics problems, that is, the dynamics at one location in the
flow are described by the same equations that apply to neighboring locations and can be solved simultaneously using the same
algorithm.

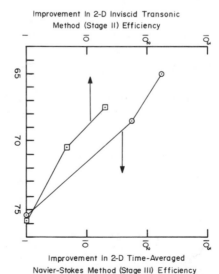

Figure 6.1   Improvements in numerical methods

LESSONS ON EFFICIENT USE OF ILLIAC IV

The introduction of the Illiac IV initiated a learning process for its efficient use in aerodynamic simulations which is still in progress. It became apparent at once that efficient use of the machine's architecture required the user to become much more familiar with its hardware capabilities than is the case with conventional serial computers. To meet this requirement and still be able to communicate with the machine in a straightforward manner, Ames developed CFD, a FORTRAN-like vector language tailored to the Illiac-IV architecture. As a result, efficient programs are generated with little more than the normal FORTRAN coding effort. However, because of the machine's primitive system software and its single-job operation, it is difficult to use the Illiac itself for program debugging. Therefore, CFD can also be translated into serial FORTRAN for code development and debugging on conventional computers such as the IBM 360/65 and the CDC 7600.

Having been provided with an efficient high-level language, the Illiac IV user concentrates on taking full advantage of the machine's parallel computation capabilities in terms of both algorithm development and coding. Again, it quickly became apparent that data management plays a key role in the efficient use of the parallel array architecture. Parallel computation also means parallel data structure because, for strictly parallel computations, PE's can only operate on data within their respective memories. Practical two- and three-dimensional computational methods call for the solution of multiple tridiagonal systems arranged in sets, each set coupling grid points in a different coordinate direction. With these so-called dimensionally split implicit procedures, maximum parallelism is achieved by initially aligning the PEM's with grid variables in one dimension, solving the systems in parallel, and then realigning the variables for the next direction. The data realignment or transpose is efficiently done using the PE routing network at a penalty of only a few percent in overhead. The maximizing of parallelism via data transposes has wide application to fluid dynamics problems and has been applied, for example, to fast Fourier transforms contained in spectral methods and to a variety of boundary conditions.

With a knowledge of the Illiac array structure and the availability of CFD, the user can efficiently program the machine with relative ease so long as the problem fits within the collective 131,072-word storage of the PEM's. Unfortunately, many problems do not fit, including three-dimensional problems and efficient two-dimensional problems that require large amounts of scratch storage. Scratch storage can increase significantly in parallel computations. These larger problems must use the 16-million word, disk memory. This memory has a 600 million bit/sec transfer rate, but the access time may be large due to the 40-msec disk rotation period. The disk may be mapped, that is, data may be stored in predetermined locations, and the user must use this unusual capability carefully to minimize access time.

EXAMPLES OF ILLIAC IV PERFORMANCE

As a measure of the Illiac IV performance for computational aerodynamic problems, a comparison of Illiac IV and CDC 7600 computational speeds for four sample problems, coded by typical users, is shown in Figure 6.2. The comparison includes two speeds for Illiac IV, one with CU instruction overlap and one without. The speeds for the CDC 7600 are those obtained using the FTN-OPT2 compiler. Without overlap, the Illiac IV shows a 3-5 times improvement over the CDC 7600 and an average gain of about 3.5. From initial test results, overlap mode (to be operational early in 1977) will provide additional improvements by a factor of 2.

BEYOND ILLIAC IV

Even though Illiac IV is classified as a supercomputer, it is not nearly powerful enough to take computational aerodynamics to the next step - timely and accurate simulations of three-dimensional flows governed by the stage III approximation. This is truly a large problem by present standards. The size of the problem is appreciated by noting that it requires about a two-order-of-magnitude increase in computed information over that needed for two-dimensional simulations performed on Illiac IV. The necessary processing capability is estimated at a billion floating point operations per second with a memory of 40 million words. This represents a 100-fold increase over the CDC 7600 and nearly as much over Illiac IV. Because of the large benefits that can be gained by such a capability, however, serious consideration is being given to the development of such a machine as the heart of a computational aerodynamic design facility to be available early in the next decade. The purpose of the facility is to provide, at reasonable cost, a steady stream of computed flow simulations to be used in aircraft design.

The stated performance goal will undoubtedly be achieved by taking advantage of the parallel nature of fluid dynamics problems. This will be reflected both in the organization of the solution algorithm and in the computer hardware. The interdependency of the two may point to a specially designed processor or an enhanced general purpose design. In either case, many critical issues involving tradeoffs between algorithm and hardware must be studied.

One issue is how to obtain the raw computing power. This is likely to come about through the design of complex hardware organizations made possible by high-density circuit technology. However, limits on circuit density and on the number of devices that can be assembled and expected to work reliably in a coherent manner imply a limit on the number of concurrent operations a processor can handle. Currently, this limit appears to be much smaller than the number of concurrent operations present in the problem. For parallel and pipeline processor, it is the number of parallel operations that count, and nonparallel operations, although concurrent, can seriously degrade performance. One solution is to design a machine with the capability of performing concurrent operations that need not be parallel; the other is to design solution methods for which the nonparallel part is insignificant. Recent developments in three-dimensional flow algorithms indicate that the latter may well be possible.

An even more critical issue is how to achieve the memory bandwidth necessary to support the raw computing power. Here, the manner in which the solution methods access data may be a determining factor. Certain implicit methods require the flow variables (five for each grid point) be accessed by successive sweeping of grid planes, each sweep in a different coordinate direction. This is done on Illiac IV, for example, by the data transpose mentioned earlier. On the other hand, explicit methods can be constructed to continually cycle through memory along the same path. Sophisticated numerical analysis is required to assess the possible tradeoffs between hardware and algorithm organization.

A final issue is the usability of the machine. To be used efficiently, the machine must be reliable in both hardware and software. The user should be able to take full advantage of the hardware through an easily manageable, rational, hierarchy of programming languages. Tasks such as disk mapping must be eliminated insofar as possible. Finally, the high cost of software development must be kept at a minimum by concurrent software-hardware design and development, keeping in mind the computer's application.

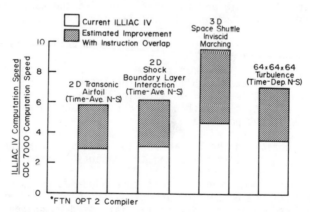

Figure 6.2   Comparison of Illiac IV and CDC 7600 computation speeds

References

1.   D. R. Chapman, H. Mark, and M. W. Pirtle, "Computers vs. Wind Tunnels for Aerodynamic Flow Simulations", Astronautics and Aeronautics, April 1975.

2.   D. R. Chapman, "Status and Prospects of Computational Fluid Dynamics", von Karman Institute for Fluid Dynamics Lecture Series 87, Rhode-Saint-Genese, Belgium, March 15-19, 1976.

C.   ILLIAC Instruction Speedup

THE MEGAFLOP GAME

Whereas computers like the Illiac are used to do a lot of floating point operations, the rate that these machines can do these
operations in a particular, special case is in some way a measure
of merit. These special cases represent absolute upper bounds on
arithmetic bandwidth and therefore can give the user some idea of
the feasibility of using a particular machine in a particular application.
     None of these measurements can give a very accurate picture
of what the final outcome will be in any application. Generally,
however, the more 'benchmarks' one has with which to measure a
machine's peak rate capabilities, the better chance one has to
understand whether use of the machine is feasible and how to
approach a particular problem to possibly take advantage of a
machine's strong points and avoid its weak points.
     With this in mind it does not seem fatuous to examine partic-
ular mechanisms in the Illiac and to increase their speed, thereby improving the peak rates and the potential speed of the machine.
     It also seems probable that some educated guessing as to the
frequency of use of particular operations might be useful in predicting the payback for any particular speed-up change. It would
be better to replace guesswork with actual measurements of interesting programs by a hardware monitoring device.

SOME SEMI-HARD CONSTRAINTS ON ILLIAC SPEED

     The control unit (CU) was originally designed to run at
25MHz (40 nsec cycle) and very early in the game the speed was
reduced to 20 MHz on paper. Some of the old memorabilia from the

---

This Section is based on an article in the IAC Newsletter by
Steve Tulloh, March, 1978.

design days show the processing element (PE) design running at
20 MHz. The processing element memory (PEM) was designed to run
at a 10 MHz (pipelined) rate and it probably can be run at 8 Mhz
now.

The PEM rate is additionally limited by the fact that the
operand select gate (OSG) in the PE is used both for sending the
address to the PE from the CU and receiving the data from the
PEM. This constrains the fetch rate to once per two cycles, which
fits well with the 8 MHz PEM rate. The current PEM access time
is about 200 nsec and with the various delays that are added in
the PE by sending the address and receiving the data into some
register, the PEM access time is probably limited to 4 cycles at
16 Mhz.

The instructions, ADRN and MLRN, seem to be the most popular
PE instructions, and indeed the PEs were designed to be floating
add and floating multiply functional units. Consequently PE
arithmetic speed-up potential is very limited. The original design called for a 7 cycle ADRN and a 9 cycle MLRN (64 bit mode).
At this moment the ADRN also takes 9 cycles because of some long
paths in the PE. A couple of extra cycles were added to give the
PE more time to process in the cycles where the long paths are
used. There is a possibility that at least one of the cycles in
the 7-cycle ADRN can be eliminated and this would reduce it to 6,
limiting the arithmetic bandwidth for this particular instruction
to 170 Mflops at 16 MHz. Again, though this is an upper bound,
it is certainly not the only one since there is no time alloted
for accumulating operands and saving away results.

REVIEW OF ADVAST SPEED-UP FOCUS

The processing of instructions in the CU starts in the Instruction look ahead (ILA) portion where blocks of 16 instructions
are fetched from the PEM as a result of either a JUMP/SKIP type
instruction executed by ADVAST or the crossing of a midblock
boundary in the program. The prefetching goes on in parallel
with other ADVAST functions but JUMP/SKIPs and IWS fetches are
executed by ILA while ADVAST waits. It's not known how much interference such waiting introduces into programs or how much
ADVAST waits for FINST queue positions.

Once the instructions get into ADVAST there are many extra
cycles in common instructions. For all simple operations such as
adding, leading ones detection, logical operations, shifts, etc.,
one clock should be enough. In the case of ADVAST local memory
(ADB) references, two cycles are enough. In the instructions
which use functional units more than once (e.g., CSB) more than
one step must be taken.

The problems faced in implementing these speed-ups are
of two kinds: (1) long delay paths and (2) excessive design
allowance for long delays which don't exist.

These kinds of ADVAST speed-ups require very little actual hardware work, but do require a great amount of engineering time which
is very difficult to estimate. They also require a fair amount of

machine time for testing to verify that the ramifications are
innocuous.

SOME EXAMPLES

The load accumulator from local memory (LDL) and the store
accumulator to local memory (STL) instructions take 3 cycles when
not indexed, and 5 cycles when indexed. The speed-up should reduce these times to 2 and 3 cycles respectively. This kind of
speed-up approaches 50% and is easy enough to take advantage of
since most programs are filled with these instructions.

Other things remaining in ADVAST for speed-up are the BIN/
LOAD instructions which are not overlapped now. SETC and LDC instructions can be speeded up somewhat since they now wait too
many cycles for the PE data.

The machine currently takes 16 cycles to execute this loop
once, which when itemized amounts to 9 or 10 cycles for the LDA
and 4 or 5 for the STA with a dead cycle (included in all FINST
instructions) between each. This amounts to a transfer rate
(which is some measure since no flops exist in the loop) of 1 row
per 1.28 usec or 3.2 gigabits.

Were the memory to be overlapped in FINST such that a new
memory cycle could be prepared before the old one finished, the
same loop could take as few as 6 cycles which is a speed-up of
2.5 times. An example of how to take advantage of such overlap
follows:

```
LOOP:   LDA X(ACO)
        LDB X+1(ACO)
        STA Y(ACO)
        STB Y+1(ACO)
        TXLTM ACO,LOOP
```

Here the effective rate is increased because the PE can fetch
the next word while the first word is coming in. The new rate is
2 rows per 8 cycles or a speed-up factor of 4. Such programming
currently buys nothing in terms of speed because the data must be
in the register before FINST will even think about executing
another instruction. The new transfer rate, with 16 Mhz added in,
would be 16.384 gigabits or a factor of 5.12. Incidentally,
ADVAST takes 15 cycles in the former loop (2 for each indexed PE
instruction and 11 for the TXLTM) and 19 cycles in the second
loop so quite a few ADVAST speed-ups would have to be installed
in order that FINST could be used effectively in these cases.
For example, a 1 cycle indexed PE instruction and a 4 cycle TXLTM
would handle it nicely.

Consider another loop:

```
STRTUP: LDS W(ACO)
    LOOPL   LDA
            ADRN X(ACO)
            ADRN Y(ACO)
            LDS W+L(ACO)
            STA Z(ACO)
            TXLTN ACO,LOOP
```

which is a rather trivial Z=W+X+Y and contains a prefetch of the
next W row to take advantage of FINST full overlap of memory operations with arithmetic. There are 4 memory operations (3 fetches and 1 store) which account for most of the 38 clocks that
this loop takes. The 10 cycles in each of the two ADRNs are
hidden. At 12.5 Mhz, the current frequency, this amounts to about
42 Mflops. If all possible improvements were made, such a loop
would require only 14 cycles at 16 Mhz or 146 Mflops or a speed-
up of 3.5.

The possible ADB extension discussed elsewhere should also
improve the speed because most likely the technology of the new
memory would allow one cycle access to ADB.

Enhancements to the instruction set for extended memory
bandwidth improvement would not significantly affect ADVAST except for the obvious changes to the control logic for those things
that ADVAST may need to do to get the instruction ready for FINST.

REVIEW OF FINST SPEED-UP FOCUS

Considering the importance of the PEM resource, an effort
has been started to streamline the use of PEM by FINST. Presently FINST overlaps a memory operation with a previous arithmetic
operation but will not overlap a previous memory operation.
Successive memory operations now take 10 clocks each. The target
is to reduce each memory operation to 4 clocks and overlap them
as well.

In the attempt to make Illiac operational certain modifications were installed which made the Illiac work, but also de-
graded the performance. In the attempt to increase performance
of the Illiac, IAC is systematically and temporarily removing the
modifications, uncovering the design errors concealed by the modifications, and installing new changes which allow the Illiac to
perform more effectively. Examples of this process are removal
of the dead time between all FINST instructions, reducing the
ROUTE steps from two clocks to one and permitting ROUTE to be
overlapped.

Presently the ROUTE instruction is not overlapped because it
inhibits the PU clocks. In an effort to produce a two-clock period data pulse with no spikes, the ROUTE instruction inhibits the
intermediate spike producing clock to the latches. An overlapping instruction would have no knowledge of this inhibited clock
and could perform its function without knowing that it had no
effect in the PU. To prevent errors of this type, no instruction

is permitted to overlap ROUTE. However, a one clock time ROUTE
would not need to inhibit PU clocks and hence could be overlapped.

SPECIAL ENHANCEMENTS

Enhancements to the Illiac's useability such as additional
instructions, bigger local memory and better route capability,
probably do not significantly affect the speed-up effort or the
memory enhancement possibilities. Some comments, however, are
probably in order.

Were the I4DM to be replaced or enhanced by a relatively
fast random access external memory it may be profitable to add
an instruction or set of instructions that would allow full advantage to be taken of the potentially high bandwidth between the
PEM and the external memory. Additional local memory in CU of
any appreciable size may suggest special move capabilities between this local memory and other memories in the Illiac system
to enhance the useability of such a memory addition.

CONCLUSION

Enhancements to the PEM could slow down the overall speed of
the Illiac because of the need for very large amounts of memory
in the Illiac system. Changes to the PEM are likely to be more
costly than replacement of the I4DM in several ways. Chips chos-
en for the job should be fairly fast and therefore more costly.
They may need refresh and page mode mechanisms in the CU which
have potentially high cost as well.

Other speed-up modifications mentioned above are not affected by memory enhancements nor do they affect each other very much.
The amount of speed-up is in the 1 to 3 times range and consequently probably does not place as significant a burden on PEM
size or I4DM size as do other aspects of Illiac problem solving.

D. The Effects of the ILLIAC IV System on Computing Technology

This section, based on an internal memo at the Institute for Advanced Computation by G. Feierbach and D. Stevenson in August 1976, outlines some of the contributions of the Illiac project to computer science and technology. Sixteen distinct advances in four categories are described.

COMPONENT AND MANUFACTURING TECHNOLOGY

A. Major Impetus to ECL Development

The I4 system was the first large scale use of ECL integrated circuits. The circuits developed for the I4 system were subsequently improved by TI and used for their ASC computer. (Of the 33 IC types used in the I4 main frame, 14 ASC parts can be directly substituted. It is questionable whether TI would have built the ASC computer had the development of the IC family not been underwritten by the Illiac requirements.)

B. Test Bed for Design Automation

The circuit cards in the Illiac main-frame were designed using a design automation system. This was the earliest successful large scale use of design automation outside of IBM. The Illiac contract provided both the financial resources and the level of difficulty to mature this process significantly. This is now a widespread practice in the computer industry.

C. New Contribution to Logic Circuitry

The barrel switch is a major circuit innovation in the Illiac that enables full word length shifts in one machine clock. This is used for floating point normalization and alignment and for shifting in general. Current supercomputer designs incorporate the barrel switch in one form or another. It has become popular enough that Fairchild has created an Isoplanar TI ECL part (F100158) which is essentially an 8 bit slice of a barrel switch.

323

D.   First Significant Use of Semiconductor Memory

The 256x1 bipolar RAMs in the I4 PE memories are the first
use of bipolar semiconductor memories in a large scale computer main memory. Since thin film memories were also considered (even prototyped) but rejected in favor of semiconductor memories, this was probably a significant turning
point for the two technologies. The memory systems developed for the Illiac IV became the father for the first
commercially available semiconductor memories offered by
Fairchild.
     A minor additional note: by using an interlocking mesh
for power and ground distribution on the memory PC boards
and judicious placing of ground strips between signals requiring isolation, it was possible to arrange the memory on
a two sided PC board for a significant cost savings. Up to
that time it was felt mandatory to have separate power and
ground planes in addition to the circuit layers.

E.   Definitive Contribution to Interconnection Technology

The system was the first to make use of extremely dense
belted cables which are soldered to paddle card PC boards
using infrared light and then covered with epoxy. These
cable assemblies are a major constituent of the system but
have been responsible for very few failures. The current
state of the art in cabling (excepting fiber optic technology) can not do better today.

F.   A Major Milestone in Multilayer PC Cards

The I4 control unit PC cards are 16" x 20" and have as many
as 12 layers. Not only was this the first successful utilization of large multilayer laminated boards, but it is
still a state of the art achievement.

MACHINE ARCHITECTURE

A.   Definitive Demonstration of Array Approach to Computation

An operational Illiac validates the design concept of array
processors; it has become the standard against which to
measure proposals for increasing computer speed through
architectural innovations involving replication of components.

B.   Synchronous Control to Focus Research on Efficiency of Computation

The Illiac demonstrates the sufficiency of a single instruction stream to control the multiple data streams encountered
in scientific computing. In a single stroke, this approach
(via the route instruction) solves the problem of synchron-

izing processor communication. This has permitted research
to focus on the efficient utilization of the array using the
single instruction stream, in contrast to the case of asynchronous, independent processors, where research has focused
largely on synchronization issues and only recently turned
to the efficiency of algorithms in such an environment.

C. First Large Scale Computer to be Microprogrammed

The I4 control unit contains a ROM driven microprocessor
which converts single instructions into a sequence of enable
signals for the PEs. At the time the I4 was designed, the
only significant machines to be microprogrammed were the
lower model numbers of the IBM 360 series. The prevailing
opinion in the computer community at the time was that micro-
programming was slow and that fast main frames could only
be designed using hardwired logic. Today, major supercomputers (including the Star-100 and ASC) contain micro-coded
control logic.

D. Synchronization of Independent Disk Drives

All the I4 disk memories are synchronized to within 2 degrees
of a revolution. This was formerly thought to be impossible
on theoretical grounds: a continuous feedback mechanism requires instantaneous acceleration and this was felt impractical to obtain without very complex detection and control
circuitry and elaborate sensors and control effectors. The
method actually used is a startlingly simple use of an oscillator as a virtual disk. Some manufacturers have shown
interest in utilizing this innovation since it makes possible very high bandwidth synchronous transfers from multiple drives.

E. Exhaustive Simulation as a Realistic Diagnostic Tool

PESO is a PE simulator that runs on the Illiac (even when
some PE's are down). The ratio of the computer power of
the entire I4 system to the simplicity of a single PE makes
it possible to simulate completely the complex operations of
a single PE in a few milliseconds of I4 time. This has
opened the door to a novel diagnostic technique not possible
on other machine architectures: exhaustive simulation of
all possible single gate faults. Over four thousand cases
can be tested at the same time so that within about five
minutes a list of possible fault locations that match the
failure symptom is in the hands of a technician. About a
third of the PE faults show up in this manner, making it a
powerful tool in system maintenance which would otherwise
be unavailable.

F.   Test Bed for Future Machines

The Illiac IV has taught some important lessons which will
have significant impact on future parallel processors. In
particular, the processor interconnection scheme has been
found to be wanting. It is both inflexible and difficult
to program.
  Research in this area has focused on the optimum interconnection scheme and on the most efficient way to use a
given interconnection pattern. All this has been predicated
on the assumptions that the connection network must be fixed
(hardwired) and that each processor can be connected to only
a few other processors (because of fan-out limitations or
cost considerations). These assumptions are no longer valid
since there are other alternatives than interconnection
schemes based on cabling, and the next generation of array
computers should re-focus the attention that the Illiac has
inadvertently misdirected.
  Further, the Illiac IV is a fixed configuration with no
self-repair capability. Current research into self-repair-
ing processors (multi-processors such as C,MMP and array
processors such as PEPE) are inadequate as a base for massive computing power required by scientific computation because those prototypes in practice admit only extremely
narrow bandwidth paths of information flow among processors.
Future systems will have modular configurations for improved
problem matching and will be able to switch ailing PEs out
and good PEs into the configuration all under software control.

SYSTEM ARCHITECTURE

To quote from Bouknight, et. al., in the Proceedings of the
IEEE, April, 1976, "It should be remembered that the Illiac
IV project was initially directed toward experimenting
with the feasibility of building a massive hardware configuration." In a word, the result is yes, it is feasible.
  The I4 system is a massive implementation of the concept of a functionally distributed operating system. It can
be viewed as the culmination of a progression which started
with early computers originally designed to execute efficiently different types of computing tasks, joined together
to execute different steps of the same computing job (e.g.,
the front end user interface preparing the job for a large
number-cruncher). Historically, these were incorporated into the main-frame design of more recent large computers.
The I4 system approaches the problem by dedicating functionally separate mini-computers and memory module buffers to
the independent functions of system support. For example,
file transfers to prepare jobs for execution are handled by
a separate mechanism from the one in charge of the movement
of program data from backing store to I4 processor memory

during program execution. The advantages of this approach
are fault tolerance (jobs which require only part of the
system can run whenever this part is available, whether or
not the whole system is working) and technology independence
(as technology advances are made, system components can be
enhanced on a module basis). An additional benefit is that
when modifications are to be made to the system to add unan-
ticipated capabilities, at most only the relevant modules
which are to interface with the new capability need be modified (or replaced); this is in contrast to the more usual
situation where the maximum system capability is determined
by the initial main-frame design.

APPLICATIONS

A. New Horizons in Solvable Problems

The size and speed of the Illiac makes feasible the solution
of many computational problems which were computationally
intractible when the machine was originally designed. The
essential reason for this is the large memory and the high
bandwidth between this memory and the processing power (more
conventional super-computers which have access to large backing store disks suffer from a narrow bandwidth between this
store and the processing unit, resulting in very large problems being essentially I/O bound -- this is especially true
of the CDC Star-100). The situation is exacerbated by the
general rule of thumb that for many scientific problems,
larger data bases (for a finer resolution of the physical
phenomenon) both take longer to pass through the data base
and, more importantly, have to pass through the data base
more often (because the iteration process converges more
slowly or because smaller time steps have to be taken).

B. Spurring the Development of New Algorithms

The concept of an array computer had provided a model for
developing parallel algorithms, but the announcement that a
powerful computer was to be based on this concept unleashed
a spate of activity in the area. At the present time, more
research has been based on the array model of computation
than on any other, save for the classic von Neumann (or
sequential random access) computer and the Turing machine.

C. Rethinking Problems for Parallel Processors Pays
    Dividends on Other Processors

A machine architecture which is a radical departure from
conventional sequential computers (as the Illiac is) encour-
ages users to re-formulate, or re-code, their problems to
make use of the additional capabilities. Before the Illiac
(and the Star) were available, some of the re-formatted
codes were debugged in a CDC-7600, whereupon it was found

that they ran faster in their new parallel-formulated
version than in the original sequential version. The
reason for this unexpected phenomenon is that parallel
formulation leads to short compact code sequences and
regular memory accessing, and these two characteristics
describe code which the 7600 is particularly efficient at
executing. As a result of this experience, the design
philosophy and algorithms originally designed for the
Illiac are being adopted as codes for the 7600.

Appendix

ASK - the ILLIAC Assembly Language

ASK is the assembly language for Illiac. It was written at the University of Illinois by Dave Grothe. ASK is a cross assembler. It runs on a Burroughs 6700.

The Illiac characteristics affect the assembly language, but not to as great an extent as the high-level languages. The existence of 64 processing elements and a control unit give rise to many different instruction formats. ASK does not attempt to remedy this by the introduction of some sort of unified syntax, and is somewhat tedious to learn and use. The major item affecting the assembler is the two-dimensional memory. This affects the assembler in two ways. First, each memory location is addressed in a different manner by different instructions. For example, the beginning of the second row of memory is word 64 to the CU. But it is row 1 to PE(0); it is syllable 128 when fetching instructions; and it is I/O word 4 when doing I/O. This creates many ambiguities. For example, in the instruction LDA 4, does the 4 mean 4 rows, 4 syllables, or 4 I/O words? The solution involves a complex set of assumptions and intrinsic functions never well-understood by the general user. Fortunately, the assumptions are sound enough that the typical user is unaware of the problem.

The two-dimensional memory introduces more storage allocation pseudo-instructions than generally encountered. Facilities exist for skipping to the next syllable which is an integral multiple of 2**N, filling with zeroes of NO-OPs. This facility frequently is useful.

Based on IAC Doc. No. PG-I8000-0062-A.

The non-machine-dependent features of ASK warrant comment. Card images are completely free format. Instructions, terminated by a semicolon, may be packed several per card or extend across card boundaries. Identifiers may be 63 characters in length. The language is block-structured using BEGIN - END pairs. Multiple allocation counters permit code to be written in an order other than that in which it is used. Macro and scanner level intrinsics are provided. Access to I/O routines and the real-time clock are provided by a set of macros included in one of the two macro libraries allowed.

Programming in assembly language for Illiac is much the same as programming in assembly language for a serial machine. It is just as tedious in spots (there is no path from $X to $A so don't write 'LDA $X') and yet permits the efficient coding available in a higher level language.

This discussion is a preliminary attempt at describing ASK, the Illiac IV assembly language, to readers not experienced in using the Illiac IV.

1. SIMPLE ASK PROGRAM FORM

An ASK program has the form:

    BEGIN
                        statement 1;

                        statement 2;

                            .

                            .

                            .

        starting-1 bel: statement i;

                            .

                            .

                        statement n;

        END starting-label.

Note that the statements are separated by semicolons (";") and that a period (".") i; required after the (optional) starting-label after the END.

2. LABELS

Each statement may be preceded by one or more labels.

Examples:

    START: statement i;

    LABEL1: I ABEL2:

                statement j;

3. <u>COMMENT CONVENTIONS</u>

After encountering a "%" in a source line, ASK ignores all subsequent characters in the line.

<u>Examples</u>:

%THIS IS A COMMENT LINE

statement i; %THIS IS A COMMENT FOR STATEMENT I

4. <u>ILLIAC IV INSTRUCTION FORMS</u>

One characteristic of the Illiac IV instruction set is the wide variety of instruction types. Not only are there both CU (ADVAST) and PE (FINST) instructions, but there are a number of types within each of these categories. This section illustrates the most commonly used types, using examples of correct ASK instructions for each type.

This material should be read in conjunction with Sections III and IV of the <u>ILLIAC IV-Systems Characteristics and Programming Manual</u> (henceforth abbreviated as "I4SCPM"), which describes the machine instructions in detail. All instruction formats given here are ASK instructions; these are accompanied by references to pages in the <u>I4SCPM</u> where the corresponding machine instructions are covered. The same general names for various entities e.g., "acar", "acarx", etc.) are used here and in the machine instruction descriptions.

4.1 CU INSTRUCTIONS

Most CU (ADVAST) instructions have the following form in ASK (see page 3-1 of <u>I4SCPM</u>):

instr(acar) adr(acarx);

where

● <u>instr</u> is the mnemonic of the instruction.

● <u>acar</u> specifies which ACAR is to be used as accumulator in executing the instruction.

● <u>adr</u> is an 8-bit CU address or value.

● <u>acarx</u> specifies which ACAR, if any, is to be used to index the <u>adr</u> field.

Example 1 (see page 3-45 of I4SCPM)

    LDL(2) $D10

where

- <u>acar</u> = "2" to specify ACAR2 as the accumulator.

- <u>adr</u> = "$D10" to specify ADB location 10 (decimal) as the address.

- <u>acarx</u> is omitted.

Note that <u>acarx</u> is optional. ASK register designators begin with a "S", and a "D" followed by a decimal number is used to indicate an ADB location. Thus the range of possible ADB addresses is $D0 to $D63.

Example 2 (see page 3-56 of I4SCPM)

    STL(1) 0(2);

where

- <u>acar</u> = "1" to specify ACAR1 as the accumulator.

- <u>adr</u> = 0.

- <u>acarx</u> = "2" to specify ACAR2 as index register.

The effective CU address is contained in the low-order 8 bits of ACAR2, since a base address of 0 is given and ACAR2 is the index register.

Example 3 (see page 3-18 of I4SCPM)

    CAND(3) $C2;

where

- <u>acar</u> = "3" to specify ACAR3 as the accumulator.

- <u>adr</u> = "$C2" to specify ACAR2 as the address.

- <u>acarx</u> is omitted.

Note that the register designators for the four ACAR's are $C0, $C1, $C2, and $C3.

Example 4 (see page 3-25 of I4SCPM)

    CRB(0) 63;

where

- *acar* = "0" to specify ACAR0 as the accumulator.

- *adr* = "63".

- *acarx* is omitted.

Note that constants are in decimal unless an alternate base is specified. Thus the *adr* value in the above example is 63:10 (63 decimal); the same value could be specified as 77:8 or 3F:16.

The second most common type of CU instruction involves the use of the "skip" field (see page 3-1 of I4SCPM). The general form of CU instructions with a skip field is

        instr(acar) adr(acarx), skip;

Example 5 (see page 3-32 of I4SCPM)

    CTSBT(0) 63,1;

where

- *acar* = "0" to specify ACAR0 as the accumulator.

- *adr* = "63".

- *acarx* is omitted.

- *skip* = "1" to specify a skip of one syllable if the test condition is satisfied.

Note that the skip field in the ASK instruction specifies the number of syllables to be skipped. Therefore, a *skip* of 0 would cause a transfer to the next instruction.

Example 6 (see page 3-67 of I4SCPM)

    ONESF(2) ,NOTALLONES;

where

- acar = "2" to specify ACAR2 as the accumulator.

- adr is omitted.

- acarx is omitted.

- skip = "NOTALLONES" to specify a skip to label NOTALLONES.

Note that if the skip in the ASK instruction is a label, ASK computes the distance from the present location to the specified label and places this distance in the skip field of the machine instruction.

Example 7 (see page 3-75 of I4SCPM)

    TXLTM(0) ,-1;

where

- acar = "0" to specify ACAR0 as the accumulator.

- adr is omitted.

- acarx is omitted.

- skip = "-4" to specify a backward skip of 4 syllables if the test condition is satisfied.

Note the backward skip of 4 syllables (a skip of -1 would be an infinite loop). The TXLTM instruction is often used for loop control.

There are four commonly used CU commands that have special formats. Three of these involve literal fields and the fourth is for JUMPing to a location.

Example 8 (see page 3-55 of I4SCPM)

    SLIT(2) LOCN;

where

- acar = "2" to specify ACAR2 as the accumulator.

- adr = "LOCN" to specify the word address corresponding to label LOCN.

- acarx is not used in this instruction.

The adr field of a SLIT instruction is a 24-bit literal (note that an "=" sign is not used). If a label is used as the adr, its word address will be assembled into the adr field of the machine instruction. The SLIT instruction places the contents of its adr field in the low-order 24 bits of the accumulator. Thus the instruction

    SLIT(0) 0;

clears the low-order 24 bits of ACAR0.

Example 9 (see page 3-12 of I4SCPM)

    ALIT(3) -1;

where

- acar = "3" to specify ACAR3 as the accumulator.

- adr = "-1" to specify the constant -1 as the literal.

- acarx is not used in this instruction.

The ALIT instruction adds the adr value to the low-order 24 bits of the accumulator; thus in the above example the low-order 24 bits of ACAR3 are decremented by 1. Note that 2's-complement arithmetic is used.

Example 10 (see page 3-48 of I4SCPM)

    LIT(1) 1,63,0;

where

- acar = "1" to specify ACAR1 as the accumulator.

- adr = "1,63,0" to specify a 64-bit literal in the form of a loop index (see below).

- acarx is not used in this instruction.

The LIT instruction places a 64-bit literal in the specified accumulator. In this example, the literal is a loop index containing an increment, a limit, and a current index value, as explained on page 3-11 of I4SCPM; the increment is 1, the limit is 63, and the current index value is 0. After this instruction is executed, ACAR1 will contain

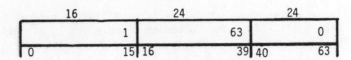

16		24		24	
1		63		0	
0	15	16	39	40	63

The following instruction illustrates a different type of 64-bit literal.

    LIT(2) -4.7@-7;

Here the literal is a 64-bit floating-point operand, which will be placed in ACAR2. The literal may also be a decimal, octal, or hexadecimal quantity:

    LIT(0) OFFFFCCC000800001:16;

Note that a "0" is used as the first character of this hexadecimal literal; if the first character were alphabetic, ASK would attempt to treat i= as an identifier instead of constant. A constant must always begin with a digit.

Example 11 (see page 3-4 of I4SCPM)

    JUMP LABEL1

where

- acar is not used in this instruction.

- adr = "LABEL1" to specify a jump to the word address corresponding to the label LABEL1.

- acarx is omitted (but may be used in this instruction).

This causes an unconditional transfer to LABEL1. Note that LABEL1 must be aligned on a word boundary. A double colon after the label will force this word alignment:

    LABEL1:: statement;

4.2   PE INSTRUCTIONS

The first thing usually done in an Illiac IV program is to enable all PE's. The following example does just that.

Example 12 (see page 4-69 of I4SCPM)

    SETE E.OR.-E;

    SETE1 E.OR.-E;

The following is an alternate way of doing the same thing:

    CLC(3);

This clears ACAR3 (see page 3-21 of I4SCPM).

    COMPC(3);

This complements ACAR3, making it all 1's (see page 3-22 of I4SCPM).

    LDEE1 $C3;

This loads the E and E1 bits in the PE's from ACAR3 (see page 4-69 of I4SCPM).

The general form for almost all PE instructions is

    instr adr(acarx);

where

- <u>instr</u> is the mnemonic of the instruction.

- <u>adr</u> is a 16-bit address value.

- <u>acarx</u> is the number of the ACAR to be used to index the <u>adr</u> field (which may then be indexed again in each PE as explained below).

Example 13 (see page 4-104 of I4SCPM)

        LDA *ROW1;

where

- <u>adr</u> = "*ROW1" to specify the row corresponding to label ROW1, indexed by the RGX register in each PE.

- <u>acarx</u> is omitted.

Note that "*" preceding a row address indicates indexing by RGX; a "#" is used to indicate indexing by the RGS register in each PE. This instruction loads the RGA registers of all enabled PE's from the locations determined by indexing ROW1 with the contents of RGX in each PE.

Example 14 (see page 4-17 of I4SCPM)

        AD ROW2(3);

where

- <u>adr</u> = "ROW2" to specify the row corresponding to label ROW2.

- <u>acarx</u> = "3" to specify indexing by the contents of ACAR3.

Note that in this case no indexing is performed in the PE's (thus all enabled PE's will access the same row of memory); however, the row address ROW2 is indexed by the contents of ACAR3 before being sent to the PE's. This instruction adds the contents of the addressed locations to the RGA registers of all enabled PE's.

Example 15 (see page 4-104 of I4SCPM)

    LDR =2(1)

where

- <u>adr</u> = "=2" to give a 16-bit literal value equal to 2.

- <u>acarx</u> = "1" to specify indexing by the contents of ACAR1.

Note that "=" is necessary to indicate a literal value as opposed to a row address. In this instruction, the RGR register in each enabled PE receives the 64-bit value in ACAR1 plus the value 2.

Example 16 (see page 4-55 of I4SCPM)

    ILE 2;

where

- <u>adr</u> = "2" to specify row 2 of memory.

- <u>acarx</u> is omitted.

Here memory row 2 is the operand. The instruction loads a word from row 2 into the RGA of each enabled PE, tests to see if it is logically equal to 0, and stores the result of the test in the I bit of the mode register of each PE.

Example 17 (see page 4-27 of I4SCPM)

    NAND $C1;

where

- <u>adr</u> = "$C1" to specify the contents of ACAR1 as a "broad-cast" address to the PE's.

- <u>acarx</u> is omitted.

Here all PE's use the same literal value, taken from ACAR1. The instruction causes each enabled PE to take the logical NAND of its RGA register and the ACAR1 value, placing the result in RGA. The following syntax is equivalent:

    NAND =0(1);

Example 18 (see page 4-41 of I4SCPM)

    DVRN $S;

where

- adr = "$S" to specify the RGS register in each enabled PE.

- acarx is omitted.

PE registers are designated $A, $B, $S, $R, and $X. This in-
struction causes the contents of RGS to be loaded into RGB; then
RGA is divided by RGB (in each enabled PE).

Example 19 (see page 4-97 of I4SCPM)

    STR #ROW3;

where

- adr = "#ROW3" to specify the row corresponding to label
  ROW3, indexed by the RGS register in each enabled PE.

- acarx is omitted.

Note that the operand in a PE register store instruction must
be a memory location. In this example, the RGR register of each
enabled PE is stored into ROW3 modified by the contents of RGS.

The PE routing instruction has the form

    RTL register distance(acarx);

where

- register is the register in each PE used to send data to
  another PE.

- distance is the distance (in terms of PE numbers) to send
  the data.

Example 20 (see page 4-77 of I4SCPM)

RTL 3(2);

where

- register is omitted (note that the comma is omitted also).

- distance = "3" to specify a distance of 3 PE's to the right.

- acarx = "2" to specify that the contents of ACAR2 are to be used to modify the distance.

If the register is omitted, the RGR register is used by default. A positive distance indicates a route to the right (i.e., the distance, modified by the contents of acarx, is added to each PE number to produce the PE number of the destination of data routed from each PE). In this example, the contents of the RGR register in each PE are sent to a PE at a distance of 3 (to the right), modified by the contents of ACAR2.

Caution: ACAR indexing of an RTL instruction may modify the Y field of the machine instruction, which specifies the PE register. See page 4-77 of I4SCPM.

Example 21 (see page 4-77 of I4SCPM)

RTL $B,-16;

where

- register = "$B" to specify RGB as the register used as the source of the routed data.

- distance = "-16" to specify a distance of 16 PE's to the left.

- acarx is omitted.

Note that a negative distance indicates a route to the left.

5. ASK PSEUDO-INSTRUCTION FORMS

Pseudo-instructions are not assembled to machine instructions, but are used to allocate, initialize, and label storage space. They are also used for symbol equating and macro definitions (DEFINE's), but these uses are not covered here. Page references in this section refer to the Reference Manual for the ILLIAC IV Assembler (ASK), abbreviated RMASK.

Example 22 (see page 9-3 of RMASK)

    ROW1: BLK 3;

This reserves 3 rows of memory, initialized to 0, with "ROW1" as the label for the first of these rows.

Example 23 (see page 9-5 of RMASK)

    WORD2: DATA 3.14159265;

This reserves one 64-bit memory location, labeled "WORD2" and initialized to 3.14159265.

Example 24 (see page 9-2 of RMASK)

    FOURWORDS: WDS 4;

This reserves four 64-bit words in memory, initialized to 0, with "FOURWORDS" as the label for the first of these words.

Example 25 (see page 9-3 of RMASK)

    BLK;

Align the instruction counter to the next row boundary, without allocating any storage. This statement is equivalent to

    BLK 0;

CATEGORIZATION OF ADVAST INSTRUCTIONS

OPERATIONS ON ACARS

- CURRENT INDEX FIELD MANIPULATION

ALIT	(add literal to ACAR (40:24))
CADD	(add operand to ACAR (40:24))
CSUB	(subtract CU register from ACAR 40:24))
SLIT	(replace ACAR (40:24) with literal)
INCRXC	(modify ACAR (40:24) by ACAR (1:15)

- WHOLE REGISTER MANIPULATION

CAND	(64-bit "and" of ACAR and CU register)
COR	(64-bit "or" of ACAR and CU register)
CEXOR	(64-bit "exclusive or" of ACAR and CU register)
CLC	(clear ACAR)
COMPC	(complement ACAR)
CROT (L/R)	(rotate ACAR left/right end-around)
CSH (L/R)	(shift ACAR left/right end-off, zero fill)
LEAD(O/Z)	(find leading one/zero in ACAR)
EXCHL	(exchange contents of ACAR and CU register)
LDI	(load ACAR from CU register)
LIT	(load ACAR with literal)
STL	(store ACAR contents in CU register)

- BIT MANIPULATION

CCB	(complement bit in ACAR)
CRB	(reset bit in ACAR)
CSB	(set bit in ACAR)

- HALF-WORD MANIPULATION

DUP(I/O)	(duplicate inner/outer 32 bits of ADB word in ACAR)

REFERENCE TO PROCESSOR MEMORY

BIN(X)	(fetch 8 words from processor memory to ADB)
LOAD(X)	(fetch 1 word from processor memory to CU reg.)
STORE(X)	(store CU reg. in 1 word of processor memory)

REFERENCE TO PE INFORMATION

LDC	(load ACAR from PE reg.)
SETC	(load each ACAR bit with mode bit from a PE)

CONTROL

CACRB	(set/reset one bit in ADVAST control register ACR)
EXEC	(execute instruction in ACAR (32:32))
FINQ	(stop ADVAST until FINST is idle)
HALT	(programmed halt; CU comes to orderly idle state)
JUMP	(jump to specified word address)

"TEST-SKIP." instructions (notes apply to "T" case in conditional skips --i.e., skip if test is TRUE. "F" case means skip if test is FALSE.)

UNCONDITIONAL SKIP

SKIP	(skip specified number of syllables forward or backward)

SKIP ON CONDITION OF CU TRUE/FALSE FLIP-FLOP (TFFF)

SKIP	(skip on pre-existing TFFF value)

SKIP ON VALUE OF BIT IN ACAR

CTSB(T/F)	(skip if specified ACAR bit is set)

ZEROS AND ONES

ONES(T/F)	(skip if ACAR (0:64 = all "ones")
ONEX(T/F)	(skip if ACAR (40:24) = all "ones")
ZER(T/F)	(skip if ACAR (0:64) = all "zeros")
ZERX(T/F)	(skip if ACAR (40:24) = all "zeros")

COMPARE ACAR CURRENT INDEX FIELD TO OPERAND CURRENT INDEX FIELD

EQLX(T/F)	(skip if ACAR (40:24) = CU reg. (40:24))
GRTR(T/F)	(skip if ACAR (40:24) > CU reg. (40:24))
LESS(T/F)	(skip if ACAR (40:24) < CU reg. (40:24))

COMPARE ACAR CURRENT INDEX FIELD TO OPERAND LIMIT FIELD

TXE(T/F)	(skip if ACAR (40:24) = CU reg. (16:24))
TXG(T/F)	(skip if ACAR (40:24) > CU reg. (16:24))
TXL(T/F)	(skip if ACAR (40:24) < CU reg. (16:24))

COMPARE ACAR CURRENT INDEX FIELD TO LIMIT FIELD OF SAME ACAR, AND

MODIFY CURRENT INDEX FIELD BY INCREMENT FIELD OF SAME ACAR

(Note: The skip is conditional, but the address modification is unconditional)

TXE(T/F)M	(skip if ACAR (40:24) = ACAR (16:24); modify ACAR (40:24) by ACAR (1:15))
TXG(T/F)M	(skip if ACAR (40:24) > ACAR (16:24); modify ACAR (40:24) by ACAR (1:15))
TXL(T/F)M	(skip if ACAR (40:24) < ACAR (16:24); modify ACAR (40:24) by ACAR (1:15))

CATEGORIZATION OF FINST/PE INSTRUCTIONS

- ### LOAD REGISTER

  LD (A/B/D/R/S/X)   (load specified register)
  LEX   (load RGA exponent)

- ### STORE REGISTER TO PROCESSOR MEMORY

  ST (A/B/R/S/X)   (store specified register)

- ### ROUTE

  RTL   (route from specified register to
                             RGR of another PE)

- ### CHANGE RGA CONTENTS

  CLRA   (clear RGA)
  COMPA   (complement RGA)
  CAB   (complement specified RGA bit)
  RAB   (reset specified RGA bit)
  SAB   (set specified RGA bit)
  CHSA   (complement RGA sign)
  SAP   (make RGA positive)
  SAN   (make RGA negative)

- ### BASIC ARITHMETIC

  AD (A, M,
    N, R variants)   (add)
  ADD   (add 64-bit logical words)
  ADEX   (add exponent fields)
  EAD   (add, extended precision results)
  SB (A, M,
    N, R variants)   (subtract)
  SUB   (subtract 64-bit logical words)
  SBEX   (subtract exponent fields)
  ESB   (subtract, extended precision result)
  ML (A, M,
    N, R variants)   (multiply)
  MULT   (multiply, 32-bit only)
  DV (A, M,
    N, R variants)   (divide)
  NORM   (normalize)
  ASB   (transfer RGA sign to RGB sign)

- ### ADDRESS ARITHMETIC

  XI   (add to RGX)
  (I/J) XGI   (same, with overflow to RGD bit I or J)
  XD   (subtract from RGX)
  (I/J) XLD   (same, with complemented overflow to
                             RGD bit I or J)

- **BOOLEAN**

(N)AND(N)	(logical AND -- operands may be complemented)
(N)OR(N)	(logical OR -- operands may be complemented)
EOR	(logical EXCLUSIVE-OR)
EQV	(logical EQUIVALENCE)

- **SHIFT/ROTATE**

RTA(L/R)	(rotate RGA left/right)
SHA(L/R)	(shift RGA left/right)
SHAM(L/R)	(shift RGA mantissa left/right)
SHAB(L/R)	(shift RGA + RGB left/right)
SHABM(L/R)	(shift RGA mantissa + RGB mantissa left/right)

- **LOAD/SET RGD BIT**

LD(E/E1/EE1/G/ H/I/J)	(load RGD bit from one bit of a literal)
SET(E/E1/F/F1/ G/H/I/J)	(set RGD bit to a function of two RGD bits)

- **LOAD RGD BIT I OR J FROM RGA BIT**

(I/J)B	(load I or J from specified RGA bit)
(I/J)SN	(load I or J from RGA sign bit)

- **LOAD RGD BIT I OR J WITH RESULT OF TEST**

  Note: Tests are indicated by G for "greater than", E for "equal to", L for "less than" O for "all ones", Z for "all zeros".

(I/J)A(G/L)	(signed floating comparison of RGA and operand)
(I/J)L(G/E/L)	(logical-word comparison of RGA and operand)
(I/J)M(G/E/L)	(mantissa-only comparison of RGA and operand)
(I/J)L(O/Z)	(test RGA logical word)
(I/J)M(O/Z)	(test RGA mantissa only)
(I/J)S(G/E/L)	(address-field comparison of RGS and operand)
(I/J)X(G/E/L)	(address-field comparison of RGX and operand)

- **BYTE-ORIENTED INSTRUCTIONS**

ADB	(add bytes)
SBB	(subtract bytes)
GB	(test for RGA bytes "greater than" operand bytes)
LB	(test for RGA bytes "less than" operand bytes)
NEB	(test for RGA bytes "not equal to" operand bytes)
OFB	(recover byte carries or test results from RGC to RGB)

●   SWAP INSTRUCTIONS

SWAP   (swap RGA and RGB)
SWAPA   (swap RGA inner and outer words)
SWAPX   (swap RGA outer word and RGB inner word)

Sources

The Fastest Computer by D.L. Slotnick, Scientific American 1971
Reaching for a Gigaflop by Howard Falk, IEEE Spectrum 1976
The IAC Computational Facility-An Overview by C.T. Markee 1977
Overlap in the Illiac IV Control Unit by E. Sternberg 1976
Overlap: Now Available on I4 to IAC Users, IAC Newsletter
Coding for Overlap Mode (Parts 1 & 2) in IAC Newsletter
Evaluation of the Illiac IV in Non-overlap and Overlap Modes by Chris
    Jesshope in IAC Newsletter
CFD-A Fortran-like Language for the Illiac IV by K.G. Stevens in IAC
    Newsletter
Glypnir-A Programming Language for Illiac IV by D.H. Lawrie et al,
    Comm. ACM 1975
A Critical Look at Some Programming Languages for Illiac IV by
    F. Richard in IAC Newsletter 1977
IAC Annual Report for FY78
Computational Aerodynamics, IAC Newsletter
Parallel Computation of Unsteady, 3-D, Chemically Reacting, Nonequili-
    brium Flow Using a Time-split Finite-Volume Method on the Illiac IV
    by W.A. Reinhardt, IAC Newsletter
The Illiac Is a Wind Tunnel for the CFD Branch at NASA/Ames, IAC
    Newsletter
TRIOIL IV, A Three Dimensional Hydrodynamics Code for the Illiac IV
    Computer, by L. L. Reed and D.R. Henderson, Report to DNA, 1975
An Illiac Program for the Numerical Simulation of Homogeneous Incom-
    pressible Turbulence by R.S. Rogallo, IAC Newsletter
Image Line Detection on the Illiac by Hough Transform by R.M. Hord,
    IAC Newsletter
Use of Illiac IV in Analysis of Landsat Satellite Data by M. Ozga, IAC
    Newsletter
Image Skeletonizing on the Illiac by R.M. Hord in IAC Newsletter
Two Dimensional Hadamard Transform on the Illiac IV by R.M. Hord in
    IAC Newsletter
IAC Support for SAR Digital Processing Research by R. Hale in IAC
    Newsletter
Computing the Singular Value Decomposition on the Illiac IV by F.T. Luk
    in IAC Newsletter
Exploitation of Parallelism in Number Theoretic and Combinatorial Com-
    putation by D.H. Lehmer in IAC Newsletter

349

A Three Dimensional Finite Difference Code for Seismic Analysis on the
    Illiac IV Parallel Processor by A.S. Hopkins, IAC Newsletter
Three Dimensional Galaxy Simulations by R.H. Miller in IAC Newsletter
Illiac Memory Speed-up by Steve Tulloh in IAC Newsletter
FKCOMB
Optimal Use of Supercomputers